Praise for *Make Life Happier*

'At a time of anxiety and division, Mark Williamson offers something rare: a wise, practical and deeply humane guide to living better and helping others do the same. Drawing on the best of modern science and years of real-world experience, this is a profoundly hopeful call to action for anyone who wants to feel happier and contribute to a better world. A timely and important book for our troubled times. We need these ideas now more than ever.'
Sir Anthony Seldon

'In a world of uncertainty, Dr. Mark Williamson brings to us a comprehensive, completely readable, and generous template for the possibility of a happier life, leading to a happier world. This is a book I will share with professionals and friends, with elders and teens, and anyone seeking to feel, despite the chaos of any one moment, a grounded and life-giving hope.' **Dr. Maria Sirois**

'Clear, actionable practices we can use in our everyday lives. This is the kind of book that doesn't just change your thinking – it changes how you live.'
Shawn Achor

'Want to be happier or to make others happier? You have to read this authoritative, science-based and enchantingly readable book by the exceptional, multi-talented leader of Action for Happiness.'
Professor Richard Layard

'I love this. It's full of helpful and practical ways to bring a little more joy and happiness into your daily life.' **Joe Wicks**

'This gem of a book is both warm-hearted and wise. It shows you how to find your footing in a shaky world, with love and inner peace along the way.'
Dr Rick Hanson

'A delightful read, perfect for anyone who wants practical tips for improving wellbeing.' **Dr Laurie Santos**

'This book is a guide for good living ... It is an inspiring book and at the same time a very helpful book. We need to read it and then put it into practice!'
Satish Kumar

'Shows us in a convincing and inspiring manner that genuine happiness, far from being a mere succession of pleasant experiences, is a skill – a way of being. This will surely help many readers in our challenging times.'
Matthieu Ricard

'Mark is one of those gentle, super-smart people who quietly changes the world while no-one is quite looking. Here he distils essential lessons from both research and practical experience in a book devoid of cliches, pat solutions or pseudoscience.' **Professor Sir Geoff Mulgan**

'A realistic how-to guide full of helpful tips and tools. If you want to feel happier and make the world a better place, read this book!' **Dr Sian Williams**

'I have been waiting for a book like this to come out! It reminds us that happiness is not merely something we experience but something we can cultivate intentionally through our thoughts, actions and relationships.'
Dr Tal Ben Shahar

'A wise and compassionate guide to help you care for yourself and for others. This book is a hopeful companion for anyone wanting to bring more calm, connection and kindness into everyday life. Insightful, reassuring and genuinely helpful.' **Julia Samuel**

'This book blends solid science with heartfelt wisdom in a way that feels like a friend showing you how life can be made better … Life changing indeed.'
Mo Gawdat

'In these days of stress and times of confusion, Dr Williamson has written an engaging, wise, warm-hearted and transformative book on how to help settle our minds and create conditions for flourishing happiness.'
Professor Paul Gilbert

'Turns the science of wellbeing into something deeply human and practical.'
Prof. Robert J Waldinger, MD

'A powerful, practical guide to a life worth living.' **Daniel Goleman**

'An uplifting, evidence-based joy to read, showing how everyday actions profoundly shape our personal happiness and the collective good. Required reading for anyone who dreams of a happier life and kinder world – one where everyone belong … This book is a warm invitation to a global movement for a kinder world and a reminder that your actions matter.'
Dr Kelli Harding

'Warm, wise and grounded in evidence, this book offers simple ideas that can make everyday life better –for you and the people around you.' **Nic Marks**

'Brilliant! A remarkably comprehensive guide to living better, feeling happier and getting more out of life.' **Dr Radha Modgil**

Make Life Happier

23 practical ways to feel better, find meaning and make a difference

Dr Mark Williamson

LEAP

First published in the UK in 2026 by LEAP
An imprint of Bonnier Books UK
5th Floor, HYLO, 105 Bunhill Row,
London, EC1Y 8LZ

Copyright © Mark Williamson, 2026

All rights reserved.

No part of this publication may be reproduced, stored or transmitted in any form or by any means, electronic, mechanical, photocopying or otherwise, without the prior written permission of the publisher.

The right of Mark Williamson to be identified as Author of this work has been asserted by him in accordance with the Copyright, Designs and Patents Act, 1988.

A CIP catalogue record for this book is available from the British Library.

Trade Paperback ISBN: 978-1-78512-474-7

Also available as an ebook and an audiobook

1 3 5 7 9 10 8 6 4 2

Design and Typeset by Envy Design Ltd.
Illustrations by Arc Studio
Printed and bound in Great Britain by CPI (UK) Ltd, Croydon CR0 4YY

Every reasonable effort has been made to trace copyright holders of material reproduced in this book, but if any have been inadvertently overlooked the publishers would be glad to hear from them.

The authorised representative in the EEA is
Bonnier Books UK (Ireland) Limited.
Registered office address:
Block B, The Crescent Building
Northwood, Santry
Dublin 9, D09 C6X8
Ireland
compliance@bonnierbooks.ie

www.bonnierbooks.co.uk

For Dad, who gave me an engineer's mindset and showed me how to be both strong and gentle.

Contents

INTRODUCTION   9

PART 1: HAPPIER INSIDE   17
Looking inwards and focusing on self-care

1. Wake Up: What am I doing and what matters most?   19
2. Look Inside: What's going on in my mind and body?   31
3. Decide to Act: How can my actions change how I feel?   47
4. See the Good: What am I taking for granted?   65
5. Keep it Real: Is staying positive always helpful?   79
6. Tame That Critic: Why am I so hard on myself?   91
7. Reframe Difficulty: Is there a different way of looking at this?   103
8. Do Experiments: How do I find what works best for me?   121
9. Build Habits: How can I keep the good things going?   135
10. Cultivate Calm: How can I be less anxious?   153
11. Find Meaning: Where am I really heading?   171

PART 2: HAPPIER TOGETHER — 189
Looking outwards and connecting with others

12. Prioritise People: Am I focusing enough on my relationships? — 191
13. Listen Actively: Do I really hear what people are saying? — 205
14. Understand Needs: Can I help resolve our difficulties? — 223
15. Remove the Mask: Can vulnerability be my source of strength? — 243
16. Heal Those Wounds: How do my past relationships shape me? — 253
17. Let it Go: How can I forgive and move on? — 271
18. Spread Kindness: How can I be helpful and inspire others too? — 285
19. Trust People: Do I see and encourage the good in others? — 305
20. Raise Resilience: How can I help the next generation thrive? — 321
21. Get Together: How can I be part of something bigger? — 339
22. Be the Change: Can I help create a happier society? — 353

PART 3: HAPPIER FOR GOOD — 373
Bringing all of these ideas together

23. Make it Last: How can we keep making life happier? — 375

References — 393
Acknowledgements — 413
About the Author — 415

Introduction

I'm not a happiness guru and this book can't change your life.

So why am I writing it – and why should you keep reading?

You're about to discover 23 life-enhancing ideas that I've road-tested in a unique way. I'll explain more, but let's start with some basics.

We all share an inner longing for real happiness. You, me, everyone. We don't just want to be happier ourselves, we want this for our loved ones and people around us too. But happiness is often misunderstood or dismissed as soft or fluffy – and many of us go through life never really feeling at peace with ourselves or each other.

By happiness, I don't just mean short-lived moments of joy. I'm also talking about that deeper sense of contentment that comes when you feel connected and purposeful. Obviously, we're all different and have our own unique life story and preferences. Yet this inner longing – to feel good and find meaning – shapes all our behaviour in profound ways, even when we're not consciously aware of it.

Unfortunately, we often respond to this instinct in unhelpful ways and seek happiness in the wrong places. Many of the hardwired instincts that kept our ancestors alive don't serve us so well in modern life. So, we overconsume and strive for wealth, status and material things. We focus on what we lack and worry about what might go wrong. Even when our basic needs are met and we're not in danger, we struggle to cope with everyday life. We find ourselves anxious, lonely or unfulfilled. We feel like we're not enough. Then, when we do face challenges, we find it hard to be resilient and make wise choices. We feel less able to support others or don't know how to help.

So how can we make life happier? This question has been at the heart of my journey and the foundation on which Action for Happiness was built. Since 2010, I've had the privilege of heading up this social movement, working closely with many of the world's leading experts in wellbeing. I've witnessed the life-changing power of simple science-backed actions to enhance happiness – not just in fleeting moments but as a sustained way of being. Not just for ourselves, but for each other.

This book is the culmination of fifteen years of this work. It's a journey of personal discovery and of collective transformation. It's for anyone who's ever felt empty inside or paused to wonder what really matters in life. It's for those who question our relentless pursuit of individual success at the expense of togetherness, or those who just want to lead a more joyful and meaningful life. At a time when our world feels increasingly fearful, confused and divided, we need these ideas now more than ever.

Thankfully, in recent years, a huge wave of new scientific research has dramatically increased our understanding of happiness and what contributes to it. Although I'm no guru, I've had a unique opportunity to work with hundreds of scientists and experts to learn what really matters. Often, the latest studies back up ancient wisdom, supporting ideas that have been passed on for generations. But I was also shocked by how many of these insights were new to me – and how few people seem to be aware of them.

For science to be helpful in daily life, it needs to be made practical. I began my career as an electrical engineer, trying to apply the science of wireless communication to help design better networks. Although my life has changed direction radically since, I still use my engineering principles – only these days I'm applying the science of wellbeing to help design better lives. My work has allowed me to try these ideas out with thousands of people in countless different ways and places. I've discovered what tends to help people most and what usually doesn't. I've also been surprised by how big a difference these actions have made in my own life too.

Make Life Happier is more than a book title – it's really an invitation to join a global movement of people who are choosing to live differently. People who recognise that happiness is not just a personal quest but a collective good that can enrich our communities and our world. It's also an invitation to shift our values. From apathy to agency. From what we can get to what we can give. From seeking validation to finding connection. From just surviving to actively thriving.

Crucially, this is about how to make life *happier*, not permanently *happy* – recognising this is a direction of travel, not a destination. The most important thing to know right now is that your actions matter. Even if you can't change your circumstances, you do have the potential to feel better, find meaning and make a difference. Whatever your situation, you can do something – and you can start today.

So I'm not a guru, I'm a happiness engineer.

This book can't change your life, but *you* can.

Why this matters

Some people see happiness just as some 'fluffy' nice-to-have, or believe that focusing on happiness is pointless, lazy or even selfish. But this isn't true. Ask parents what they want above all for their children and most say, 'I just want them to be happy.' This is what we want most for the people we love – to avoid unnecessary suffering and thrive as much as humanly possible. It's also the key to a better world for us all.

Research shows that when people are happier they tend to be healthier overall and live longer. They're less likely to catch a cold or experience a cardiovascular event such as a heart attack or stroke. Happier people also have stronger relationships and tend to be more reliable and productive colleagues at work. They're also more likely to be prosocial. They tend to do more acts of kindness, engage in less risky behaviour, be more financially responsible and care more about social issues or the environment.

Another popular but misleading idea is that 'aiming to be happier makes you unhappy', so we're better off hoping it simply comes as a by-product. Again, this isn't true. Yes, there are lots of unhelpful ways to pursue happiness, such as chasing fame or money. But there are unhelpful ways of pursuing any worthwhile goal. For example, obsessing too much about health might make us anxious, but aiming to be healthy is still a good idea. We just need to find more helpful ways of getting there – and as we'll see, there are lots of proven and successful paths to happier living that really do work.

But don't just take my word for it. This book gives you the chance to become a 'happiness scientist' and try things out yourself. You can discover what works best for you and then find ways to make these actions a lasting part of your daily life.

Beyond 'smiley-happy'

Before going any further, we need to clear up something important. This book is not about trying to be happy all the time. A life of only good feelings is neither possible nor desirable – and it would be pretty shallow and one-dimensional. Nothing in this book, or elsewhere, can prevent those inevitable times of unhappiness that we will all encounter at some stage in our lives – the failure, loss, sadness, health issues or heartaches.

Aiming to make life happier isn't about denying our negative emotions or pretending to feel joyful when we're not. We all encounter adversity and it's completely natural to feel anger, sadness, frustration and other uncomfortable emotions. To suggest otherwise would deny our humanity, with all its complexity, messiness and imperfection. Rather, this is about trying to make the most of the good times while also coping effectively with the unavoidable tough times in order to experience the best possible life overall. We can't avoid some hardships, but we can learn how to respond more wisely to them.

Although we tend to seek out pleasurable experiences, a happy life is also one which is meaningful, not just enjoyable. Aristotle referred to this as *eudaimonia* or a 'life worth living'. This is why the happiest people in the world aren't necessarily the stereotypical image of 'smiley-happy'. For example, Finland regularly tops the world happiness rankings, but most Finns don't consider themselves particularly smiley. However, they do have a sense of contentment and positive relationships in a culture with high levels of trust and mutual support. That sense of purpose and togetherness is vital.

Practical happiness

Scientists have done extensive research into which actions tend to make us happier and we'll cover many of them in this book. However, it's important to remember that we're all different, so what works for someone else may not necessarily work for you.

Since launching Action for Happiness I've had the opportunity to meet and work with hundreds of experts in fields relating to happiness, from spiritual teachers like the Dalai Lama to scientists working at the cutting edge of research in neuroscience, psychology, economics, mental health and behavioural science. I've then spent years sharing the insights from these experts and adapting them for use by people in their different everyday lives – including in organisations, schools, local communities and online too.

I learned that happiness doesn't just happen to us, it can be cultivated with deliberate actions and choices. These in turn build our sense of agency and hope, helping us to make the best of things, including in really difficult situations. Even small actions can have a big impact and stop us feeling helpless.

Along the way I also became an amateur 'happiness scientist' for my own habits too. I began doing personal experiments, with my everyday life as the research lab. Yes, there were lots of mishaps along the way. No, I haven't reached some ultimate pinnacle of happiness that spares me from the unhappy times. However, there is one big thing I kept discovering repeatedly through it all . . .

Self and others

The most important overall message from this book is that *lasting happiness comes from combining self-care and caring for others.*

If we think of 'wellness' only as a form of personal optimisation, we miss something vital. Just chasing personal happiness is not enough. Nor is just trying to be virtuous. Personal development and ethics must go hand in hand.

When we care for ourselves, we're more likely to have the capacity to help others. As they say, 'You can't pour from an empty cup.' When we care for others, we're much more likely to find meaning in our own lives too. Doing good feels good.

So looking after your own wellbeing is essential, but not sufficient. You need to care genuinely about others too. The beauty of this is that wise self-care gives us greater capacity for others, while the added 'bonus' of helping others is that it gives us a boost too. Doing both together is better for everyone.

This is ultimately an ethical project. It's about paying attention not only to how we feel inside but to the effect our choices have on others. We're deeply interconnected and the way we behave shapes the culture around us. In countless everyday moments we each have the chance to make life a little better for the people we share it with.

Your invitation

This book covers 23 practical ways to make life happier. Before we dive into the ideas, it's worth knowing how the book is structured. The first part (Happier Inside) covers core skills for your own wellbeing, like how to build helpful habits or be a 'realistic optimist'. The second part (Happier Together) covers wider social wellbeing, like how to have great relationships or be part of something bigger. The brief final part (Happier for Good) brings it all together in a way that lasts and contributes to the greater good. We start with the personal, but towards the end we'll zoom out to the wider picture, including the role of government, measuring wellbeing, the economy, health, education, work and other important areas of society.

Along the way, whenever I refer to research you'll find the relevant studies listed in the references for that chapter at the end of the book. I'll also share my insights from road-testing these actions with lots of people, including how they've helped in my own life, often in unexpected ways. So you'll learn about the surprising way I cured my chronic pain, how I eventually recovered from being a lifelong 'people pleaser' and the sweary acronym I now use as my daily reflection!

As you turn these pages I invite you to engage not just with your rational mind but also with your heart. Think of this less as a passive reading experience and more as something you actively try out in your life. Your journey to happier living is as unique as you are, yet I hope many of the ideas and stories you discover here will be helpful signposts along your path. So, let's get going.

PART 1:
HAPPIER INSIDE

Looking inwards and focusing on self-care

Chapter One:

Wake Up

What am I doing and what matters most?

Twenty years ago, I woke up, sprang out of bed, got dressed and – halfway through my morning coffee – realised something incredible: I actually felt good.

Considering that just two months before a doctor had told me I was likely to be in a wheelchair before I turned 40, this first pain-free moment in years qualified as something of a miracle.

Even more incredible is what saved me.

There was no magic pill, no surgery, no mystical cure. Instead, to my great surprise, my healing had come from learning to shift my focus. I'd begun to unwind the stress and pressures of my life and prioritise wellbeing. I'd started being more present in everyday moments and more willing to appreciate the extraordinary in the ordinary.

Waking up, it turned out, was about tuning in.

My wake-up call

When I was first told that my chronic back pain was the result of a hereditary and degenerative spinal disorder, I was angry and frightened – but not yet ready to accept the grim prognosis.

My wife Kate, who was retraining to be an osteopath, offered an alternative explanation: could it be that my back problems were related to the stress of my high-pressure job as a business consultant?

I wanted to dismiss her suggestion just as badly as I wanted to dismiss my diagnosis. Surely this was new-age nonsense?

I had a background in engineering and I was certain my back problems were structural – it was the only logical explanation. The doctor had shown me an MRI scan with my 'bulging discs' and misaligned spine.

I was in constant pain and it affected everything. There were days when I couldn't get out of bed, days when I couldn't walk. I was missing out on life. Yes, I was stressed at work, but there was simply no way pain this debilitating could be 'all in my head'.

As it turned out, I was right about the pain (definitely not imagined), but wrong about the causes. So were the doctor and orthopaedic surgeon I had consulted. Modern healthcare is incredible, yet for certain conditions, like back pain, it turns out there's often more going on than can be explained just by scans and physical causes.

That's when Kate recommended a book which completely changed my life. It was called *Back Sense* and used rigorous research to explain how most back pain actually comes from muscle tension, and the underlying cause of this is often stress and anxiety. After years of suffering I was willing to try anything, and reluctantly opened myself up to the possibility that something deeper might be causing my problems.

As I read, I felt the penny drop. There it was – the truth, my 'eureka' moment and wake-up call: I was deeply unhappy at work, but because I wasn't acknowledging this, my mental tension and pain were appearing as physical symptoms instead.

Breaking the cycle

By revealing the rational, scientific links between unhappiness and pain, that book helped me take early steps to break the much more emotional cycle of chronic pain in my life, which I'd been blind to.

First, I learned to simply become more aware of my discomfort. Where previously I'd done everything I could to avoid feeling pain (this never actually worked, by the way), I chose instead to practise noticing when and where I felt it.

I started small: I learned a simple breathing exercise, which helped me become aware of my body. We now call it mindfulness – but this was long before that word went mainstream. I began to bring my attention to the tension and just let it be, rather than trying to ignore it or 'fix' it. This also helped me to be more present in moments of joy and pleasure rather than constantly worrying about the pain.

I learned to put myself in environments where I was more likely to feel calm, spending less time at work and more time with loved ones. I started to rebalance my life and rethink my priorities. I woke up from living on autopilot and began to make intentional choices to live more mindfully and meaningfully.

The biopsychosocial model

Back pain is an example of a biopsychosocial condition. In addition to biological components, wider psychological and social aspects also play a significant role in how pain is experienced and our overall health.

Although pain can be related to structural or anatomical issues, it can also be exacerbated by psychological factors such as stress and wider social factors such as our workplace conditions or situation at home.

Clinical research from the Netherlands Study of Depression and Anxiety (NESDA) found that chronic pain is common in up to 70 per cent of patients with depression or anxiety. This link also runs in the other direction: people with chronic pain are more likely to be experiencing mental health challenges.

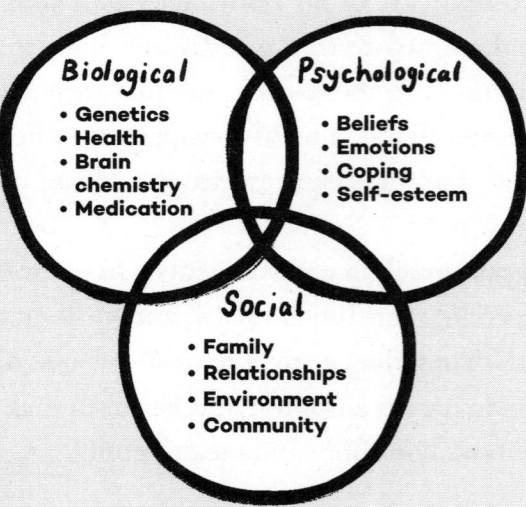

Understanding these biopsychosocial interactions means we need to think holistically about our wellbeing. Our bodies, minds and social context all matter.

Turning off autopilot

We're all on autopilot much of the time, and in fact, we often need to be. Relying on our habitual instincts is essential for our survival. We're bombarded with more information and stimulation in our daily lives than we can cope with. If we didn't tune lots of this out it would be too much to handle. The stress of trying to take everything in would leave us completely overwhelmed. But so too does the stress of living mindlessly.

The alternative is to wake up and consciously aim for the things that are really worth pursuing, like more meaning, more experiences, more joy, more connection.

By being attentive to my pain, I allowed myself to become more aware of the situations and activities that helped, and those that left me uncomfortable. Not just physically but also more broadly: the things that made me happy and the things that didn't. Then, I started using that information to guide how I lived my life.

In other words we can learn to turn off autopilot, to make intentional choices that prioritise wellbeing from moment to moment, instead of simply going through the motions. Aiming to thrive, not just survive.

Over time, my small changes led to tectonic shifts: that first pain-free day, taking time off to study, starting a family, pivoting from consulting and the stock exchange to focus on climate change initiatives, and then setting up Action for Happiness as a charity – to help other people create more happiness, for themselves and across society.

In this book, you'll discover the most important lessons I've learned along the way. But it all begins with waking up.

Many of our autopilot behaviours and habits are rooted in our survival instincts. We aren't consciously aware of them, but they're powerful, shaped by what we've come to believe will help us survive and succeed. Much of what we do on a daily basis links back to these instincts.

The problem is, when we act from an unconscious perception of what's good for us we often end up behaving in ways that don't actually serve us or bring fulfilment.

Take me, for example. Growing up in a 'good Christian family' I had a strong sense that 'we're good people'. In my mind, I wanted to live in a way that pleased others, whether it was my parents, friends, teachers or bosses. I sought external validation. To me, being 'good' meant being seen that way by others. I was smiling on the outside but sometimes it felt superficial, like I was trying to keep up appearances. My subconscious was telling me: I'll be happy when I pass my exams, when I land that job, when I get more successful – when I, when I, when I . . .

Although I was incredibly blessed to grow up in a loving, stable and supportive home, I had created a certain tyranny for myself by striving to always be seen as a 'good guy'. I still feel this drive even now – to help more people or make a bigger impact in the world. The difference today is that this comes more from a sense of inner conviction rather than a hunger for external recognition.

When we learn to let go of this need to be happy based on other people's standards we can focus more on what truly makes us feel fulfilled.

> 'Happiness is . . . a deep sense of flourishing. This is not a mere pleasurable feeling, a fleeting emotion, or a mood, but an optimal state of being.'
>
> **– Matthieu Ricard**

Finding inner motivation

Psychologists describe two different types of motivation that guide our decisions and actions. The first type is 'extrinsic' motivation, which comes from outer factors like status, achievements or rewards.

Until I woke up and realised happiness was not something I'll find 'when . . .', my life had been built around extrinsic motivators. On the outside I may have been perceived as happy and successful and 'good', but inside it didn't feel that way.

I was climbing up the ladder, achieving what I thought I should, playing along with the story I wanted people to buy into about me. And yet it was never enough. I was always struggling on towards that mythical 'when . . .' It was relentless and exhausting. My life was full, but it felt empty of real meaning.

The second type of motivation is 'intrinsic', which comes from inside us when we do something for its own sake, for example because it's enjoyable or meaningful.

Deciding to leave my job and pursue things that truly mattered to me – especially with Action for Happiness – changed everything. I discovered my intrinsic motivation and gave myself permission to choose work that felt fulfilling, even when friends told me I was crazy leaving a respected job to do 'some weird happiness project'. This marked the beginning of my ongoing recovery from people-pleasing. The transformation I've experienced since has been both surprising and profound.

You can go on your own version of this journey. It may already be underway.

To make life happier, we need to release ourselves from the endless quest for future success and postponed joy. Rather than staying on the hamster wheel, always waiting for happiness to come later, we can wake up to prioritise what matters and find satisfaction in the present.

But in my case, there was another vital shift needed too.

From fear to hope

We've all heard of the placebo effect, where patients experience improvements from a treatment or medication despite not receiving the 'real thing'.

But the part we often take for granted is that these are genuine benefits which people have created for themselves – based on their expectations! In fact, because most major medical trials use a placebo-controlled study, this is possibly the most widely replicated effect in the whole study of human behaviour.

Yet we usually focus on the new pill or procedure and ignore this incredible fact: that our expectations shape our reality much more than we realise. In my case, my expectations about my back were a bigger block than the pain itself, or the stress that had caused it.

After hearing scary news from doctors, I told myself, 'I have a damaged back; it's painful, and it's only going to get worse.' This mindset completely shaped my outlook on life. Pain and fear don't just affect our body – they can seep into everything, from our relationships to the simplest tasks, like going downstairs or making tea. Anyone who has experienced chronic pain knows just how debilitating it is.

So, the stories we tell ourselves about our pain and unhappiness matter. If we fear the pain, we reinforce its hold on us.

> ⭐ 'There is nothing either good or bad, but thinking makes it so.'
>
> **– Shakespeare (*Hamlet*, Act II, Scene 2)**

When I opened up to the idea that my pain might not be permanent, I was able to let go of that constant fear. I became much more hopeful and purposeful, which in turn helped my recovery. It was a major turning point. As well as helping me realise that my life was out of balance, it taught me a powerful lesson about the power of expectations.

Many of us fail to recognise how much our mental state affects every aspect of life – our physical health, our ambitions, our relationships. I came to understand that my inner emotional health isn't a 'soft and fluffy' nice-to-have. In fact, for someone like me with an analytical, engineer-like mindset, it's even more crucial.

As well as letting go of the stress from seeking outer validation, I was also able to let go of fear and find a greater sense of hope. Looking back now, I realise that I experienced a form of 'post-traumatic growth'.

And you can too.

> **Post-traumatic growth**
> Post-traumatic growth (PTG) refers to the positive changes that some people experience after going through very stressful or traumatic events. These changes can include feeling more appreciative of life, developing stronger relationships, finding personal strength, seeing new possibilities or experiencing spiritual growth. In other words, people who come out the other side of devastating events sometimes end up happier.
>
> In contrast to post-traumatic stress disorder (PTSD), people who experience PTG often report feeling more fulfilled or that life seems more meaningful, even though

> they may still struggle with significant distress at times. Post-traumatic growth often brings a richer emotional life, where feelings like gratitude emerge alongside the challenges of dealing with adversity. Although trauma never feels good at the time, and no one would wish it on anyone, it can help put things in perspective and bring a greater sense of purpose to life.

Begin your Good Life Crisis

Painful life experiences often give us the chance to reevaluate and change in positive ways. Thankfully, although this growth can happen after a major life crisis, I also believe it doesn't necessarily require one.

We all have the potential to wake up and make life happier today, and we don't need to wait for a devastating diagnosis, the loss of a loved one or any other traumatic event as the trigger. You can start right now, firstly by giving yourself permission to switch off autopilot and opening up to the possibility of change.

What might be your own personal wake-up call?

Are you chasing other people's approval or allowing fear to shape your expectations? Invite yourself to become more conscious of what would make you feel happy and fulfilled – on the inside rather than the outside.

One helpful way to wake up, without needing an actual crisis, is to listen to the wisdom of your 'future self'.

After my back-pain recovery, a memorable moment that finally helped me take a new direction came when I worked with a coach called Aidan. One day he asked me to look ahead and visualise myself many years in the future, looking back on my life. He even asked me to sit in a different chair, so I could really try to 'be' my future self and speak from this perspective.

You could try this yourself right now too. Imagine being yourself in the future, looking back over all your highs and lows, all your opportunities and achievements.

Take a moment to really get into that future perspective and try to visualise a positive situation where things have generally worked out well.

When you feel ready, try asking yourself the same question I was asked:

'What advice would your future self give you about what really matters now?'

It seems so simple, but I found this brought me surprising clarity. What would your wise 'future self' say? I found mine saying, 'Spend more time with people you love, doing things you really care about.' It was so obvious, yet so different to how I'd been living!

We all have this potential to appreciate how precious our life is while there's still time to make the most of it.

I call this a Good Life Crisis. And this book can facilitate yours. I hope you'll join me on this journey. The next chapter introduces one of the most vital tools to guide our way – one we'll return to many times over the course of this book.

WAKE UP: CHAPTER SUMMARY

Ask yourself:

❓ **What advice would my 'future self' give me about how to live today?**

Don't just:

✗ Keep ploughing on without thinking about what really matters.

Try this out:

✔ Focus on the things that matter most. Let go of other stuff.

Chapter Two:

Look Inside

What's going on in my mind and body?

On a grim January day in Scarborough in 2011, I found myself in an unfamiliar room, sitting in a circle with a random mix of local people I'd just met. There was a binman, a butcher, an artist, a belly dancer, a shop worker, a marine biologist and a retired couple. We all had our eyes closed, yet somehow it didn't feel weird!

To explain what brought this odd group together, it might help if I told you about the other two people in the room: they were David Sillito, the BBC's culture correspondent, and Andy Puddicombe, a mindfulness teacher who would soon go on to create the Headspace app used by millions.

Together, we were about to embark on the 'Happiness Challenge'. This was a week-long exploration of science-backed ideas for happier living – broadcast on the BBC *Breakfast* television show in the run-up to the launch of Action for Happiness.

Day one began with mindfulness, and that's where this chapter starts too.

> ### 🧠 What is mindfulness?
> Mindfulness is simply paying attention to what's happening right now. Instead of being pulled into worries about the future or replaying things from the past, we bring our awareness back to the present moment. It's a practical skill anyone can learn; for example, by noticing the sensations in our body, what's around us, or our thoughts and feelings as they come and go. Importantly, we do this without judgement, noticing how things are without labelling them as good or bad.
>
> Mindfulness is not a rigid routine or complicated ritual. You don't need incense, chanting or a perfectly calm mind. It can be done anytime, anywhere and doesn't have to involve meditation (although meditation is a great way to learn the skill initially). Having a busy mind is completely normal. Mindfulness helps us see things more clearly so we can respond more wisely rather than react on autopilot.

Today, mindfulness is a fairly mainstream idea, and many of us have heard that things like breathwork and meditation can be good. But back in 2011 it was still a fringe topic, and I could sense that David, with the scepticism of a good journalist, thought it was quirky – he wasn't sure our participants would even be willing to give it a try.

But as the session unfolded, something remarkable happened. As Andy guided the group through simple exercises – paying attention to our breath, the sensations in our bodies and the sounds in the room – I watched these people take their first tentative steps into experiencing something profound. The energy shifted and the usual noise quietened, and for a few minutes we simply paused and paid attention. By the end of the session, even David seemed moved and less sceptical.

What I saw that day was people from all walks of life discovering a different way of relating to their thoughts and feelings. It reminded me of the shift I'd been through when I turned to mindfulness while dealing with my chronic back pain. Desperate for relief, I'd started experimenting with it, beginning with a simple breathing exercise. At first it was just about coping with the physical discomfort, but as I practised I started seeing something deeper: I was learning a skill that changed how I related to the world.

Fast forward five years and there I was, watching others learn what I had: that becoming more aware of what's going on in our bodies and minds is an important first step towards being calmer and happier. It may begin with a simple breathing exercise, but it opens up a richer way of experiencing daily life.

The benefits of mindfulness

Research shows that mindfulness can alter both the structure and function of the brain, enhancing wellbeing and reducing stress. Functional MRI studies show that regular mindfulness practice increases activity in the prefrontal cortex, the part of the brain responsible for higher-order thinking, self-awareness and emotional regulation. It also reduces activity in the amygdala, the brain's 'fear centre', which is often overactive during stress and anxiety. This combination helps people manage difficult emotions and build greater emotional resilience.

Mindfulness can also promote 'neuroplasticity' – the

brain's ability to change and adapt over time. A Harvard University study found that after just eight weeks of mindfulness training, participants showed growth in brain regions associated with memory, learning and compassion.

Mindfulness-based interventions (MBIs) have also been shown to reduce symptoms of depression and anxiety, manage chronic pain, support recovery from addiction and improve overall wellbeing.

What does mindfulness involve?

For some people, the word mindfulness brings to mind new-age mysticism or wellness clichés. If that's you, don't worry — you don't need to sit cross-legged on a mountain to benefit from this. What we're talking about here is much simpler and more down to earth: the everyday skill of paying attention.

In the previous chapter, we asked: What am I doing and what truly matters? Maybe that helped you recognise you'd like to change some things in your life. We'll come back to that soon, but first we need to hone our core skill of mindful awareness. This is the foundation we'll build on later. Once we become more fully aware of what's going on inside us and around us it becomes easier to notice which actions genuinely help.

If this still sounds a bit abstract or you're unsure about the idea of mindfulness, that's okay. One helpful way to describe it comes from the All Blacks rugby team, who use the mental conditioning mantra: 'Be where your feet are.'

During a match, the players train themselves to be fully present and focus on their body, their breathing, their position and what's directly in front of them. This helps them perform at their best and stay 'in the zone' rather than being distracted by the scoreboard or the crowd.

So it works for elite athletes, but what about the rest of us? In the next few sections we'll learn some basic mindfulness skills together. If you already do this daily, feel free to skip ahead. If you don't, I hope these ideas will help you make mindfulness a habit that leaves you feeling less stressed and more in control. Nothing needs to change on the outside – only how we pay attention on the inside. As we develop this awareness and start noticing more, we gradually shift from mindless survival towards mindful living.

Having a busy mind is natural

What happens if I ask you to pause for a moment, sit still and not focus on anything?

I don't know about yours, but my mind almost immediately rushes off. I start thinking about what I'm doing later today or remembering what happened earlier. I'll wonder what that noise is outside or why on earth I haven't changed that wallpaper. These thoughts – and many more – arise involuntarily, as if from nowhere.

This relates to a common misunderstanding about mindfulness and meditation. We often associate these practices with having to sit in an uncomfortable position while trying to 'clear our mind'. We discover this is impossible and say things like, 'I tried meditating but I couldn't do it, my mind was too busy!'

Fortunately, this is missing the point. Rushing off is what our minds naturally do – they're constantly busy making connections, processing what's happening and helping us work out what to do next. Being mindful is simply noticing what's going on for us – including our busy thoughts – rather than trying to clear things away.

> **→ Mindful 3-2-1: Try this now**
> This is a 10-second reset that can be done anytime, anywhere and helps bring your attention back to the present.
>
> Pause, take a few deep breaths and gently bring your attention to:
> - 3 things you can see around you
> - 2 sounds you can hear
> - 1 thing nearby you can touch
>
> This exercise uses an amazing capacity we all have but usually take for granted: the ability to choose where we place our attention. In this case we're bringing our awareness to our senses of sight, hearing and touch. There are countless things going on around us and inside us at any given moment, and choosing where to place our attention is like shining a torch on one specific part of our experience.
>
> You can try it again now, by simply noticing the sensations in a particular part of your body, like your left thumb or right foot. What's going on there right now?
>
> Take a moment to recognise this powerful capacity you have to direct your attention somewhere that you choose.

Building our attention 'muscle'

Fifty years ago, hardly anyone went to the gym – it just wasn't a thing. Yet these days we all accept that doing a repeated exercise, like a bicep curl, builds that muscle. Lifting weights transforms your body over time.

The same principle holds when it comes to transforming your mind. Each time we bring our attention back to the present it's like doing a bicep curl for our attention. As we keep practising this over time, our attention 'muscle' builds and we get off autopilot more often. This is the basic building block for mindful living.

Many people find the easiest way to learn this is through meditation, which really just involves creating a quiet space, away from distractions, where we can focus on developing this skill.

I first learned this with a simple breathing exercise. I made time each day to sit still and try to keep my attention on my breath. With hindsight this was 'meditating', but it felt very straightforward and doable. No mantras or incense were needed.

Each time I noticed my thoughts had wandered off, I simply tried to bring my attention back to the present and focus on my breathing again. Rather than giving myself a hard time for my mind being distracted or busy — which it almost always was — I learned to simply smile to myself, notice where my mind had drifted and gently bring my awareness back to my breathing.

Maybe you'd like to try this now?

> **➜ IPSO breathing (in, pause, slowly out)**
>
> Here are three easy steps I use to become aware of my breath and practise mindfulness. You can say these words in your head as you repeat the steps:
> - **In** (breathe in)
> - **Pause** (briefly hold your breath)
> - **S**lowly **O**ut (breathe out, more slowly than your in-breath)
>
> See if you can focus your attention on your breathing for just one minute. When you realise your mind has

> wandered off, simply bring it back to repeating the IPSO steps. You may also notice yourself gradually relaxing as your rate of breathing slows. This activates the parasympathetic nervous system, which helps us to 'rest and digest' and feel less stressed.

Focusing on the breath is the ideal way to learn the basic mindful skill, and we can then use this to expand our awareness. A helpful next step is to focus on the body and on becoming more aware of what's going on physically.

Take a moment now to bring your attention to the feelings and sensations in your body as a whole. What do you notice?

I suspect that even in just a few seconds of doing this you may identify something you hadn't been aware of. Perhaps some feelings of tightness or tingling, or a part of your body that feels warm or cold. Maybe some areas of discomfort.

Turning towards rather than away

One of the most helpful aspects of mindfulness is the principle of accepting things just as they are. So we notice our experience and acknowledge it rather than judging it as good or bad. Mindfulness also helps us to see more clearly when we're suffering, for example with pain. Rather than pushing these feelings away, we turn towards them. This is actually quite a radical idea and takes a bit of practice.

When we experience pain, we naturally want to avoid it because it's unpleasant. So we try to ignore it, distract ourselves or numb the discomfort. But avoidance doesn't work in the long run – and can even make things worse.

If we fight our pain, we still feel it. But we also unleash further distress with thoughts like, *Why has this happened to me?* or *What if I never recover?* So this adds self-inflicted wounds that compound our suffering. Buddhists call this the 'second arrow', referring to the extra suffering we create in our minds on top of the original pain.

Acceptance doesn't mean we're giving up or resigning ourselves to how things are. It's about just being present with what's going on from moment to moment. It sounds counterintuitive, but the intensity of physical pain – or difficult emotions – often reduces when we allow ourselves to feel this fully.

I saw this first hand when I met Jasmine, who'd been battling for years with chronic fatigue and fibromyalgia. She'd tried all the usual treatments, but nothing had worked and she was stuck in a cycle of pain and exhaustion. Then she came across our Action for Happiness course and learned about mindfulness from Jon Kabat-Zinn – the pioneering doctor who developed 'Mindfulness-Based Stress Reduction'.

Jasmine found she could approach her pain differently – rather than trying to fight it, she began to accept it and observe her discomfort. Although the pain was still there, her relationship with it shifted and it became less debilitating. She told me how it had given her a new sense of control and she felt more hopeful about the future.

With my own chronic back pain, I was surprised to find that when I consciously brought my attention to the painful areas, the pain began to feel less intense. I noticed the 'shape' of my pain and how this changed as I became more tuned into it. I learned to do a body-scan exercise each night and found that it helped me to relax and sleep more easily, with much less discomfort.

→ Body scan: try this tonight

Sit or lie down in a comfortable position. Take a few deep breaths.

You can close your eyes if you like (although you may want to read this first!).

Start by just noticing the sensations in your toes and your feet.

Then slowly begin to move your attention up your body, noticing the feeling in your ankles, then your lower legs.

Keep noticing as you move your attention up to your knees and upper legs.

Continue to move on to the sensations in your pelvic region and lower back.

Notice how your abdomen rises when you breathe in and falls as you exhale.

Now experience the sensations in your chest and then your upper back.

Next bring your attention to the feelings in your fingers, hands and wrists.

Notice the sensations in your forearms, upper arms, shoulders and neck.

And then on to the feelings in your face and head.

Finally, bring awareness to your whole body, from your toes to your head.

Take a few breaths as if you are breathing in and out with your whole body.

Your inner 'weather'

Once we've developed our basic awareness of breath and body, we're ready to start going deeper to begin exploring our thoughts and feelings.

When I learned to be more aware of my body, it didn't just help to relieve my back pain, it also helped me uncover the truth about my underlying stress and how this contributed. The biggest shift came when I realised that my physical pain was really just a signal. Underneath the surface was a deeper emotional weight I hadn't fully acknowledged: fear, frustration and anxiety about my condition.

As I brought my attention to these feelings, I began to see them clearly for what they were. I learned not to push them away but to observe them. And over time, both my physical and emotional pain began to lose their grip.

In the coming chapters we'll focus more on inner feelings, including how you can get comfortable with them and some helpful ways to shift your mood. But before that I'd like to share a simple question and metaphor, which I find really helpful:

What's the 'weather' inside you like at the moment?

Much like the weather outdoors, we have a sort of inner weather pattern that changes each day as our thoughts and feelings come and go. Maybe today is like a bright spring morning, with a feeling of freedom and lightness? Or perhaps it's more 'dark and stormy' inside, with feelings of worry or frustration? Learning to notice what's going on inside us is vital, especially in difficult times.

The other thing about weather is that it's always changing. Even when today feels rainy or stormy, it won't be that way forever and the sun will come out again.

I also find it helpful to remember that above the clouds there's always blue sky. You may have noticed this while flying on a plane, when it rises above the grey into beautiful clear air. Similarly with our inner weather, when we learn to observe and move beyond our 'cloudy' thoughts, we find more clarity and things can feel brighter.

More on that later, but in the meantime, let's explore more benefits of mindful living.

Attention in a world of distraction and convenience

It's more difficult than ever to live mindfully. As influencers, advertisers and apps compete for our attention, it can be hard to stay focused on anything. We're bombarded with notifications 'pinging' and new alerts or ads popping up to take our focus away. This battle for our attention means we're less able to just sit quietly with a book or be alone with our thoughts. It feels like our attention spans are getting shorter and we're 'always on', all the time.

Meanwhile, lots of us also now have the fortune to be surrounded by incredible abundance and convenience. Take food, for example. Many people now have access to a vast range of tasty snacks and other indulgences at almost any time, often just at the touch of a button or swipe of a card.

As a result there's a mismatch between our survival instincts and this modern environment. Our ancestors evolved to seek out food whenever possible, so this could be stored away to survive times of scarcity. But now, as we're confronted with near-limitless readily available calories, our ancestral impulses often leave us consuming more than we need, leading to obesity and health problems.

When we rush through life on 'autopilot' we're less likely to notice what's behind our everyday choices. We miss the richness of our experiences and can easily slip into unhealthy habits. Learning to live mindfully can help us break free from this cycle of distraction by engaging more consciously with our thoughts and actions. In fact, I want to suggest a radical idea:

How you attend to the world actually changes what you find!

I don't mean the physical world literally changes according to your thoughts, I mean that by developing your ability to pay attention you can change your relationship to the situations and people around you. And you can make wiser choices as a result.

This ability to notice is your ultimate superpower in a world of distractions.

> **The power of 10 minutes a day**
>
> In a randomised controlled trial, researchers found that just 10 minutes of mindfulness a day can improve wellbeing and motivate people to adopt healthier habits like exercising more regularly, eating better and improving sleep quality.
>
> One participant noted, 'I am more patient, and I take more joy from the present moment.' Another reported that daily mindfulness had 'shown me a different lens through which to look at the world.'

Everyday mindfulness

The great news is that we don't have to meditate to live more mindfully. In the same way we can bring our attention back to our breath or body during a meditation, we can also learn to pause and do this at any time during the day.

We can notice the physical sensations while sitting at our desk. We can appreciate that beautiful tree on the way to work, or how we're feeling inside while waiting for the kettle to boil.

Again, each time we take a tiny pause to notice, we're building that attention 'muscle' and beginning to live with more awareness.

Mindful living is about bringing this present-moment awareness into all our daily tasks, whether that's walking down the street, enjoying a meal, using our phone or having a conversation. Each of these moments offers an opportunity to connect with the here and now – and to get 'below the surface' of what's happening.

I'd definitely recommend meditation as a great way to learn mindfulness, but don't give up if you find meditation isn't for you. Instead, try looking for creative ways to bring mindfulness into your everyday life. One of the biggest barriers to this is simply remembering to notice, especially on busy days.

> **Remembering to be here now**
> In the ancient Indian language of Pali, the word for mindfulness is sati, related to the verb sarati, which means 'to remember'. In this sense, remembering doesn't mean dwelling on the past, it means remembering to come back to the present moment. This is the core skill of mindful living, especially when so much of modern life is designed to hijack our attention.

My personal favourite tip is to turn everyday events or sounds into reminders to be mindful. For example, although I now keep all notifications off on my phone, I still often hear the sound of other people's devices alerting them to new messages. So I try to use these pings as a cue to slow down.

If I hear a bell or alert, I simply pause. I take a breath and observe my body and my surroundings. I may notice something I haven't seen before – like the way the light shines on a certain part of the room or something new outside my window.

> **Mindful reminders**

Here are some everyday activities and spontaneous events you could turn into your own reminders for a mindful pause:
- When your feet first touch the floor in the morning
- Clock chimes or church bells
- Waiting for the kettle to boil
- Putting on your shoes
- Hearing the ping of a phone notification
- Sitting down at your desk for the first time
- Pausing before replying to a question
- Hearing a siren or car horn
- Using your payment card
- Pouring a drink
- Switching the lights on or off
- Brushing your teeth
- When your head hits the pillow at night

Being less judgemental

By being present with our experiences – the comfortable and the uncomfortable – we learn to accept ourselves and our lives as they are. We give ourselves permission to get off that 'I'll be happy when . . .' hamster wheel and draw our focus to the only thing we really have: not the when, but the now.

And when we let go of judging everything for its immediate benefit or harm, we're more likely to experience moments of joy and appreciation.

> ⭐ 'There is no other day. All days are present now. This moment contains all moments.'
>
> – **C.S. Lewis**

Remember, this is not about achieving a particular state of mind or reaching perfection. It's about being present with whatever arises, without judgement. By letting go of self-criticism, you create more space for growth.

So allow yourself to experience thoughts and feelings as they come and go – and recognise that every moment of awareness is a step in the right direction. Each time you return to the present moment, you're building that attention muscle and cultivating a deeper connection with yourself and the world around you.

The good news is that you don't need to have mastered any of this to keep moving forwards. The remainder of this book brings lots more opportunities to apply your mindful skills in new ways to make life happier.

LOOK INSIDE: CHAPTER SUMMARY

Ask yourself:
❓ **What's going on for me beneath the surface?**

Don't just:
✗ Live on 'autopilot' and stay disconnected from your mind and body.

Try this out:
✔ Choose to live mindfully and learn to 'tune in' and be more present.

Chapter Three:

Decide to Act

How can my actions change
how I feel?

As a child, I loved riding bikes – from learning on my Raleigh Bluebird with stabilisers, to doing 'bunny hops' on my BMX. As a teenager I was out on my bike early each morning delivering newspapers, and even spent a summer on a cycling adventure in Germany. I enjoyed the freedom my bike gave me to get around and to earn pocket money doing the paper round. But above all I loved the physical sensation itself: speeding down hills with the wind on my face, feeling *alive*.

And yet two decades later, although I'd recovered from my back-pain drama, the only cycling in my life was an occasional journey to the local station or shops. My exercise, if I managed any, involved jogging once a week. But I didn't love it.

Despite my vague memories of childhood cycling, it didn't really seem appealing as a grown-up. Driving was so much quicker and less weather-dependent. And when we moved to Kingston, I felt intimidated by the Lycra-clad cyclists who went flying past around the park on their flashy bikes. Maybe it could be fun, but proper cycling would need new equipment and clothing I didn't own. It just didn't feel viable.

Then unexpectedly that summer, while on holiday in France, everything changed. I was keen to get some exercise, not least because my doctor had recently warned me I was overweight and my cholesterol was too high. However, I found myself unable to jog, due to a sore knee. Kate was doing lengths of the pool, but I'm not a keen swimmer.

Suddenly I spotted a bike leaning against the wall of our holiday rental. On a whim, I decided to hop on. I had no grand plan, no big goals – I just thought I'd give it a try and went off for my first ride in years. It was a bit awkward at first, but wow it felt *good!*

Cycling around the French countryside provided the usual buzz that comes with being active. But more profoundly, I felt reconnected to the simple joy and freedom cycling had offered in my childhood. From there, my love for cycling was rekindled. On returning home, I continued to take that small action: getting out on my bike. The more I decided to do it, the more I found myself enjoying it and pushing past those excuses that had kept me off a bike for years. And yes, I did end up getting some Lycra!

That one simple act of getting on the holiday bike didn't just solve my exercise dilemma, it changed how I felt. I noticed ripple effects for my mood and overall energy. The way I could clear my mind while heading out into the world – it transformed what had been an intimidating idea into something that brought me more joy and clarity.

Ever since that summer, cycling has been a huge part of my life again, all thanks to that spontaneous decision to just get back on a bike.

Take action, feel better

Most of us think we need to *feel* a certain way before we act – whether it's waiting for motivation to start exercising or wanting to feel confident before trying something new. But science shows we've got this the wrong way around. Our actions shape our emotions more than we realise. Psychologists use the term 'behavioural activation' to describe the insight that changing what we *do* changes how we feel.

Studies show that taking action – even when you don't feel like it – can lead to changes in your mood, energy and wellbeing. Whether it's going for a walk, calling a friend, or simply smiling at someone, these small actions change how we feel by creating positive feedback loops. Each tiny step has a ripple effect, making it easier to keep going.

Put simply: We don't just do what we do because of how we feel; we feel the way we feel because of what we *do*.

That's what I experienced when I finally just got on that bike after years of thinking about it. The act of *doing* changed everything. Once I started, I began to feel different and my outlook shifted.

> **Positive feedback loops**
> Neuroscience shows that when we engage in behaviours that are beneficial – like taking a walk, helping someone or showing gratitude – the brain activates its reward and motivation systems, including the release of dopamine. This neurotransmitter signals that an action is worth repeating, helping to reinforce the behaviour. This creates a positive feedback loop: each helpful action

> leads to a positive feeling, which in turn motivates more action. Over time, repeating these actions strengthens neural pathways in the brain, making it easier to keep going and enhancing our wellbeing.

From awareness to action

In chapter one we talked about the Good Life Crisis and how we have the potential to 'wake up' and decide to make life happier. Then in chapter two we explored how mindfulness allows us to tune in to the present moment, helping us become more aware of our thoughts, emotions and sensations.

Now we're going to take this one step further. Our focus will shift from simply observing to taking conscious action, using what we've noticed to guide our decisions in the real world. Your mindful awareness becomes a tool to shape your behaviour.

Each time we decide to take action, even something as simple as stretching or stepping outside for fresh air, we reclaim a sense of agency. It's not about committing to huge life changes or pressuring yourself to feel good. It's giving yourself permission to try something and then notice what happens as a result. Every intentional action is a tiny reminder that we have the potential to make life happier.

And remember, we're aiming for 'happier' rather than expecting to feel happy all the time, which is unrealistic. This is about finding ways to feel good, both in the moment and also about life in general. But rather than thinking of it as a *feeling* to chase after, it's more helpful to see this as a *skill* that can be cultivated through your actions.

> ### 🧠 Happiness is not 'one size fits all'
> Scientists have done lots of research into what makes us happier and we'll explore many of their discoveries in the coming chapters. One of the most important findings is that it *is* possible to become happier through conscious choices and actions. Although some happiness strategies reported in the media turn out to be less effective than claimed, certain factors are consistently linked to greater wellbeing – particularly our relationships and practising gratitude. At the same time, it's also important to remember that we're all different, so what works for someone else may not work for you.
>
> One surprising finding is that we aren't very good at predicting what will make us happier. We tend to overestimate the impact of things like possessions or appearance and underestimate the value of things like helping others or having a sense of purpose. But while our predictions may be unreliable, we all have the potential to learn from experience.

By staying mindful, we can track how different actions impact our mood and wellbeing. Just as mindfulness helps us tune into our emotions, it can also help us reflect on the outcomes of our actions. We may notice that some boost our mood or help us feel more energised, but others leave us feeling depleted or uncomfortable – and that's okay.

The key is to start experimenting, to take action and to learn from each step.

> **→ Don't just read this book!**
> You may have already noticed that at the end of each chapter I encourage you to put what you're reading into practice. These simple prompts invite you to ask yourself questions, consciously consider stopping things that aren't serving you and try specific actions that relate to that theme. If you haven't taken action on the prompts at the end of chapters one and two yet, I encourage you to try them out now and to keep doing that as we continue through the book.

Getting the basics right

People often talk about 'the basics' for health and wellbeing, like eating healthily, exercising regularly and getting enough sleep. We've all heard them, perhaps so often they don't even register any more. Blah, blah, whatever.

When I began my work on happiness, I'll confess I initially ignored these basics as if they were obvious platitudes. I felt drawn to exciting new research in areas like resilience and purpose (more on these later). But as I learned the skills of mindful living, I discovered just how essential these basics are too. In fact, when it comes to deciding to act, this is the best place to start. They are the foundations everything else builds on.

I was embarrassed to discover that my own approach to movement, sleep, nutrition and tech use all left a lot to be desired. So I started taking these more seriously and found that even small changes made a big difference. Let's look at each of these briefly.

Movement

When we move our bodies we not only stay fitter and healthier, we also feel better emotionally. Physical activity gets the blood pumping and releases those feel-good endorphins, which lift our spirits, lower stress and research shows can even reduce symptoms of depression.

You don't need to run marathons or take up a punishing gym regime – there are so many ways to stay active, from walking to yoga or even dancing in the kitchen! The best way to make movement a habit is to build it into your daily routine, for example by including a walk as part of your usual journey or turning chores into exercise.

Above all, try to find a form of activity that you actually enjoy, as you'll be so much more likely to keep it up. My gym routine had fallen by the wayside years ago, but when I took up cycling it became a lasting habit because I genuinely enjoyed it – and this then transformed my mental health as well as my fitness.

> **→ Tips for movement**
> - Build movement into your daily routine
> - Find ways of being active that you enjoy!
> - Leave your exercise kit out ready in advance
> - Treat chores as opportunities to 'work out'
> - Choose the stairs or get off a stop earlier

Sleep

Sleep is another essential piece of the wellbeing puzzle. I'd never been good at going to bed early and would still be working or pottering around after midnight most nights. But as I persevered with daily mindfulness, my self-awareness seemed to grow and I reluctantly noticed that when I go to bed earlier, I tend to sleep better and everything else seems to go a bit better too.

Having a good night's sleep can make all the difference in how we handle the day ahead. When we're well-rested, we think more clearly, manage our emotions better and tackle challenges with a fresh perspective.

There are lots of tips on 'sleep hygiene' these days, so I won't repeat them all here. Being mindful with our intake of caffeine or alcohol can help, as can turning off screens. Also, establishing a calm bedtime routine, like reading a book or some gentle stretching, helps signal to our bodies that it's time to rest.

Simply creating a bit more space for rest – like winding down a bit earlier – can support better sleep. And when sleep comes more easily, we're more likely to wake up feeling refreshed and better able to engage with the day ahead.

> **Tips for sleep**
> - Establish a regular sleep routine
> - Get daylight early in the day, dim lights in the evening
> - Avoid caffeine intake after midday
> - Finish eating several hours before bedtime
> - Ensure calm, screen-free time before sleep

Nutrition

Like sleep, nutrition is another huge topic, and this certainly isn't a food or diet book! But I was amazed to find that simple changes to my eating habits made a huge difference to my energy and mood. Again, mindfulness really helps here.

Eating mindfully helps us pay closer attention to our food

choices and notice how different foods make us feel. Also, when we take the time to savour our meals and notice the flavours and textures, it makes eating way more enjoyable. So with a bit of experimentation, we can choose more of the foods that nourish us rather than leave us feeling sluggish or depleted.

For instance, when I tried replacing sugary and processed foods with more natural ones, I found I was much less likely to go on that rollercoaster of highs and lows in energy. When I chose more fibre and gut-friendly foods, my digestion and general health improved significantly. And to my surprise, when I tried leaving bigger gaps between meals I noticed myself feeling much calmer and less 'hangry'.

But we all have different nutritional needs — and some of us struggle with disordered eating. So if mindful eating feels like a big ask right now, you might find it helpful to speak to your doctor or a trained dietician or nutritionist to get the right advice for you.

> **→ Tips for nutrition**
> - Notice which foods help you feel good (and which don't!)
> - Choose natural food over sugary or processed food
> - Eat more fibre and foods which support gut health
> - Try leaving longer gaps between meals
> - Remember to stay hydrated by drinking water regularly

Tech use

Finally, in our tech-dominated world, there's another 'basic' we could all do with getting better at: how we use our digital devices and their impact on our attention.

Despite good intentions, I really struggle with my tech use and often find myself staring at a screen instead of being there for my kids, listening to someone, enjoying a meal or noticing my surroundings. I've picked up my phone in the middle of the night, looked at it while driving and texted while sitting on the loo – all terrible ideas!

Although I still haven't cracked this, I've got much better at staying present and ignoring digital distractions. And each time I reach for my phone I now try to ask myself:

Why am I looking at this screen?
What else could I be doing?
Do I really need to do this now?

It's understandable that we find this hard – these devices and apps are designed to grab our attention at all costs. That's why many tech company bosses don't even let their own children use the products they developed. But with intention and practice we can discover what works for us and become less dominated by our devices.

> **➜ Tips for tech use**
> - Turn off notifications and alerts on your devices
> - Unsubscribe from unwanted emails or unhealthy group chats
> - Do 'single-tasking' and focus on one thing at a time
> - Set aside tech-free places and times (e.g. meals)
> - Be mindful with your consumption of news and social media

The antidote to autopilot

We established in previous chapters just how easy – and natural – it is to live on autopilot, rushing through our days and tasks without much conscious thought, often reacting automatically.

Taking deliberate action is a powerful way to disrupt this cycle. When we consciously choose to do something – whether it's getting up for a stretch or starting a conversation – we interrupt the automatic flow of the day. Action pulls us out of our default patterns and reminds us that we have control over what we do next. It doesn't need to be a huge effort; even small actions can bring back our sense of agency.

By stepping out of autopilot mode, we regain control of our time and our attention. And the more we practise this, the more we break free from the cycle of reactivity. By choosing to act with awareness, we re-engage with our lives in a way that brings clarity.

In this sense, action becomes the antidote to autopilot. You can step into the driver's seat of your life, shake up your routine and bring yourself back into the present, allowing you to see new possibilities for whatever comes next.

> ⭐ *'You don't have to see the whole staircase, just take the first step.'*
>
> **– Martin Luther King Jr**

Try it and see

When we think about doing something new, it's easy to lack confidence or get overwhelmed by the idea of trying to build a lasting habit. We can end up putting so much pressure on ourselves that we stop before we even begin.

So the best way to take on a new action is to start small. Instead of feeling the need to sustain a new behaviour, we can simply allow ourselves to experiment with tiny one-time actions – without any pressure to repeat them.

Trying an action just once, without commitment, can be liberating. Whether it's a five-minute walk, writing a quick message to a friend, or simply pausing for a few deep breaths, these little steps make a difference to how we feel right now. There's no requirement to turn it into a new routine if it doesn't work or feels overwhelming.

> **→ Mindful action checklist**
> When you decide to try something, consider the following questions:
> - How do I feel physically while doing this action?
> - How do I feel emotionally while doing this action?
> - How do I feel after doing this action?
> - Would I be willing to do this action again?

The key is to notice how you feel afterwards and this is where mindfulness can be so helpful. By tuning in to your body and mind after trying a new action you can see what impact it had. Some actions may go brilliantly and be worth repeating, while others may not. Either way, you're learning more about what works for you. We'll also dive more deeply into happiness experiments in chapter eight.

Growth mindset and the power of 'yet'

Our fear of failure or inadequacy is often a barrier to action. You might find yourself doubting your ability to change: What if I can't do it? What if I mess it up or make a complete fool of myself?

Many of us assume our abilities are innate and unchangeable, something psychologist Carol Dweck refers to as a 'fixed mindset'. But in reality we all have the potential to develop new abilities through effort and persistence. This simple but vital idea is what Dweck calls a 'growth mindset'.

In other words, we need to be willing to be 'bad' at something in order to learn and grow. That old phrase 'practice makes perfect' is more helpful when we rethink it as 'practice makes *better*'. There is no 'perfect', and every small action is a step forwards.

The simplest way to adopt this mindset is with a small three-letter word: *yet*. So, 'I can't do this' becomes 'I can't do this . . . yet.' 'I'm not good at this' becomes 'I'm not good at this . . . yet.' And so on.

With this subtle shift, we can try stuff out with a playful and experimental attitude, which acknowledges our worries or inadequacy, but also reminds us that when we give something a go it usually ends up becoming more natural and doable with a bit of perseverance.

There's a common belief that if we just think positively or visualise success, good things will come to us. While wishful thinking can certainly bring us a brighter outlook, it's not enough to merely *hope* for the best. Wellbeing isn't something that passively arrives – it's something we create by making intentional choices, even in small ways.

The most important action of all?

This first part of the book (Happier Inside) is focused on ways to feel happier within yourself. But happiness is not a solo pursuit and we are a social species. In part two (Happier Together) we'll explore relationships in a lot more detail, including topics such as listening, kindness, forgiveness and love. Meanwhile, as we reflect on how taking action can make life better, it's worth noting the number-one thing that tends to predict long and happy lives, according to Professor Robert Waldinger: the quality of our *relationships*.

So keep this in mind as you try out some new happiness ideas – and maybe include a few simple actions to reconnect with friends and loved ones or let others know you care. When it comes to happier living, the positive psychologist Chris Peterson put it beautifully and simply: 'Other people matter.'

What do you love doing?

You will probably have had times when you felt happier in the past and it can be really helpful to bring some of these to mind. For example, which activities, people or hobbies brought you the greatest sense of joy or meaning in the last few years? Often the simple things can be the best. Is there a way you could bring more of these into your life now, or restart something helpful that you stopped doing?

Another great way to find actions that work for you is by reconnecting with activities that brought you joy when you were younger. Take a moment to reflect on the hobbies or experiences that really made you feel alive or energised. Perhaps something you loved as a child, like drawing, playing music or spending time outdoors.

Ask yourself: What did I love doing before life became so busy? Was it visiting friends, reading novels or being creative? When you've identified one of these happiness triggers, why not experiment with reintroducing it into your life now. Try it once, see how it feels and go from there. The goal here is to discover what naturally lifts your spirits, not to create another to-do list.

> **→ Simple daily action ideas**
>
> Action for Happiness provides monthly calendars with daily actions designed to boost wellbeing. By trying out just one small action each day, you can experiment with a variety of ideas and see which ones are most helpful or motivating for you.
>
> Here are 10 of my favourite small happiness-boosting actions to try:
>
> - Do a small act of kindness for someone to brighten their day
> - Get back in contact with an old friend
> - Do something active you enjoy, ideally outdoors
> - Pause for a few minutes to sit still and just breathe
> - Try a different route today and see what you notice
> - Plan a fun or exciting activity to look forward to
> - Ask someone for help with a difficulty you're facing
> - Thank someone you're grateful to and tell them why
> - Talk kindly to yourself, like you would to a friend
> - Find three reasons to be hopeful about the future
>
> These actions are inspired by the '10 Keys to Happier Living', developed by Action for Happiness and Vanessa King.
>
> For new actions every day check out: actionforhappiness.org/calendar

Take one step towards a bigger goal

We all have larger goals we'd like to work towards, whether it's improving our health, strengthening relationships or pursuing a creative passion. Often these goals feel intimidating and it's easy to put them off. The key here is not to overthink it. Rather than waiting for the perfect time, just take the next small step.

If you've been meaning to improve your physical health, rather than planning a whole fitness regime, start by simply going for a short walk, stretching for five minutes or cycling into town. If you've been wanting to reconnect with someone, send a quick text or make a short phone call. Then check in on how you feel.

Although we're trying to keep this simple, don't be afraid of some discomfort. The modern world encourages us to take the easy option wherever we turn – from prepackaged meals to auto-playing videos. Companies make huge profits trying to sell us more comfortable lives. But a bit of discomfort can be liberating! By choosing to get outside and walk, cook your own meals or connect with someone new in your neighbourhood, you are reclaiming a sense of agency and control over your life and building your resilience. Think of every small action as another positive step towards that longer-term goal to make life happier overall.

> *'Happiness is not something ready-made. It comes from your own actions.'*
>
> **– The Dalai Lama**

As we'll discover in more detail later, when you're happier this doesn't just benefit you, it helps others around you too. So don't just take action for your sake, do it because feeling happier will also help you be the best you can for others: as a reliable friend, a loving partner, a supportive colleague, a wise parent or a responsible citizen.

> **DECIDE TO ACT: CHAPTER SUMMARY**
>
> Ask yourself:
> ? **Which actions actually leave me feeling happier?**
>
> Don't just:
> ✗ Try to feel differently without doing anything differently.
>
> Try this out:
> ✔ Do something positive, however small, and notice how you feel

Chapter Four:

See the Good

What am I taking for granted?

Keep a *gratitude journal*? You have got to be kidding me!

When I was first introduced to the idea of focusing on gratitude, I was sceptical. As a British bloke, in midlife, the idea of sitting down to write about what I was thankful for each day seemed contrived, even cringey. I remember thinking, *How could this help?*

However, when I saw the research on the benefits of gratitude, I became more open-minded. Scientists had found evidence that a simple daily gratitude practice can help people feel happier, improve their sleep and reduce their stress. So I got curious – maybe it was worth trying out?

I began to explore the connection between my mindfulness practice and gratitude. Maybe choosing to see the good stuff wasn't about pretending everything was fine . . . perhaps it could simply be taking a few moments to recognise that even on bad days there's always something to be thankful for.

So I put my wannabe 'happiness scientist' hat on and decided to give it a try – just as an experiment, nothing serious. For a few minutes each evening, I'd jot down three good things about my day: stuff I felt pleased about, little things I enjoyed, friendly conversations, seeing something that made me laugh or smile. That sort of thing.

Like many of my experiments to make life happier, this new focus on gratitude felt unnatural at first. Although I'd always considered myself an upbeat person, I was surprised to discover how rarely I had been paying attention to what was good. I just wasn't used to sitting down and reflecting on the positives when my mind was racing away with the challenges of the day.

But after a few days, that awkwardness faded and something else started to take its place: appreciation. Instead of focusing on what had gone wrong or worrying about tomorrow, I found myself remembering lots of little good things I would normally have overlooked. This also encouraged me to keep more of an eye out for things that gave me a boost during my days, too: like the view across the park on my way to work, a good cup of coffee or a kind word from a colleague.

Why not take a moment to try this yourself now.

→ Three good things

Think back over the last 24 hours and bring to mind something that was good. It might be a big thing, like an achievement or event. Or it could be something tiny, like a shared smile or a moment outdoors.

Next, grab a pen (or your preferred device), write down your good thing and include a few words about why it was good. Perhaps what it meant or how it made you feel. Don't worry, no one else needs to see what you write.

Now, try to repeat this and expand your list to three

> good things that have happened recently. Notice how it feels to bring these back into mind.
>
> Why not set an intention to try this every evening for just one week? Repeating this simple exercise for just a couple of minutes daily has been linked to greater happiness and a lower likelihood of depressive symptoms.

My own gratitude experiment seemed to prove the science right. I started seeing the world a bit differently. On difficult days, when everything felt heavy, making time to still find three good things helped me see that not everything was falling apart. Even on the worst days, good things still happen.

At night, instead of lying awake with thoughts of what hadn't gone to plan, I found that reflecting on those positive moments helped me unwind and get to sleep more quickly.

This wasn't just about me, though. I began to see how this practice could help others around me too. I started experimenting with asking my loved ones and colleagues questions that encouraged them to look for good things too.

So instead of asking my kids the usual 'How was your day at school?' (to which the usual answer was 'Hmm, okay I guess'), I'd ask, 'What went well today?' Or instead of starting a work meeting with a long list of issues, we'd ask, 'What's gone well recently?'

These subtly different prompts sparked more meaningful conversations. My kids actually started sharing funny and memorable things from their day. And my colleagues began to shift their focus to include things that were going well, not just problems that needed fixing.

Crucially, none of this was about *avoiding* the difficult stuff or pretending everything was fine. My kids still complained about boring teachers and our team still had lots of issues to get through. But we *also* made time to recognise the good stuff.

Resetting our negativity bias

It's natural *not* to be in the habit of focusing on good things. We all have a built-in tendency to pay more attention to the difficult parts of being alive, rather than fleeting lovely moments. We're hardwired to focus on what's wrong.

This instinct, known as the 'negativity bias', was crucial to our ancestors' survival. Paying attention to danger in an unpredictable world – from predators to rival groups – often meant the difference between life and death. If they hadn't focused on the risks, we wouldn't be here now.

Today, this same tendency helps explain why our minds still fixate on what's wrong – whether it's a harsh email, a challenging meeting or something we said that didn't go down well. Meanwhile we often overlook what's gone well, especially when we're on autopilot. We get stuck in cycles of worry and frustration, automatically jumping to the negatives without stopping to appreciate the good stuff.

> **The negativity bias**
> The negativity bias is our natural tendency to register bad things more readily than good things and to dwell on negative events more than positive ones. This psychological asymmetry explains why bad first impressions can be so difficult to overcome and why past traumas can have lingering effects. In most interactions,

> we're more likely to notice negative things and remember them more vividly later. We tend to recall insults more than praise, react more strongly to negative stimuli and make decisions based more on bad news than good news.
>
> This tendency is a helpful evolutionary trait. Throughout human history, those who were more attuned to danger were more likely to survive. They were also then more likely to hand down genes that made their offspring more attentive to risk too. This evolutionary perspective suggests the negativity bias is simply a way that the brain tries to keep us safe.

Choosing to actively see the good in our lives helps us disrupt our autopilot mode and counteract the negativity bias. Alongside our natural focus on what's wrong, we can also consciously direct our attention to what's going right. We can choose to notice, and even celebrate, small moments of joy or kindness that we'd otherwise take for granted.

Gratitude also plays a role in reshaping how we process experiences. Dr Rick Hanson, a psychologist and neuroscientist, once explained to me that our minds are like Velcro for negative experiences but Teflon for positive ones. In other words, the bad stuff sticks, while the good tends to slide away.

But by practising gratitude, we're essentially training our brains to hold on to positive experiences for longer. As gratitude becomes a regular part of our lives, we find it easier to notice and stay connected to positive moments, even in stressful times.

> **🧠 Gratitude in the brain**
>
> Practising gratitude can shape how our brains respond over time. Thanks to the brain's neuroplasticity, regularly noticing what's good can strengthen neural pathways associated with positive emotion and attention.
>
> Expressing gratitude also engages the brain's reward and mood-regulation systems, involving neurotransmitters such as dopamine and serotonin, which contribute to motivation, emotional balance and general wellbeing.
>
> Over time, practising gratitude can also support a process known as 'cognitive restructuring', where we become more aware of our automatic thoughts and purposefully choose to reflect on what is good or valuable.

Expressing gratitude

Feeling thankful isn't just something to experience in our heads. One of the best ways to build gratitude is to notice the good things other people do and to let them know.

Although our nearest and dearest usually do the most to support us, we often take them for granted and forget to let them know how much we appreciate them. There's an easy way to put this right: make a point of noticing and thanking them!

One lovely way to do this is to send a message to thank someone for what they did and let them know how much this helped you and why. Research has found that expressing gratitude in this way can really boost wellbeing, both for the recipient and the person doing the thanking. It doesn't need to be complicated or embarrassing. If you'd prefer not to write, just take a moment to say thanks in whatever way feels natural.

Everyone benefits when we regularly show appreciation – whether through a simple 'thank you' or something really heartfelt. If you're not sure what to say when writing a birthday card, focus on gratitude. Mention something you value about them or a shared experience you're thankful for. It makes your message so much more meaningful.

Also, when someone thanks you, don't minimise it. If you say 'oh, it was nothing', you're discouraging them from showing gratitude. Take a moment to really hear them and recognise that they're thanking you. You could even reply with something like 'I really appreciate you saying that, it means a lot', which in turn gives them a boost too.

Ordinary moments are precious

Gratitude isn't just about special times. When life feels mundane or difficult there are things we can do to keep hold of our appreciation. Sam Harris, the author and podcaster, introduced me to a powerful practice to reliably shift my focus and reconnect with what's really valuable. Maybe you could try this with me now?

First, think of something you do that you really enjoy. For me this might be something simple like riding my bike or having a family meal.

Once you've got something in mind, here's a thought that may be a bit painful to acknowledge, but is simply the truth of the matter . . .

At some point there will almost certainly be a *last time* you get to do that thing.

There will be a last time I'm ever able to ride my bike. Perhaps it'll be in my 80s when I start feeling too wobbly; or maybe I'll have an accident while commuting tomorrow? The point is, I probably won't realise it's the last time until afterwards.

This turns out to be true for most things in life – there will be a last time, but we usually don't know this until we're looking back. One day a meal will be missing someone who's been there for years, or something we rely on will be gone.

This perspective reminds us that life is unpredictable and we never know how the future will play out. Yet to my surprise, thinking like this actually leaves me feeling more appreciative of this moment and the time I have right now.

I remember this particularly on one car journey where the traffic was a nightmare and our kids were arguing. I felt tense and annoyed, despite the music playing and the countryside gently whizzing past outside. I just wanted to get home.

But then I remembered: one day it will be the *last time* I ever get to drive my family back along country roads, chatting and listening to our favourite tunes. And for all I know, this might even be it!

In that moment, I was able to let go of my frustration and recognise that everyday situation as something precious. Not perfect, but something that I could appreciate. I suddenly felt an overwhelming sense of gratitude for life – and even shed a few tears.

Okay, so maybe I got a bit carried away there, but nevertheless it was a powerful reminder that I had so much to be grateful for.

> ⭐ 'Enjoy the little things in life, for one day you may look back and realise they were the big things.'
>
> – Robert Brault

Gratitude and hope in difficult times

I was also surprised to discover how a grateful attitude can help those living through very tough times, facing far more serious challenges than I have.

I saw this first-hand through the DIY Happiness project, supporting women in disadvantaged communities. I met Nicolette, who was dealing with real hardships: unemployment, domestic violence, local antisocial behaviour and daily struggles to make ends meet and feed her children. Understandably she didn't see how reflecting on good things could possibly make a difference.

But after trying it out for a few weeks, something shifted. 'My circumstances haven't changed yet,' she told me, 'but my ability to deal with them has.' Gratitude helped her recognise the small things that were already supporting her and gave her more capacity to take steps to improve her situation. She still needed urgent improvements in her surroundings, but a subtle shift in her inner attitude made a meaningful difference.

Nicolette's words have stayed with me ever since. She's right: gratitude doesn't magically fix our problems, but it can shift our focus. It allows us to hold on to the small moments of light, even when the bigger picture feels heavy. It's not naive wishful thinking – it helps us see things clearly and stay hopeful.

As we look at the state of our world, it can be easy to feel hopeless. It seems like there's so much to despair about, from war and injustice to the climate crisis. Constant negativity in the media shapes our perception of the world and it can be difficult to hold on to the reality that there are positive things happening too. Yet all around us countless good things happen every day, from new scientific breakthroughs to millions of daily acts of kindness, creativity and friendship.

As well as facing up to – and standing up against – what's wrong, gratitude can help us look for and encourage constructive ways forwards. Yes, it takes effort, but when we hold on to the potential for good things to emerge we lay the groundwork for better outcomes. This isn't about pretending everything is okay, and gratitude is not a substitute for change. But rather than just complaining about what makes us angry we can promote what we love – and help ourselves and others feel more hopeful.

How gratitude builds on mindfulness

In chapter two we explored how to become more aware of our thoughts, feelings and surroundings. Practising mindfulness gives us the ability to observe what's happening *without* judgement, creating a foundation of greater awareness. Gratitude builds on this by inviting us to pay closer attention to what's supportive or life-enhancing – and to cultivate a habit of active appreciation. The more we practise this, the more we're able to notice the small moments of goodness we might previously have overlooked.

Gratitude expands our mindfulness from awareness into appreciation, allowing us to live with more of a sense of abundance rather than scarcity. By combining these two skills, we get an even richer experience of each day. Mindfulness allows us to pause and be present, while gratitude helps us see the good within that moment. Together, they help us really be there for life's small moments and get more out of them.

By adopting a 'gratitude attitude' we become more attuned to the joys in everyday life – whether it's noticing the beauty of a flower, the warmth of the sun or a friendly conversation. This in turn creates a ripple effect. By noticing more of the little good moments as they happen we can become more optimistic about the future, knowing that even on challenging days there will always be something to appreciate.

Begin your gratitude experiment

There are various tried-and-tested ways to include more gratitude in your daily life. So, following on from that invitation in the last chapter to 'take action' I recommend experimenting with a few of the ideas below.

> **→ Ways to see the good**
> Here are some different approaches you can try out:
> - **Start a daily practice**. Try doing the 'three good things' exercise every night. Treat it as an experiment and see how it feels. You may be surprised.
> - **Use good questions**. Help your loved ones, friends or colleagues experience gratitude. Ask, 'What went well?' or 'What's been good?'
> - **Really thank people**. Bring to mind someone you feel grateful to. Then get in touch to let them know and to really thank them. Messaging is a great start. Or to show how much it means, you could try writing them a card or letter and giving it in-person.
> - **Begin with what's good**. Start a meal, gathering or meeting by inviting everyone to share something they feel grateful for. Don't worry – there will still be time to focus on the issues too!
> - **Share positive stories**. Spread good ideas by passing on inspiring stories you've heard or uplifting articles. In a world focused on bad news, help to remind people there's good happening all the time too.

Advanced-level gratitude

Once you've mastered the basics of bringing more appreciation into everyday life, you might even want to explore some more gritty or demanding ways to be thankful, even when things don't seem great at first glance.

If you're feeling up for a challenge, think of something you're finding hard or where you feel dissatisfied – perhaps a difficulty in a relationship or with your work.

Got something in mind?

Now, challenge yourself to come up with at least one good thing about it. For example, can you appreciate that your work at least provides a source of income or you like one of your colleagues? Or maybe a relationship challenge helps you appreciate someone else in your life? See how many potential good things you can uncover about this difficult situation.

The balanced perspective

Although there are huge benefits to moving beyond our negativity bias, it's vital to remember that practising gratitude isn't about ignoring life's problems or pretending everything is okay. Gratitude allows us to hold two truths at once: life is hard *and* yet there are still things to be grateful for.

It's natural to highlight what's wrong. We all want things to be better. Being grateful isn't about tolerating injustice or being naive about tough situations. And it doesn't magically turn bad things good. But it *does* help us keep things in perspective.

There's an important difference between critical thinking – asking questions or challenging assumptions – and cynicism, which tends to assume the worst. Cynicism often masquerades as intelligence, but it's really a form of detachment or a defence against things not going well. Gratitude is more vulnerable and courageous. It takes strength to stay open-hearted in a messy world.

Keeping things in perspective also means avoiding forced or misplaced gratitude. If someone is feeling low, encouraging them to feel grateful could bring up feelings of inadequacy. Or after a traumatic event, trying to focus on the positives should not overshadow the need to address what happened.

So it's not a cure-all. Gratitude needs to be used as a constructive tool rather than a superficial remedy. Yet by intentionally noticing the good alongside – not instead of – the bad, we create a more balanced and resilient perspective: one that helps us navigate both the joys and difficulties of life with greater clarity and grace. Even in the darkest times, there are still glimmers we can hold on to.

In the next chapters we'll explore more deeply what it means to make life happier when we're living through difficult times – and how to balance seeing the good with acknowledging the hard stuff.

SEE THE GOOD: CHAPTER SUMMARY

Ask yourself:
? **What am I thankful for (or taking for granted)?**

Don't just:
✗ Focus only on what's wrong or what might go wrong.

Try this out:
✔ Appreciate precious moments rather than taking them for granted.

Chapter Five:

Keep it Real

Is staying positive always helpful?

'There's literally nothing good in my life right now!'

We were standing together at the back of a big auditorium where I was running a workshop on the science of happiness. Shortly before, I'd invited the participants to try out the 'three good things' action from the last chapter.

I'd done this many times and, as usual, there was a warm buzz as people turned to their neighbours to share something good. Maybe it was the funny thing their child did at breakfast, the unexpected compliment from a friend, or the kind stranger who held open the door so they made their train on time.

As the room filled up with enthusiastic noise, I spotted a woman towards the back who hadn't found anyone to talk to, so I wandered over to say hello. As I approached I could already sense she seemed annoyed and like she just wanted to be somewhere else. Anywhere else!

'Honestly,' she said, 'there's nothing to be thankful for. It's all awful. I don't need to be told to look on the bright side, like that will somehow magically fix my problems.'

I took a breath. I felt a bit defensive, but also sensed a learning opportunity – for both of us. Rather than trying to help her see things differently, I listened and reassured her that her feelings made sense. I shared that, although I was here promoting the benefits of gratitude, I too had dreadful days and I agreed that forced positivity isn't helpful.

Too often, happiness is presented to us as a picture-perfect life – the kind that's impossible to live up to. We've all seen those cheesy stock images of people leaping joyfully on beaches and memes telling us to 'just think positive'. These simplistic nudges can feel more like insult than inspiration, especially in tough times. Equating happiness with contrived positivity doesn't leave room for the imperfect reality of life.

Sometimes, seeing the good feels truly impossible – like it did that day for the woman I met, or for me when I was struggling with chronic back pain, or for countless people around the world who are facing real and painful hardships.

As the exercise drew to a close, I thanked her for being honest and said, 'It sounds like things are really tough right now.' To my surprise, she looked up with a brief, but genuine, smile and replied: 'Well, I guess I can be thankful my liver is still working.' Even on a dark day, she'd found a tiny ray of light. But it was grounded in realism, not wishful thinking.

I returned to the front of the room and reminded the audience how, alongside all these positive things they'd shared together, many of us probably also had moments of frustration and difficulty going on right now too. We agreed that for gratitude to be authentic, it must leave room for the reality of the situation, allowing for honest emotions rather than trying to force ourselves to feel happy.

Realistic optimism vs forced positivity

In real life, good things and bad things coexist. Small moments of joy live alongside other moments of struggle, pain or heartache. These pleasant moments are important, but they don't magically fix things.

To make life happier, we need to see the good while also recognising what's wrong. It's about practising 'realistic optimism' – a balanced approach that acknowledges challenges while still finding hope, rather than blindly sugar-coating every situation.

Forced positivity invalidates people's struggles and discourages emotional honesty. Although well-intentioned, if we encourage someone to brush aside their pain or frustrations, this can leave them feeling isolated or unheard, compounding the very feelings they're struggling to process.

Take, for example, those popular platitudes: 'Good vibes only!' 'Everything happens for a reason' or 'You're exactly where you need to be.'

If, like me, you find sayings like this uncomfortable, don't worry – that doesn't make you a pessimist. These clichés misrepresent the reality of life, including its inevitable ups and downs. They may appear uplifting, but they ignore the complexity of the real world. Pain and disappointment are as much a part of our human experience as joy and hope. To suggest otherwise is dismissive, even alienating, especially on the difficult days.

→ Wishful thinking vs realistic optimism

Here are some more helpful and grounded versions of common platitudes:

Wishful thinking	Realistic optimism
Good vibes only	Sometimes life sucks. But even on tough days, good things can happen
Everything happens for a reason	You can't control what happens, but you can choose how to respond
You're exactly where you need to be	Appreciate how far you've come and focus on the next step forwards
Just follow your dreams	Focus less on validation from others and more on your inner motivation
You can do anything you put your mind to	Set motivating goals, but make sure they're realistic too

Imagine telling someone reeling from a painful loss, cancer diagnosis or significant setback that 'everything happens for a reason'. What may be intended as encouragement can instead feel hollow – like their suffering isn't being acknowledged. If we sideline people's emotions in favour of positivity, we're not helping them move forwards – we're asking them to ignore the very feelings they need to process to heal.

Pain doesn't disappear because we pretend it isn't there. It lingers, often growing if it remains unaddressed. To create the space for healing, we need emotional honesty – where frustration, sadness or anger can be acknowledged. Being able to process our emotions is the first step towards finding clarity and building hope.

Many of us have internalised cultural narratives that associate positivity with strength and sadness with weakness. This can lead to feelings of guilt or shame when we inevitably face struggles. We may find ourselves thinking, *I should be over this by now* or *Why can't I just stay positive like everyone else?*

However, as the psychotherapist Julia Samuel explains, painful emotions don't disappear when we try to push them away. They need to be felt, expressed and understood in order to heal. Real resilience comes not from bypassing suffering, but from allowing it to be part of our story – and learning how to live alongside it.

Thankfully, in recent years, we've seen encouraging shifts – and less stigma – in how people talk about mental health. More of us are opening up about our 'inner lives' and acknowledging the struggles that lie beneath the surface. Topics like anxiety, grief and depression are more commonly discussed and less taboo, which has been a big step forwards in creating space for deeper and more honest conversations.

> **➜ Get mental health support**
> If you're struggling with grief, anxiety, depression or just finding it hard to cope, you're not alone. One in four of us will have problems with our mental health at some time in our lives. Here are some actions you can take:
> - **Tell someone you trust how you feel**. Talk about it with friends or family. Or call a helpline for a friendly chat (see findahelpline.com).

- **Focus on the basics**. Look after yourself, with small steps around healthy meals, regular sleep, staying active and connecting with loved ones.
- **Seek professional help**. Ask your doctor about potential support, such as counselling, therapy or medication.

'Manifesting' isn't the answer!

One fascinating example of forced positivity is the so-called 'Law of Attraction' – as promoted by Rhonda Byrne in her bestselling book *The Secret*. This claims that you can 'attract everything that you require' in life if you just wish for it in the right way. According to Byrne, 'you do it through your thoughts'.

Although our beliefs do shape how we interpret the world, it simply isn't true that just wishing for something will change the physical reality around us. However much I try to 'manifest' a desire for my loved one to recover from cancer, this won't magically make it so. It's almost certainly better to help them seek the medical care they need.

Byrne also describes how 'thoughts of fear and powerlessness' can attract people to 'being in the wrong place at the wrong time'. This feels like victim-blaming to me. Although I do believe that our attitude makes a big difference, we also need to recognise the reality of our situation. This includes the fact that lots of people end up in difficult, unfair and dangerous situations through no fault of their own.

Active Hope

In challenging times, it's natural to look for a way out. While visualising goals and focusing on what we want can help us stay motivated, the concept of 'manifesting' usually falls short. Coping requires more than just hoping – it requires action.

This is where the work of Dr Chris Johnstone on 'Active Hope' comes in. Johnstone is a medical doctor and resilience expert who worked for years as an addictions specialist in the National Health Service. He's found that we get hope all wrong.

Chris observed that people often want a *feeling* of hopefulness that their preferred outcome is likely. But if we wait for this before taking action, we get blocked, especially in areas where we don't rate our chances highly. Rather than just wishing for certainty, which depends on external outcomes, Active Hope is something that we can create intentionally, regardless of whether success is guaranteed.

Having helped lots of people recover from challenging life situations, Chris has seen first-hand that we can regain a sense of purpose by focusing on small, consistent actions that align with our values. He suggests three specific steps.

> **→ Active Hope in three steps**
> In his book on Active Hope, co-authored with systems-thinking expert Joanna Macy, Chris Johnstone outlines three simple steps to build Active Hope when facing an overwhelming or uncertain situation:
> 1. **Acknowledge your reality.** Take in a clear view of how things are, noting your fears, struggles and concerns rather than suppressing them.

2. **Choose your direction.** Identify what you hope for, in terms of the direction you'd like things to move in or the way you'd like to behave.
3. **Take steps forwards.** Start to make progress, however small, with purposeful actions that move you or your situation in that direction.

As Active Hope doesn't require optimism, we can apply it even in areas where we feel hopeless. It doesn't guarantee the outcome, but it turns despair into motivation. By taking small steps we make the future we want more likely.

Active Hope acknowledges the reality of our circumstances while focusing on what we can do to create change. It's not blind optimism – it's a way to accept life as it is and still move forwards with purpose. So we're combining acceptance and action.

Acceptance doesn't mean resignation or tolerating a bad situation – it's about seeing things clearly and honestly, without glossing over or denial. By focusing on small, achievable actions, we can move towards our goals while building resilience and momentum. Whether we're dealing with personal problems or worried about wider social issues, this helps us to be part of the change we want to see.

'Courage doesn't always roar. Sometimes courage is the quiet voice at the end of the day saying, "I will try again tomorrow."'

– **Mary Anne Radmacher**

Consider someone navigating a difficult job market. Active Hope begins with them acknowledging the reality: 'This is tough and it's going to be hard to find the right role.' From there, it shifts to action: updating their profile, contacting people or applying to one job each day. Each step, however small, contributes to a sense of progress and builds the capacity to keep going.

Instead of relying on the universe to deliver outcomes, we can meet life where it is and ask, 'What's one thing I can do today to make this situation better?' We're rooted in reality but powered by possibility. Even in the face of adversity, we can do something.

> 🧠 **There is beauty in the broken**
>
> 'Kintsugi' (which means 'to join with gold') is the Japanese art of mending broken pottery with gold, so that a repaired vase can become more 'imperfectly beautiful' than it was before the break. Rather than trying to hide the damage, this highlights the repair.
>
> Our imperfections are what make us unique and valuable. By being willing to see our flaws, face our difficulties and put ourselves back together, we are being more real. Like the mended vase, we're stronger, more authentic and more resilient than something that has stayed 'perfect'. We'll talk more about accepting ourselves and facing difficulties in the next two chapters.

The possibility of 'and'

When faced with hardship, we often get stuck in negative thought patterns, like catastrophising, taking things personally or feeling that we're a failure. Trying to suppress these thoughts isn't healthy, so we need to acknowledge them. Yet we also need to make space for possibility too.

One of the most powerful ways to do this is what the psychologist and resilience expert Dr Maria Sirois calls the 'possibility of and'. This mindset encourages us to hold two truths at the same time, reflecting the complexity of real life. So after acknowledging the reality of our situation, we also make room for what she calls a 'balancing truth'.

For example:
- *'I'm struggling* **and** *I'm doing my best.'*
- *'Life is hard* **and** *there is beauty in it.'*
- *'This is not what I wanted* **and** *I can find a way forwards.'*

Using this 'and' mindset helps us stay realistic while maintaining a sense of momentum. We develop more 'cognitive flexibility' by recognising that difficult feelings and positive outcomes are not mutually exclusive. Instead of being trapped in all-or-nothing thinking – where we're either thriving or failing – it gives us permission to exist in the messy, in-between space of being human.

This approach also pairs beautifully with Active Hope. So let's explore how we can combine these ideas in practice, to respond to a difficult situation in a healthier way.

Take a moment to reflect on a challenge you're currently facing. Perhaps it's a difficult relationship, a setback at work or certain worries about the future.

Name the challenge
Start by stating the situation or feeling honestly. Avoid minimising it. For example:
- 'I'm feeling overwhelmed by work deadlines.'
- 'I'm struggling with feeling lonely right now.'

Identify the 'and'

Now, add a balancing truth to the statement. What else is true about your situation? What strength or opportunity can coexist alongside the challenge? We're not after forced optimism, this is about broadening our perspective. For instance:

- *'I'm feeling overwhelmed by work* **and** *I've met tough deadlines like this before.'*
- *'I'm struggling with feeling lonely* **and** *I've got someone I could reach out to.'*

Choose your action

Consider what small but meaningful next step you can take to move forwards. This isn't about 'fixing' the problem instantly but rather acknowledging the power you have to influence your situation. For example:

- If you're overwhelmed, you might prioritise one task to do today.
- If you're feeling lonely, you might plan to call a friend.

This simple but powerful technique trains the mind to hold space for both struggle and hope, ultimately strengthening our resilience. It lets us acknowledge that life isn't always either terrible or wonderful – it's often both.

Keep it real *and* see the good

The last two chapters have looked at the power of gratitude and the importance of realism. This combination is vital because holding two opposing thoughts in our heads at the same time is one of the hardest yet most important skills for happier living.

Here are four contrasting statements which seem at odds with each other:

- Things were difficult
- Things went well
- Things will be difficult
- Things will go well

Yet all four of these statements can be – and usually are – true at the same time. Focusing on just one of them is incomplete. The messy, grey areas of life are where the real growth happens – and this discernment is crucial to making wise choices.

Living a happier life isn't about avoiding struggles, it's how you navigate them. So if someone tries to suggest how you can feel happy all the time, they're either selling snake oil or they've misunderstood how life really works.

In the next chapter we'll look at another vital skill to help us find this balance: learning how to treat yourself as you would a friend.

KEEP IT REAL: CHAPTER SUMMARY

Ask yourself:

❓ **How can I respond constructively to this situation?**

Don't just:
✗ Believe positive thinking will bring you everything you want.

Try this out:
✔ Be a realistic optimist. See life as it is and respond with Active Hope.

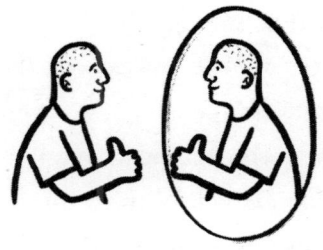

Chapter Six:

Tame That Critic

Why am I so hard on myself?

Before we dive into this chapter, I want you to pause and consider this scenario:

Imagine someone you love is having a hard time. They feel like they've failed or messed up in some way. Or they've let themselves or someone else down. What would you say to support or comfort them? And how would you want to respond to them in terms of your tone or body language?

Take a moment to think of the words you'd use and how you'd behave towards them.

*

Now, let's flip the situation: what do you say to *yourself* when you mess up?

Is it similar to how you'd talk to your friend or family member – or perhaps not?

When I was introduced to this exercise by self-compassion expert Dr Kristin Neff, I found the first question fairly easy to answer. I knew I would want to reassure my loved one by saying something like, *'You're doing the best you can in a difficult situation.'* And I'd try to use warm words and supportive body language.

But when I flipped the scenario back to me, it was another one of those monumental wake-up moments. I realised – perhaps for the first time – just how harshly I often speak to myself. On the outside, I present myself as upbeat, warm and caring. But on the inside, my inner critic was much nastier than I'd been willing to admit.

That second question helped me see that I was bombarding myself with criticism. I'm not normally a sweary person, but I realised I'd often called myself an 'F-ing idiot' (or worse), even for little mistakes. I'd been berating myself when I failed to meet impossible standards – using uncharacteristically foul language!

I may have appeared calm and content on the outside, but by tearing myself down like this, I was undermining my peace of mind on the inside.

Does this sound familiar to you at all?

Kristin's exercise revealed a disconnect between my personal values around kindness, acceptance and mindful living – and how I actually spoke to myself. It was a turning point – and that day I resolved to try to retrain my inner critic.

> ⭐ *'Changing the conversations we have with ourselves has the potential to change our lives.'*
> **– Ethan Kross**

Before looking at some solutions, let's take a moment to explore why many of us are so harsh on ourselves so often.

The harsh inner critic

Being aware of an inner voice in your head is a near-universal experience. The majority of people report having some kind of internal monologue – a stream of verbal thoughts running in their mind, a bit like a narrator. Scientists believe this helps us recall ideas, mentally rehearse situations, process information and make decisions.

Often our monologue can be cautious or critical – and for understandable reasons. This stems from a natural instinct to protect ourselves from danger or failure or embarrassment. However, in some cases that critical voice overreaches, moving from being a 'protective friend' towards becoming a voice of unrelenting judgement. It may also reflect how we were spoken to as children.

Our culture then amplifies this problem. Marketing messages target our insecurities, relentlessly telling us that we're not enough – not successful enough, attractive enough or happy enough – until we buy the product or adopt the lifestyle that promises to fix us.

Meanwhile, social media bombards us with highlight reels of others' lives – polished, curated and filtered to perfection. Our own messy, imperfect reality feels inadequate in comparison and the inner critic seizes this as proof that we're failing. As a result, many of us are harder on ourselves than we would ever be on someone we love.

We also often berate ourselves about our interactions with others – for saying the wrong thing, not being kind enough or failing to be a 'perfect' friend. We set unattainable standards for our own behaviour, which we don't expect of others. So if a friend says something careless, we forgive them – but if we do, we judge ourselves more harshly.

The costs of self-criticism

Living with a harsh inner voice comes at a high price. When we take the hurtful things our critic tells us as facts we're more likely to struggle with low self-esteem. Even our successes can feel hollow when the inner critic starts nitpicking flaws or imagining ways we could still have done better. Carrying around this 'bully in our brain' erodes our ability to fully appreciate our achievements or the good things in our lives.

Also, this isn't just a problem for our inner life. The way we treat ourselves sets the tone for how others treat us too. That cycle of negativity in our heads can also affect our relationships. If we approach ourselves with self-contempt we may inadvertently allow, or even invite, poor treatment from those around us. This can become a vicious cycle.

The critic also undermines our growth. Fear of failure becomes an unhelpful companion, whispering, *What if I mess up?* or *What will they think of me?* This keeps us stuck in our comfort zone, unwilling to take risks or try new things – it narrows our outlook.

> **The science of negative self-talk**
> Research shows that talking harshly to ourselves doesn't just feel bad in the moment – it's also linked to longer-term mental health difficulties. Habitual inner criticism is associated with rumination and increased symptoms of anxiety and depression. It also reinforces limiting beliefs and engages the brain's threat-response system. These patterns are linked to heightened stress responses, including changes in levels of cortisol (the stress hormone), making it harder to cope when things go wrong.

> The good news is that engaging in more realistic and encouraging self-talk can really help. The work of clinical psychologist Paul Gilbert shows that learning to respond to yourself with compassion helps to calm the threat system and supports emotional regulation. Studies also show that there are ways to step back from automatic criticism and shift our inner dialogue – for example, by describing feelings in neutral language or reframing thoughts constructively.

Can the critic be helpful?

Although the inner critic can be destructive, it's not inherently bad. It evolved as a survival mechanism, aiming to protect us from mistakes or harm. Like a poorly trained coach, it may deliver its feedback in ways that hurt more than they help. But with practice, we can retrain this coach to be more constructive.

By helping us to reflect on our mistakes, the critic can offer insights that help us grow, sharpen our skills or deepen our understanding. So, rather than getting caught up in self-recrimination, we can extract the wisdom behind our inner judgements and then use this to move forwards with clarity and purpose – and a bit more kindness.

Having a healthy relationship with our inner thoughts is a vital part of resilience, which we'll explore in the next chapter. Learning to handle setbacks with curiosity instead of condemnation strengthens our ability to bounce back. Each challenge becomes an opportunity to practise self-care and perseverance. Over time, this can actually build a sense of inner stability that no external validation can provide.

The key is balance: training the critic to be a wise coach instead of an unfriendly bully. Although we can't silence it – because let's face it, the voice never goes away – we can work on transforming it.

That's what I tried to do after realising how unhelpful my own inner narrative had become. Whenever I caught the voice in my head turning nasty, I simply tried to speak to myself more like I would a friend.

And I stumbled on a memorable way to reframe my sweary voice!

> **→ F*** me**
>
> Having noticed that I regularly used the F-word to berate myself when I messed up (e.g. 'You f-ing idiot', etc.), I needed a way to disrupt this. So I started using my inner 'F-word' insults as the trigger for a daily mantra (with a handy acronym!) for how I want to treat myself and others:
>
> *Friendly, Useful, Calm and Kind*
> Now, when my inner voice is about to criticise me for having 'f***ed up', I use this mantra. It makes me smile and reminds me how I want to show up in the world.
>
>   **F**: How am I being **friendly**? (Including to myself)
>   **U**: How am I being **useful**? (Even when I make mistakes)
>   **C**: How am I staying **calm**? (Even when things go wrong)
>   **K**: How am I being **kind**? (Including to myself)

By softening my inner voice and replacing judgement with curiosity, I became better at navigating setbacks without being undone by self-criticism. That's really what this chapter is about: not silencing your inner voice, but turning it into an ally.

The power of self-compassion

We started this chapter with Kristin Neff's work on self-compassion and that simple exercise to explore the way we usually talk to ourselves. Now, let's focus on how self-compassion works in practice – and why it can be so transformative.

Self-compassion isn't about giving ourselves a free pass to do what we want – it's about responding to our struggles with care instead of condemnation. This shift calms the brain's stress system and engages its soothing response, redirecting us from cycles of threat and punishment to a state of safety and warmth.

According to Neff, self-compassion combines mindfulness, self-kindness and a sense of shared humanity. *Mindfulness* helps us recognise the critic's voice without letting it consume us, by observing our inner dialogue with curiosity rather than judgement. *Self-kindness* transforms harsh inner narratives into supportive ones. So instead of thinking, *I'm so bad at this*, we might think, *This is hard, but I'm learning*. This gentler approach reduces shame and fuels motivation. *Shared humanity* reminds us that imperfection is part of being human. When we view mistakes as universal rather than personal failures, they become opportunities for connection and growth rather than isolation.

Neuroscience shows that the brain can develop new habits through repetition. So consistently practising self-compassion can reshape the way we process setbacks. Each time we choose to respond to self-doubt with kindness instead of harshness we strengthen those neural pathways. Over time, this changes our default response.

Ultimately, self-compassion equips us to move through life with less inner drama. Growth doesn't come from berating ourselves into change but from supporting ourselves through the process, with the same patience we would offer a loved one.

'Treat yourself as you would treat a good friend.'
— **Kristin Neff**

How to tame your inner critic

Self-compassion is not just an abstract idea – it's a practice that can transform the way we engage with our inner narrative. So here are some practical ideas to do this.

💡 *Talk like you care*

Whenever you're feeling down on yourself, imagine a loved one has come to you facing something similar. Most of us would instinctively comfort and reassure them. Yet often, this kindness we extend to others is absent from our own inner dialogue. This contrast is our opportunity: when we notice self-critical thoughts, we can pause and ask, 'What would I say to someone I care about in this situation?'

💡 *Create distance from harsh thoughts*

The words we use to describe our emotions hold power. Phrases like 'I'm a failure' merge our identity with temporary setbacks, making them feel insurmountable. Instead of labelling yourself, try describing the emotion you're experiencing. For example, replace 'I'm so bad at this' with 'I'm feeling frustrated right now.' This subtle adjustment creates space between you and the criticism, allowing you to see it as a passing feeling, not a fixed truth. Psychologist Ethan Kross calls this 'self-distancing', and has shown that it helps us regulate emotions more effectively and avoid getting stuck in inner criticism.

Writing down self-critical thoughts can also help. By externalising the voice in your head, it becomes easier to evaluate it objectively and reframe these thoughts into something constructive.

So, 'I'm terrible at this' might become 'This is new and I'm still figuring it out.' Another way to create distance is to use your own name when you're struggling – for example, I might say to myself, 'Mark, you're feeling overwhelmed right now.' This shift into an observer-like stance helps us speak to ourselves in the same supportive way we would to a friend.

Time travel for perspective

When you're feeling self-critical, it can help to step back, consider the bigger picture and reflect on how you might view this moment in the future. A week from now, will this mistake still linger? What about a year from now? Even the most difficult feelings and situations will change. Thinking from the perspective of your future self – who has moved past this moment – can offer more clarity and reassurance.

Reframe your inner critic as a coach

For all its harshness, the critic often carries a good intention – trying to protect us from failure or embarrassment. By reframing the critic as a coach, we can extract its insights without letting it undermine our confidence. So instead of resisting criticism, ask yourself: 'What's the wisdom here?' Perhaps your inner voice is pointing to an area for growth or highlighting a genuine risk. A phrase like 'I'll never succeed at this' might signal the need for more preparation, while 'I'm not good enough' could be an invitation to reach out for support. So take on board the helpful coaching – but leave the rest.

Use humour to disrupt negative loops

Sometimes the best way to handle the inner critic is to disarm it with humour. A light-hearted approach can interrupt spirals of self-doubt, replacing tension with a sense of playfulness. For example, using a favourite encouraging phrase or light-hearted reminder can help reframe criticism in a way that feels approachable. My own 'Friendly, Useful, Calm and Kind' mantra is said tongue-in-cheek, but also genuinely cheers me up and shapes how I behave. So you could come up with your own light-hearted phrase to remind you to smile and take your self-criticism less seriously.

> ⭐ 'To be beautiful means to be yourself. You don't need to be accepted by others. You need to accept yourself.'
>
> – Thich Nhat Hanh

Choose kindness over criticism

As we've seen, taming your critic is not about eliminating it but learning to work with it. By reframing your inner dialogue, stepping away from harsh judgements and practising those self-compassion ideas, you'll start to feel more at peace with yourself.

This transformation doesn't happen overnight. It's a practice that deepens each time you choose kindness over criticism, balance over perfectionism or growth over fear. So treat the ideas in this chapter as starting points to experiment with. I hope, like me, you'll find ways to shift your inner critic to be a warmer and more supportive voice – one that gently nudges you forwards rather than putting you down.

You may have heard of the 'Golden Rule', which is common to many faiths and wise traditions. It reminds us to 'Treat others the way you want to be treated.' (And in chapter 18 we'll see how we can upgrade from Golden to the Platinum Rule!)

I'd now like to encourage you to try an adapted version, known as the 'Internal Golden Rule'. This says: 'Treat yourself the way you wanted others to treat you.' So, even if others haven't treated you well, you can still show yourself the love you deserve.

Ultimately, the way we speak to ourselves shapes the way we move through the world. Cultivating a more compassionate inner voice isn't just an act of self-care – it's a foundation for living with greater resilience and purpose. The next time your inner voice gets critical, consider it an invitation – not to scold yourself, but to show yourself some understanding. That small shift can make a massive difference.

> **TAME THAT CRITIC: CHAPTER SUMMARY**
> Ask yourself:
> ❓ **What would I say to a self-critical loved one? (Now say it to yourself.)**
>
> Don't just:
> ✗ Use a harsh inner voice to motivate or punish yourself.
>
> Try this out:
> ✔ Show yourself the same kindness and care you'd give to a good friend.

Chapter Seven:

Reframe Difficulty

Is there a different way of looking at this?

'What a f***ing idiot,' I called out instinctively.

I don't usually swear at other people like this! But my heart was racing and I was really shaken up. I'd been commuting to work on my bike and the target of my unusual outburst was a driver. Their car had just swerved across lanes in front of me, causing me to brake and veer sharply to the side to avoid getting hit.

I was fine, but genuinely angry. That had been such a dangerous moment and I'd been lucky to stay upright and avoid a serious accident. The driver was clearly in a hurry and in that moment I just wanted to chase after them to vent my anger.

They sped off, seemingly unaware of the near accident – but my emotional reaction didn't flee the scene so quickly. The incident haunted me for the rest of my journey. Even when I sat down at my desk I was still feeling it. Why was I so furious? I had reason to be upset, but the intensity of my reaction felt disproportionate.

So I took a moment to tune in to that feeling of anger and I found something deeper. I'd been knocked off my bike the previous year, leading to broken ribs, a broken bike and months of pain and insurance hassles. I was angry because today's driver had put me – and possibly others – at risk. It wasn't just a near-miss – I'd felt disrespected, unsafe, frightened. This person was being intentionally reckless; they probably hated cyclists and they needed to be taught a lesson!

Once I named those feelings, something shifted. I could see the story I was telling myself wasn't necessarily accurate. Sure, the driver had been careless, but this may not have been intentional. Maybe they were distracted, stressed or in a hurry. Perhaps I'd been in their blind spot or they were rushing to get their partner to hospital.

I will never know what was going on for them that day. I couldn't control their behaviour, but I could still choose how to respond. So I made a mental note to keep an eye out for cars doing similar dangerous moves in future. And I also decided to give a wave of thanks to all those drivers who *do* behave respectfully and safely towards me and other cyclists – something I've been trying to do ever since. Then I took a deep breath and let the whole thing go. I felt calmer and the rest of my day went well.

> 'Everything can be taken from a man but one thing: the last of the human freedoms – to choose one's attitude in any given set of circumstances.'
>
> **– Viktor Frankl**

This is an example of a vital lesson, which took me quite a while to learn: when I step back and examine my emotions, I gain more perspective. I have the potential to let go of anger and frustration, rather than letting them spiral or consume my day.

We can't change what happened, but we can reclaim control over our emotional response.

Emotions as signals

People often label emotions as 'good' or 'bad', but this isn't accurate. While some emotions do feel more pleasant than others, labelling them as positive or negative can be unhelpful. Every emotion we experience is a *signal* – our body's way of alerting us to something important. These signals operate rapidly, often below the level of conscious awareness, to help us navigate the world and respond to our environment.

Each emotion carries valuable information about our inner state or external environment, guiding us towards actions that align with our values and needs. For example, anger can spur us to confront unfairness, fear can help us avoid danger and sadness can prompt us to seek comfort or connection. Because emotions carry important messages about what we need, it's really important we don't ignore them.

> **The problem with suppression**
>
> A 2013 study published in *Health Psychology* followed a nationally representative sample over 12 years and found that people who regularly suppressed their emotions had significantly higher risk of all-cause mortality compared to others.
>
> Why does this happen? Suppression can keep the body in a state of low-level stress, impacting the immune system, increasing inflammation and disrupting everything from sleep to cardiovascular function. In short:

> what you don't express, your body may internalise.
>
> Bottling up our emotions may help us avoid short-term discomfort or social friction, but over time it can undermine both mental and physical wellbeing. Activities like therapy, expressive writing or open-hearted conversations can help shift the pattern – letting things out before they take a toll.

When emotions are buried, they don't disappear – they linger and resurface in other ways. They may escalate into outbursts or appear physically through tension, fatigue or illness. They can amplify our inner critic or foster resentment towards others. Think of unacknowledged emotions like a pressure cooker, building in intensity until released.

The power of acknowledging emotions

When we give our emotions the space to share their message, they're more likely to pass naturally. Accepting our feelings doesn't mean letting them take over or indulging them indefinitely – it means recognising their presence and purpose.

Susan David, a Harvard Medical School psychologist, suggests that we aim to build 'emotional agility'. Rather than suppressing them, this involves embracing all our emotions with curiosity, including the challenging ones, and treating them as valuable information rather than burdens.

To practise acknowledging your emotions, you can draw on the mindfulness skills we've been cultivating throughout this book so far.

Pause and notice: When you feel an emotion rising, take a moment to notice and, if possible, name it. For example: 'I'm feeling angry' or 'I'm feeling sad.'

Allow the emotion to exist: Remind yourself that it's okay to feel this way. This is an understandable response. Emotions are temporary visitors – they come and go.

Get curious rather than judgemental: Rather than telling yourself not to be angry, sad or afraid, step back and ask yourself, 'What is this emotion trying to tell me?'

By viewing emotions as temporary signals rather than absolute truths, we can hear their message without letting them dictate our actions. For example, is there a boundary that needs reinforcing? Am I worried about something important? Am I grieving a loss or yearning for something missing? This practice of noticing and questioning our emotions is a cornerstone of emotional resilience.

> **➜ If your emotions could talk**
>
> So what are your emotions really trying to tell you? Here are some ways you could interpret their messages once you've noticed how you're feeling...
>
> **ANGER**: I am showing you something's wrong and your boundaries have been crossed
>
> **FEAR**: I am here to warn you of danger and protect you
>
> **GUILT**: I am reminding you of your values and helping you take responsibility
>
> **SADNESS**: I am here to help you slow down and process what happened
>
> **SHAME**: I am trying to protect you from rejection and help you feel accepted
>
> **ANXIETY**: I am trying to keep you prepared and help you stay safe

> **OVERWHELM**: I want to help you get through this and to slow down
>
> **GRIEF**: I am here because you loved, to help you honour what's been lost

Dr Tal Ben-Shahar, an expert in positive psychology and leadership, has a great concept about giving yourself 'permission to be human'. He notes that when we allow ourselves to feel the full range of emotions and welcome them as temporary 'visitors', they lose their power to overwhelm us.

Resilience: bouncing forwards

Psychologists define resilience as the capacity to adapt well in the face of stress, trauma or significant challenges. But this isn't about toughness or endurance. Research shows that resilience involves emotional flexibility, self-awareness and connecting to others – not simply gritting your teeth and pushing through.

We sometimes hear resilience described as the ability to 'bounce back' after hardship, but true resilience isn't about returning to who you were before adversity. It's about *bouncing forwards* – emerging wiser and stronger. Psychologist Shawn Achor describes this as learning how to 'fall up' rather than fall down: treating setbacks not as failure, but as information to help us grow.

What helps us recover us isn't perfection or positivity – it's the ability to meet difficulty with awareness, to name our feelings rather than bury them and to use them as a guide rather than a threat. We don't just survive the storm, we learn to navigate it with greater self-knowledge, stronger relationships and a clearer sense of what matters most.

Feelings are not facts

Although it's crucial to respect the signals our emotions offer us, it's equally important to recognise that our feelings may not be accurate reflections of reality. They are shaped by past experiences, personal beliefs and survival instincts. Sometimes, they can act as false alarms – warning us of danger that isn't actually present or exaggerating the severity of a situation.

> 'Just as thoughts are not facts, feelings are not facts either. Emotions are information.'
> **– Dr Julie Smith**

To help us respond well in difficult times, while remaining open to the thoughts and feelings that come up, we can look to cognitive behavioural therapy (CBT), one of the most well-researched and effective approaches in psychology.

CBT shows us that it's not just the situation that shapes how we feel, but the *story* we tell ourselves about it. A core principle of CBT is 'reframing', which involves stepping back to examine those stories and choosing to view our situation through a more helpful lens. Reframing helps us reduce unnecessary suffering and find constructive ways forwards. That's what I'd managed to do, eventually, after that near-miss on my bike.

When something happens to us, it's easy to assume that the event itself causes our emotional reaction. In moments of heightened emotion, we might think: *That argument with my partner made me furious*, or *My boss's criticism ruined my day*.

But CBT teaches us that emotions don't actually arise directly from events, but from how we interpret them. These interpretations, or beliefs, are often automatic and unconscious.

They're shaped by our past experiences, habits of thought and biases.

Imagine, for example, that your partner forgets your birthday. One interpretation might be, 'They don't care about me.' This belief can lead to feelings of hurt and resentment. But another interpretation might be, 'They've been really stressed at work lately, and this doesn't mean they don't care about me.' This belief, in turn, leads to a calmer and more compassionate emotional response.

CBT helps us to uncover these hidden interpretations, challenging unhelpful ones and replacing them with something more constructive. This reframing process, sometimes referred to as 'cognitive restructuring', helps us navigate challenges more wisely.

Reframing and resilience

When we reframe a difficult situation, we're not pretending it didn't happen or brushing off how hard it felt. Instead, we're shifting from seeing ourselves as powerless to recognising opportunities for growth and action.

For example, a missed deadline might initially feel like a failure, if you interpret the problem as proof you can't handle your workload. But, reframed, it becomes a learning opportunity: missing that deadline may prompt you to seek out support or set more realistic expectations with those who are asking you to deliver in the future.

This shift from helplessness to agency is the core of resilience. By reframing our adversity, we can approach it with a mindset geared towards growth rather than defeat.

> ### → The ABC model
> One of the simplest tools in CBT for understanding and reframing our emotional responses is the ABC model:
>
> **A: Adversity**. The situation or event we're facing.
> Example: *A friend cancels plans at the last minute.*
>
> **B: Beliefs**. The story we tell ourselves about the situation.
> Example: *'They don't really value our friendship.'*
>
> **C: Consequences**. The emotions and actions that result from our beliefs.
> Example: *Feeling hurt, angry and withdrawing from the relationship.*
>
> It's not the adversity itself that creates the consequences, it's how we interpret it – and the way our beliefs shape how we feel and respond.
>
> By learning to question and adjust our beliefs, we can create more helpful emotional and behavioural outcomes. For example, if our interpretation had been 'Something must have come up for them', our response would be different.

CBT can help us to recognise common unhelpful beliefs, sometimes known as 'cognitive distortions'. Once we spot these we can challenge them and replace them with more constructive interpretations. Here are some frequent ones:

- **All-or-Nothing**: seeing things in black-and-white terms, either all good or all bad.
  Example: *'If I fail this exam, I'm a total failure.'*
  Reframe: *'This doesn't define me. I can try again.'*

- **Overgeneralising**: making sweeping conclusions based on a single event, often using words like always or never.
  Example: *'I always mess things up'* or *'I'll never succeed.'*
  Reframe: *'Yes, sometimes I make mistakes, but I also do things well.'*

- **Catastrophising**: expecting the worst outcome, blowing things out of proportion.
  Example: *'They'll think I'm incompetent and I'll lose my job.'*
  Reframe: *'What's the most realistic outcome here?'*

- **Personalising**: believing you are the cause of negative events.
  Example: *'My friend didn't reply, she must be mad at me.'*
  Reframe: *'Actually this might have nothing to do with me.'*

- **'Should'-ing**: placing unrealistic expectations on yourself or others.
  Example: *'I should be more productive'* or *'People should treat me kindly.'*
  Reframe: *'My best is enough'* or *'People are dealing with things I can't see.'*

Timeless wisdom, modern tools

Stoic philosophy, which dates back over two millennia, aligns surprisingly well with the insights of modern cognitive therapy. At the heart of both approaches is a shared truth: While we can't control what happens to us, we can choose how we respond.

For the Stoic philosophers, this was the key to living a good life: achieving peace and purpose by mastering our thoughts and reactions. In the same way, CBT – often considered a scientific descendant of Stoicism – teaches that our inner state isn't determined by external events but by the interpretations we bring to those events.

> 'You have power over your mind, not outside events. Realise this and you will find strength.'
> – **Marcus Aurelius**

One of the most enduring lessons from Stoic philosophy is the importance of distinguishing what is within our control and what isn't. The Stoics emphasised that we often have no power over external events – such as how others behave or the circumstances we find ourselves in. But we do have influence over our interpretations and responses. This shift in focus from external to internal helps reduce unnecessary suffering and gives us a sense of agency, even in difficult situations.

Make life happier: Stoic edition

The Stoics didn't just philosophise – they used practical techniques for managing life's challenges. These remain as relevant today as they were in ancient Greece and Rome – and they align well with modern CBT.

Mentally rehearse challenges

The Stoics used 'negative visualisation' to prepare for adversity by imagining possible difficulties in advance. For example, before a big presentation, you might envision potential obstacles – like tough questions or technical difficulties – and rehearse how you'd respond calmly.

In CBT, similar ideas appear in approaches such as 'stress inoculation', where mentally rehearsing stressful situations can help reduce anxiety and build confidence.

Embrace impermanence

Marcus Aurelius, a Roman emperor and Stoic philosopher, often reminded himself that everything in life is fleeting. This wasn't meant to depress but to inspire gratitude and perspective. By embracing the impermanence of life, the Stoics encouraged living in the present and appreciating what we have while it lasts. Likewise CBT helps people let go of attachment to outcomes, recognising that change is an inevitable part of life and not something to fear.

Zoom out to keep perspective

When life feels overwhelming, the Stoics recommended taking a step back and viewing challenges in the broader context of our lives. By 'zooming out' we remind ourselves that today's struggles may not seem as significant in a month or a year. This is mirrored by CBT's focus on challenging catastrophic thinking. For instance, instead of saying 'This is a total disaster', we can ask ourselves, 'Will this really matter in six months?'

Together, Stoicism and CBT offer us timeless and proven strategies for navigating challenges with clarity and resilience. By combining Stoicism's philosophical depth with CBT's practical methods, we get a roadmap for managing life's difficulties.

How to SHIFT your situation

Over time, I've developed my own approach to responding to challenges — called **SHIFT**. It covers the four steps I've found most helpful when I'm trying to shift my perspective in a difficult situation: Something Happens (although sometimes I say 'Sh*t Happens!'), Interpretation, Feeling, Takeaway.

These steps are based on my own experience, drawing inspiration from the ABC of cognitive behavioural therapy and Stoic philosophy. SHIFT is a way to slow down, make sense of what's going on and choose a response that aligns with your values. Let's walk through how you can use it for an emotionally charged situation.

SH: Something Happens

Begin by describing the situation that triggered your emotional response. Be as factual as possible — this step is just about identifying what happened.

To try this out: think of a recent situation where you felt really frustrated or upset.

- **Example:** 'I didn't get a reply to my email about this important project.'

I: Interpretation

Bring your attention to your immediate beliefs about this situation. What's your story about why it happened or what it means?

So for your recent situation, what beliefs or interpretations came up? Write them down without judging whether they're true or false.

- **Example:** 'They think my ideas are worthless, or they don't take me seriously.'

F: Feeling

Notice how your interpretation of the situation is making you feel. Labelling emotions can help you process them and reduce their intensity.

For your example, what emotions have come up from the story you're telling yourself? Take a breath and name them.

- **Example:** 'I feel disrespected and embarrassed.'

T: Takeaway

In this final step, you have the opportunity to reframe the story and choose how best to respond to this situation.

For your situation, is there a more balanced and helpful way of seeing it? What small action could you take to move forwards?

- **Example:** 'Maybe they're swamped right now and this isn't about me. I'll follow up with a friendly nudge to make sure they saw my email.'

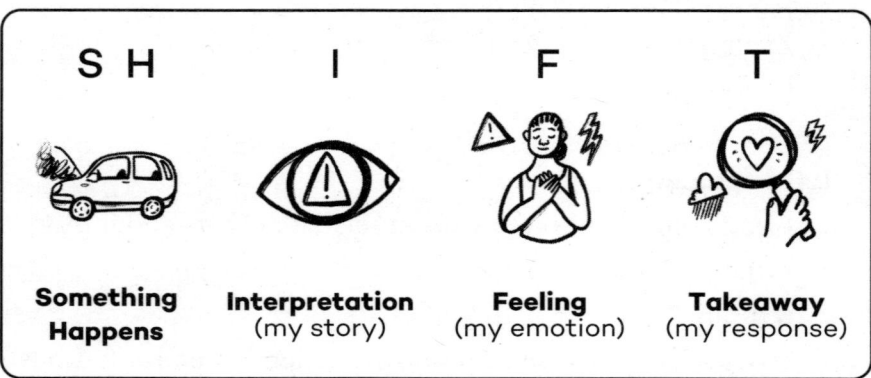

I find the SHIFT model incredibly helpful in difficult situations because it combines reflection and action. It's not about trying to rationalise away difficult emotions or stay positive; for example, in a genuinely dangerous situation, fear and evasive action may be the most appropriate response. But crucially, the 'I' in the middle reminds me that, although the situation is usually outside of my control, I am ultimately responsible for how I interpret it and what I do.

So the next time you feel stuck or overwhelmed, pause and try to SHIFT your perspective – you might be surprised by how much it can change the way you feel and how you respond. You can use it for everyday frustrations and also with bigger challenges where reframing can bring much-needed clarity and calm.

> **Watch out for emotional spillovers**
>
> Research shows that our emotional states have spillover effects: they don't just affect how we feel, they can cloud our judgements. We tend to be influenced by the mood we happened to be in at the time. For example, we may end up with a favourable view of a restaurant because we went there when hungry. Or we may remember not liking a town because it was raining when we visited.
>
> We need to be especially aware of these spillover effects in our relationships. When we're feeling a certain way, we often view others' behaviour and intentions through that emotional lens. For example, if we're frustrated, we may interpret our friend's neutral response as a hostile one. Or if we're in a good mood we may give someone the benefit of the doubt, even if they've let us down. The well-known expression 'Don't shoot the messenger' comes from ancient times, when a ruler received bad news and their anger spilled over so they took

> it out on the person delivering the news, even when they had nothing to do with it.
>
> So when responding to a situation – especially an emotionally charged one – it helps to check in with your emotional state and notice how this might be affecting your response. It's often helpful to come back to a challenge or relationship difficulty when you're in a calmer emotional state and you have more clarity.

Reframing difficulty when you feel truly helpless

Sometimes, the challenges we face feel far beyond our control. Global crises, wars, environmental disasters or just the weight of ongoing uncertainty can leave us feeling powerless, anxious and helpless. In these moments, reframing might seem impossible. How can we reframe something as vast and overwhelming as climate change, social injustice or a global pandemic?

Although the SHIFT model aims to help you change the narrative in your head when something happens to you, the same principles can actually apply to reframing difficulties that feel far beyond the scope of your influence. The key is to acknowledge the reality – including your limitations – without losing your sense of agency. No matter how big or small the problem, you always have some control over how you respond.

Consider the following lessons from this chapter, as a guide for reframing how you can respond to overwhelming global issues.

💡 Start with compassionate awareness

When the world seems awful, the first step is to recognise that it's understandable to feel sadness, fear or anger. These emotions are signals that reflect our deep care for the world around us. Rather than pushing them away or resigning ourselves to inaction, we can acknowledge these feelings and recognise our desire to see things change. With compassionate awareness we can look at the situation with empathy for others and reframe our discomfort as a sign of our shared humanity.

💡 Focus on what you can do

The next step is to identify what is within our control. While we might not be able to change the course of a global event, we can choose our response – how we engage with the world, what we say to others and what actions we take, however small. For example, you aren't able to stop a war, but you can take steps to support those affected, whether through donations, advocacy or simply offering support to those in your community. The key is acknowledging that even when you can't solve the big problem, you can contribute in meaningful ways, within the limits of your resources and abilities.

💡 Reframe helplessness into shared action

Feeling helpless is a natural response to overwhelming situations. Rather than seeing our inability to fix everything as a personal failure, we can remind ourselves that our small actions, when combined together, create ripple effects. For example, when confronted with systemic injustice, it can feel paralysing to realise how entrenched the problems are. While none of us can fix these systems alone, we can still act in ways that align with our values, through learning, speaking up, supporting affected groups or getting together with others and contributing to change where we can.

> ☆ 'Do your little bit of good where you are; it's those little bits of good put together that overwhelm the world.'
> **– Desmond Tutu**

We all suffer – it's an inevitable part of being human. But as my colleague and friend Alex Nunn likes to say about any situation, 'It's either good, or good practice.'

By focusing on what we can control, embracing even small actions and maintaining compassion for ourselves and others, we build resilience not just in our personal lives but in the world around us too. Learning to respond constructively to hardship or trauma without harming others or berating yourself – this is true strength.

REFRAME DIFFICULTY: CHAPTER SUMMARY

Ask yourself:

❓ **Is my interpretation of this situation helpful?**

Don't just:
✗ Push away uncomfortable feelings or pretend things are fine.

Try this out:
✔ Let go of things outside of your control, focus on what you can change.

Chapter Eight:

Do Experiments

How do I find what works
best for me?

'No way! Giving up snacks would be miserable,' I huffed as I scanned the article about the health benefits of leaving gaps between meals.

I was a total sceptic when I heard about the idea to eat in shorter 'time windows' each day – a concept sometimes called time-restricted eating or intermittent fasting. Skipping snacks? No, thank you. My mid-morning energy bar and the afternoon break for some cake or fruit – these were some of the highlights of my usual routine. Sure, I sometimes felt a bit sleepy – or hungry again! – soon after, but the thought of spending longer each day without food felt like a punishment, not a way to feel better.

Yet I was still curious – and the research seemed fairly compelling. Could changing my approach to *when* I ate help me be healthier, or even happier? I was aware my eating habits could probably do with some attention. I'd been neglecting my health as I focused on supporting our young family while trying to run a charity full-time. My energy levels were down, I wasn't sleeping well and my recent BMI score had me in the 'overweight' category for the first time. To top it all, my doctor had started warning me about my worryingly high cholesterol levels!

So, with some reluctance, I thought I'd give it a go. What was the worst that could happen? I asked myself. If it didn't work I could just go back to my normal approach. I decided to try for just a week initially: starting my breakfast a bit later, finishing dinner slightly earlier and dropping the snacks in-between.

The first day was predictably uncomfortable. By mid-afternoon, I was gazing longingly at a box of biscuits – convinced the whole idea was a terrible mistake. But I'd committed to giving it a go for a week, so I persevered. And as I continued my experiment, something surprising happened: I noticed shifts – not just physical, but also mental.

I began experiencing less of the usual rollercoaster of spikes and crashes in energy, which I'd often had when snacking. Meals became more intentional and mindful. And with time, I found a sense of balance I hadn't expected, both in my body and my mind. I felt calmer, more centred. I even started sleeping better. What began as a sceptical experiment turned into something that genuinely improved not just my health but my quality of life. It made eating feel more – not less – joyful.

> ### ➜ Do what's right for you
> Our bodies are all different and the path to good health isn't the same for everyone. So before experimenting with changes to your own eating habits it's good to consult a doctor or certified nutritionist. Please note that intermittent fasting isn't suitable for everyone and

> is unlikely to be right for those with a history of eating disorders, type 1 diabetes or for people who are pregnant, breastfeeding, undergoing fertility treatment or have low BMI.

This experience wasn't my first adventure in trying new habits and it certainly hasn't been the only one that surprised me. As you already know, some experiments I've tried – like mindfulness, gratitude or hopping back on a bike – have led to unexpected and transformative changes, despite my initial scepticism.

Testing out – and then adopting – these new ideas has played a critical role in helping me make life happier. And in my work at Action for Happiness I've seen hundreds of people adopt a wide range of different changes in their own lives too. The results can be amazing. But of course, not every experiment has a happy ending.

Cold-water swimming, for example, was a total failure for me. Everyone I knew seemed to be raving about its benefits – the mental clarity, the energy boost, the sense of exhilaration. My wife loves it. My friends swear by it. So I thought I'd give it a try.

The truth? I hate the cold. I always have. So I get out in the water, shiver miserably and, despite putting on a brave face, can't wait to get out and warm up again. While others emerge feeling euphoric, I just end up cold, miserable and a bit resentful. I gave it a fair shot, but it wasn't for me – and that's okay. Now I know.

Over the years, I've run all sorts of experiments. Some have been small tweaks – like taking a different route to work or picking up my guitar again. Others have involved learning more about myself, like wearing a sleep tracker or glucose monitor. Others have been bigger changes, like local volunteering, switching to alcohol-free beers or cutting back on sugar. Some experiments have stuck, like going to bed earlier, getting back in touch with old friends and cycling regularly, while others ended in frustration – like high-intensity interval training (HIIT), which hurt my knees. And some just didn't really work for me, like positive affirmations or that cold water!

The key point is this: some things will work, some won't and that's perfectly fine. Each experiment has taught me more about myself.

Become a happiness scientist

The scientific method is one of humanity's greatest tools for discovery: observe, question, hypothesise, test and learn. It's unlocked the secrets of our universe, but it can also help to unlock something much closer to home – our happiness.

> **The scientific method**
> Scientists use a structured approach to figure out how the world works. It starts with curiosity and involves finding answers, not by assuming or guessing, but by testing ideas and making sense of what they find. Experiments usually begin with a question, like 'What happens if I change this?'
>
> Researchers form a hypothesis – an educated guess – and then design an experiment to test it. They collect data, look for patterns and keep track of what happens. If the results don't fit, they adjust and try again. Crucially, even if an experiment 'fails' it still teaches something valuable by showing what doesn't work. Scientists stay open-minded, aware their first idea may not be right.

> So they repeat experiments and build on previous ones to get closer to the answer.

This spirit of experimentation – of trying out and adapting – is something we can all apply in our own lives. You can approach life like a scientist: by asking good questions, running little experiments and staying curious about what works for you. You don't have to have the answers straight away. Each tweak you try out is a test and every result – whether success or failure – teaches you something valuable.

Applying the scientific method has contributed significantly to how we understand happiness at the population level. For example, studies show that close relationships, physical activity and gratitude consistently tend to support people's happiness.

However, scientists rely on large studies to identify general trends – what works for most people, most of the time. But the reality is that *you're not 'most people'*. What works in a study of thousands may not work for you.

When reporting their experimental results, scientists report the 'N number' – the total number of participants, or sample size, for the study. But when it comes to what works for us individually, the most important experiment is the one you conduct on yourself – what we call an 'N=1 experiment'. In this case, there's just one participant: *you*.

Think of it like this: if a large-scale study says that morning runs boost happiness, but every time you try running you feel miserable, the study doesn't matter. What matters is *your experience*. The key is to identify the general areas that science shows are helpful – like movement or mindfulness – and then experiment to see how they fit into your life.

We're all different

Although the experience of feeling good is universal, what makes us happy varies hugely depending on our situation and preferences. These personal differences are what make this journey endlessly fascinating and varied. Some people love socialising in large groups, while others feel happiest in more intimate settings. Some folks recharge by running marathons, while others find peace in gardening or cooking.

Our genetic make-up and upbringing also influence what we enjoy and how we respond to new experiences. Take sleep, for example. Some people feel their best when they go to bed early and wake up with the sunrise. Others are night owls who find creative inspiration in the quiet hours of the evening. Neither approach is right or wrong. The trick is to observe your natural patterns and adjust accordingly.

So, while there are universal themes that generally support wellbeing, the specifics are ultimately up to you. Science can point you in the right direction, but only *you* can determine what works for your unique situation.

> **Scientific determinants of happiness**
> Research by Professor Sonja Lyubomirsky and colleagues investigated how variations in happiness are explained by different factors. They concluded:
> - **Genetics** tend to determine the greatest variation in happiness, reflecting our innate temperament and personality traits.
> - **Life circumstances** contribute, too, including factors such as income, marital status and where

we live. But these often have less lasting impact than we expect, as we adapt to changes (known as 'hedonic adaptation').
- **Intentional activities** then play a bigger role than we might imagine, including our choices, how we relate to others and the habits we build.

The proportions attributed to each of these categories are debated by researchers and may vary considerably. For example, people in poverty or facing trauma are likely to be more affected by circumstances. But importantly, although we may have a happiness 'set-point', our genes don't define our destiny. Our habits can shift our baseline, like strengthening muscles at the gym. Genes set the stage and circumstances provide the context, but our intentional choices are the most powerful lever we have to make life happier.

Enter the experiment

I'd now like to invite you to become your own 'happiness scientist'. The idea is to experiment with action ideas that research suggests tend to make people happier. But crucially, you're going to figure out if – and how – each idea works for you. Not everything you try will bring you joy or fulfilment. That's okay – the goal isn't to get it right every time, it's to explore, observe and learn. If something doesn't work, you can let it go. If it does work, you can choose to bring more of it into your life.

Experimentation also doesn't need to be grand or time-consuming. In fact, the most impactful experiments are often small and manageable adjustments that subtly shift the rhythm of your day. These changes allow you to test new approaches without getting overwhelmed, keeping the process feeling light and doable.

> **→ How to run your experiments**
> - **Try one new thing each week:** Choose something small but meaningful. Order a dish you've never tried, listen to a genre of music you usually avoid, or take a different route home from work. Treat it as a game and pay attention to how it makes you feel.
>
> - **Start with areas that intrigue you:** If you've always been curious about yoga or want to learn how to paint, try your first class or online tutorial. Think of it as a one-off exploration, not a lifelong commitment.
>
> - **Reflect regularly:** At the end of each day or week, ask yourself, 'What worked? What didn't? How did I feel during and after trying this?' You could even keep a simple experiment journal to track your findings and see patterns over time.
>
> - **Use curiosity as your guide:** Instead of approaching experiments with pressure to succeed, adopt a mindset of curiosity. Ask yourself, 'What might be interesting to try?' Let that question lead your choices.
>
> - **Focus on small tweaks:** Not every experiment has to involve a new activity. You can try adjusting the timing of something you already do, like eating lunch outside

instead of at your desk, or calling a friend instead of texting. Sometimes the smallest shifts can have the biggest impact.

- **Practise intentionality:** Begin each day by asking, 'What's one thing I could try today that might make me feel happier, or calmer?' Set that as your experiment for the day and then reflect on the outcome that night.

Remember, the goal isn't perfection or radical transformation – it's simply to invite a little more variety, playfulness and mindfulness into your everyday life.

Ideas to experiment with

This book is full of ideas you can try out and adapt to make your own. We've covered some already – including getting the basics right and reframing difficulties. There are lots more ideas coming up later, too, including tips to manage anxiety and listen deeply. Plus there are some challenges to try out around kindness, vulnerability, forgiveness and trust. But to help you get underway in your 'happiness scientist' mindset, here are some insights from the science of wellbeing that you can try experimenting with now:

💡 Experiences vs things

Research shows that people tend to be happier when they spend money on experiences rather than material things. So instead of buying that latest product, item of clothing or accessory, could you use your funds on a social event, healthy activity or cultural experience instead?

💡 The joy of anticipating

Studies suggest that when it comes to enjoyable events and activities it's not all about the experience itself – the anticipation beforehand also makes us happier. So could you take time now to book in something for a few months down the line, like a short break, special night out or a get-together with old friends?

💡 Talking to strangers

Many people imagine they will find it difficult or even embarrassing to talk to strangers. However, studies show that when people actually try this it tends to give them – and others – a real boost. So could you stop for a friendly chat next time you're in a queue, on public transport, out in the park or at the shops?

💡 Set your intention for the day

One of the best ways to make good use of our days is to keep focused on the things that matter most, especially at busy times. So could you try including a short reflection or journaling activity in the morning, where you plan your day ahead and make a mental note of the most important thing to do that day?

💡 Valuing your time

We tend to undervalue the importance of our time and we miss opportunities to free up time for the things that matter for our wellbeing. So is there an upcoming commitment that you could let go of, without impacting others too much? Or could you get some help with everyday chores to free up time for friends and family?

💡 Changing your phone habits

We're spending more time staring at our screens, and studies suggest this isn't great for our wellbeing. Rather than giving up our devices, we can change our relationship with them. So could you leave your phone downstairs at night or try a 'no-screens' rule when you're together with family or friends, for example at mealtimes?

💡 The happiness of generosity

Research has found that people are happier when they spend money on others rather than on themselves. But generosity doesn't require money – we can also give our time, attention and enthusiasm. So what could you give or do for someone else this week to bring them some joy or let them know you care?

> 💬 'The best way to cheer yourself up is to cheer somebody else up.'
>
> – Mark Twain

Make discovery the goal

At its core, experimenting is about discovery. It's leaning into the unknown with an open mind and a willingness to see what happens. The beauty of this approach is that every attempt brings something valuable. Failures are not setbacks, they're data points.

When high-intensity workouts didn't do it for me, I didn't give up on exercise altogether. I shifted my focus to other activities. Likewise, experiments that bring joy often reveal surprising truths. My experiment with intermittent fasting wasn't just about food, it taught me more about mindfulness and balance.

Through experimenting, you'll also uncover hidden assumptions about what makes you happy. You may discover that it isn't the thing itself that brings you joy but the ritual or environment surrounding it. Or you may find that something you thought you needed doesn't actually matter as much as you believed.

Experimentation reminds us that, while there's lots we can't control, there are countless small ways to boost wellbeing. And the cumulative effect of these small changes? A life that feels richer, lighter and more attuned to what matters.

Motivation tips

If trying new ideas feels a bit overwhelming, here are some tips to make your experiments even easier:

- If it feels daunting, break it down into the smallest possible steps.
- When you want to do more of something, make it *easier* – for example, leave your running kit by your bed.
- When you want to stop doing something, make it *harder* – like turning notifications off on your phone.
- Don't wait for motivation – trying the thing *is* the motivation!

Get your DOSE of brain chemicals

Here's another science-based way to explore different actions to try. The author and neuroscientist T.J. Power came up with the acronym DOSE as a helpful way to remember four of the key brain chemicals that influence wellbeing.

• D: Dopamine is the 'reward chemical', which drives motivation, goal-setting and pleasure. It encourages us to repeat behaviours. So instead of constantly checking your phone or having a junk-food binge, try creating something, ticking off a meaningful task or celebrating an achievement.

• O: Oxytocin is the 'love hormone', which fosters trust, empathy and connection. It helps us build healthy relationships. So instead of chasing social media likes or isolating alone, try making more time for loved ones and friends, showing affection, sharing a hug, cuddling a pet or giving compliments.

• S: Serotonin is the 'mood stabiliser', which regulates our mood, sleep and appetite. It can support self-esteem and may help us avoid depression. So instead of staying indoors, ruminating or comparing yourself to others, try getting more sunlight exposure, doing mindfulness or being active out in nature.

• E: Endorphins are the 'pain relievers', which alleviate stress with feelings of euphoria. They act like the body's natural painkiller. So instead of turning to alcohol or substances, or pushing yourself to burnout, try exercising, having a laugh with friends or enjoying your favourite music, comedy or movie.

Above all, get curious

This chapter isn't about getting it right. It's about getting curious – stepping out of your usual patterns, trying something new and seeing where it takes you.

Remember, there are no wrong answers. Whether it's something small like smiling at a stranger or something big like signing up for a dance class, every experiment holds the potential to show you something meaningful. Trying out is where the magic happens.

So, what will you try out next? What small shift could you make today to feel a little happier tomorrow? Let this be your call to action: step into the unknown, do some new experiments and enjoy the discoveries that come your way.

DO EXPERIMENTS: CHAPTER SUMMARY

Ask yourself:

❓ **What positive change do I want to try out today?**

Don't just:
✗ Assume your existing habits are the best way forwards.

Try this out:
✔ Experiment with new behaviours and find what works best for you.

Chapter Nine:

Build Habits

How can I keep the good things going?

My dad always had a list of things to do, scrawled on the back of an old envelope.

As kids, my sister and I were often on the lookout for the latest list which he'd mislaid, or amused to find old ones hidden down the back of the sofa. We were also a bit confused as to why these complex – and often unintelligible – creations were even needed.

Yet years later, if you'd asked me how I spent my time, it would have been all about my own to-do list. Busy in corporate life, I'd found myself following in Dad's footsteps with my own illegible lists, initially scribbled in notebooks and later added to devices. Like many of us I had picked up the habit of writing down what had to be done each day, so I could prioritise my time and avoid forgetting things.

I took rather too much satisfaction in crossing items off that list and regularly updating it. But as productive as I seemed, something crucial was missing. My lists were all about *doing*.

They were full of work tasks and life admin but had no real connection to my values or wellbeing. They said nothing about who I wanted to *be*.

Then one busy day, when I'd been struggling to find time to even step away from my desk, I had an unexpected turning point. I put 'Get outside and breathe' at the top of my list. For once, I gave myself permission to take this as seriously as everything else on there. It made a huge difference, not just that day but ever since.

I began to realise that I could harness my desire to get stuff done to profoundly shape my mood and the wider direction of my life. Alongside reminders to send a work email or book an appointment, I started to include actions that supported my mental wellbeing and reflected the person I wanted to be.

That's how my 'to-do' list started to become more of a 'to-be' list.

It started small, with simple reminders to do things like get to bed in good time. Then, as I saw the benefits, those daily and weekly nudges began to grow. These days my routine includes lots of habits that have genuinely enhanced my life, bringing more joy not just more admin. Reminders to start the day with mindfulness, make time to check in with loved ones or write down three good things at the end of the day.

My list also includes a reminder of values I care about – like trying to be *Friendly, Useful, Calm and Kind* (see chapter six). Naturally, I still often fail to live up to these, but rather than just being good intentions they've become part of daily life.

> **→ Your 'to-be' list:**
> Take a moment to think of things you'd want on your 'to-be' list.
> - Which one or two daily habits really help you be at your best?
> - What core value are you trying to bring into your daily life?

Focusing on *simplicity* really helps. After various flawed attempts to make things last, I discovered the power of having a 'one-minute version' of any helpful habit I'm trying to build. For example, although I sometimes find space to meditate for 30 minutes, this isn't always feasible. Rather than giving up, I keep my daily intention by just pausing for one minute of deep breathing. Or if a busy day means I can't be with a loved one, I still take a minute to send them a message and let them know I care. These micro-habits lower the bar, making it easier to keep going.

Another powerful way to simplify has been learning to say 'No' to things that don't align with my priorities. I've always hated the feeling of letting someone down, but I discovered that when I say 'No' with honesty and clarity, people understand. Saying no to unnecessary commitments frees up time for the stuff that really matters.

Over time, this blend of intentionality and simplicity has helped me sustain various changes in my life. The beauty of habits is, once they're established, they require less and less effort. Like brushing your teeth, they eventually happen automatically.

Experimenting with habits

In the last chapter we became 'happiness scientists', experimenting with new actions to see how they made us feel, without any pressure to keep them up. This allows us to discover what genuinely works for us, free from the expectation of forming habits immediately. Once we've found *actions* that are helpful, the next step is turning these one-off experiments into lasting *habits* that become automatic.

In this chapter we're moving from the *what* to the *how* – to find the best ways to get our actions to stick. I like to think of this as 'happiness engineering'. Just as engineers find ways to turn scientific breakthroughs into practical solutions for everyday life, so we can take what we've discovered from our one-off experiments and find ways to make them work in the messy reality of our daily lives.

Habits are 'autopilot' in action – an incredible ability we all have to remove the strain of consciously deciding or remembering to do something. When an action becomes a habit, it frees our mental energy for other things. Take brushing your teeth as an example. For most of us, this is something we instinctively do each day without thinking. It's so automatic that going to bed without brushing feels unthinkable.

If millions of us can establish a lifelong habit for our *dental* health, surely we can create similar habits to support our *mental* health too!

> ⭐ 'The purpose of a habit is to remove that action from self-negotiation. You no longer expend energy deciding whether to do it. You just do it.'
>
> – **Kevin Kelly**

When an action becomes a habit it can reorganise our neural pathways thanks to the brain's neuroplasticity. In studies at MIT, researchers found that once new habits are established, the neural activity patterns associated with them can persist and be re-engaged later, even after a period of non-use. So once you form a new habit, the brain can retain a trace of it – making it easier to return to in the future.

But . . . habits don't form overnight. Tooth-brushing didn't become automatic the moment we got our first baby teeth. It took months or years of repetition – often with plenty of encouragement (or nagging!) from parents – to build that habit until it stuck.

This is the challenge of habits: how do we take something we want to do and transform it from a novel, effortful action into a seamless, natural behaviour? The answer lies in taking our 'happiness scientist' mindset one step further. Once we've found an action that works, we take intentional steps to make it last. Each time we do that action, we reinforce our neural circuits and build our 'muscle memory'.

> 'We are what we repeatedly do. Excellence then, is not an act, but a habit.'
>
> **– Will Durant, summarising Aristotle**

The science of habits and the habit loop

Why do some habits stick while others slip away? Thankfully, researchers have explored this extensively and found some key principles for habit formation. By understanding the science of habits, we can harness these insights to create routines that feel sustainable and enjoyable.

At the core of habit formation lies the 'habit loop' – a concept

popularised by Charles Duhigg and expanded by James Clear. It consists of four stages:
1. **Cue:** a trigger that prompts the habit.
2. **Craving:** your motivation or desire to act.
3. **Response:** the action or behaviour itself.
4. **Reward:** the benefit or satisfaction you get.

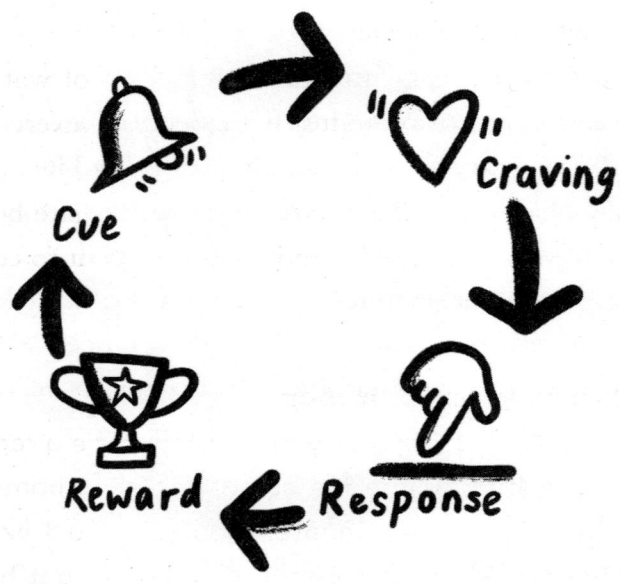

To see the loop in action, let's take an example of a common habit many of us do rather more than we would like to: checking our phone! Here the *cue* is a notification which draws our attention to the phone, triggering the *craving* to see a new message or just relieve our boredom. As a *response,* we stop what we're doing to check our apps and the *reward* is finding out what's going on. This also brings a small release of dopamine which in turn reinforces the habit.

For a habit to stick, the loop must be both satisfying and repeatable. The more appealing and rewarding the habit, the more likely it is to stick. In his book *Atomic Habits*, James Clear explains how to use this loop to build habits that last:

- **Cue**: make it **obvious**. If you want to drink more water, leave a full bottle on your desk. If you want to exercise more, put your running shoes by the door.
- **Craving**: make it **attractive**. Connect the action with what you're looking forward to – such as feeling refreshed and hydrated, or becoming fitter and healthier.
- **Response**: make it **easy**. Just take a small sip of water when you see the bottle, or commit to just five minutes of exercise to get started.
- **Reward**: make it **satisfying**. Notice the immediate benefits – feeling more alert or energised – and take a moment to celebrate, which helps reinforce the habit.

> ### → Enhance your habit loop
>
> What's a helpful action that you'd like to make a regular part of your life? Maybe it's something that came up for you in the previous chapter. Perhaps you'd like to start meditating, spend more time outside or get home earlier?
>
> Now, let's personalise your habit loop for this behaviour:
>
> 1. What is the **obvious cue** that will trigger you to do this?
> 2. What is the **attractive craving** that will motivate you to act?
> 3. What is the **easiest response** that you can commit to?
> 4. What is the **satisfying reward** you'll get from doing it?

> For the next few days, really focus on using and enhancing your loop and try to find ways to make this habit feel as effortless and rewarding as possible.

Understanding the habit loop can also help us to break or change habits that we want less of in our lives. One way to do this is to take an *existing* cue and craving and link these to a *different* response and reward. For example, when I hit a mid-afternoon slump and I'm craving a snack, I could reach for an apple (which I've left nearby) rather than a bar of chocolate (which I've intentionally left in the cupboard). As a result I feel healthier or proud of myself, rather than having a sugar crash or feeling bad.

In other cases we can just remove an unhelpful cue. When it came to phone-checking, I found turning off notifications significantly reduced the habit and made life calmer. I still check my phone more than I'd like to, but removing this cue helped enormously.

James Clear also makes a helpful distinction between our *goals* and *systems*. Aiming for a vague goal is usually less effective than focusing on the systems and behaviours that will get you there. For example, I had a *goal* to 'use my phone less' but it was my *system* of keeping all non-essential notifications off which made all the difference. Also, although my long-standing *goal* to 'write a book' helped to set my direction, having a *system* of 'writing for 30 minutes each morning before checking emails' was much more effective. Without that system, this book wouldn't exist.

⭐ *'You do not rise to the level of your goals. You fall to the level of your systems.'*

– James Clear

The power of small changes

Even when we understand how habits work, it can still feel really hard to keep up our desired actions. Thankfully, it doesn't have to be hard work. In his book *Tiny Habits*, Professor B.J. Fogg emphasises starting small and explains how successful habits are born from simplicity and immediate success. Rather than starting with big aims, begin with tiny versions of the habits you want to build.

For example, to build a habit of daily mindfulness, begin with just pausing for a few deep breaths as soon as you get out of bed each day. Or if you want to work out regularly, begin with just a few stretches or push-ups. This lowers resistance while building confidence. Over time, these tiny actions grow into larger routines as you experience success and build momentum.

The key here is to take your desired habit and create a version of it that is so simple you can always make time for it, even on busy days. So when time gets in the way, you still do the mini version. Establishing the habit is more important than doing the full action.

The other vital insight from B.J. Fogg is that emotions are even more powerful than repetition for creating habits. It's not just doing a habit over and over that wires it into your brain – it's the positive feeling you associate with it. That's why celebrating matters.

Our brains are wired to seek gratification, so there's a real benefit in rewarding yourself each time you do a desired action. Celebrations could simply include saying 'nailed it' to yourself with a smile, or the satisfaction of ticking an action off your list, or taking a moment to appreciate that you feel calmer or happier.

Behavioural research has also shown that our memory of any experience is especially shaped by the last part of what happened. So by adding a relaxing cooldown or a favourite drink at the end of a workout, we remember it as more enjoyable. This is another great reason to celebrate after doing a desired habit.

Bundle your habits

One of the most effective ways to build new habits is to link them with existing habits or things you already enjoy doing. Let's explore two different science-backed versions of this: 'habit stacking' and 'temptation bundling'.

In habit stacking you link a new habit you want to build with a current habit you already do reliably. For example, when you make your coffee in the morning, use this as a cue to do some mindful breathing. Or when you brush your teeth at night, use this time to think of things you're grateful for. By using an existing routine as a cue for the new habit, you make it much easier to remember.

> **→ Which habit will you stack?**
> Think of a *new* daily habit you'd like to build. What does the smallest, simplest version of this look like? Now bring to mind an *existing* habit you already do reliably (ideally at a similar time each day). Use the formula below to link them:
> *After I [current habit], I will [new habit].*
> For example: After I get out of bed in the morning, I will drink a glass of water.
> Or: After I sit down at my computer, I will take a breath and relax my shoulders.
> Then find a way to remind yourself to link your new habit to your existing one each day and remember to celebrate each time you do it. Before long, your new habit will naturally keep going.

In her book *How To Change*, Professor Katy Milkman introduces a different way of linking habits, which she calls 'temptation bundling'. This involves pairing a habit you want to do with something you really enjoy. This works especially well when pairing a habit that feels effortful with one you naturally find tempting.

For example, you might only allow yourself to watch your favourite show while working out. Or you only treat yourself to your favourite drink or snack after finishing your weekly review. By combining an enjoyable activity with the less appealing one, you create a reward system that reinforces your new habit and makes it more likely to stick.

> **→ Which temptation will you bundle?**
> Bring to mind a helpful habit you'd like to build but feels hard to get started. Now think of something you really love doing that could be paired with your new habit. It could even be a 'guilty pleasure' or something you feel tempted to do too often! Now, use the formula below to link them:
>
> *I will only do [tempting activity] while doing [helpful habit].*
>
> For example: I will only listen to my favourite podcast while out walking.
>
> Or: I will only check social media after I've done my morning routine.
>
> Find a way to remind yourself to only do your tempting activity after or along with your desired habit. Again, remember to celebrate each time you do it.

When something feels pleasant, we're more likely to repeat it. If it feels unpleasant, we're far less likely to – even if it's 'good for us'. So we can expand this idea to enhance any habit. For example, you could add your favourite music to make chores more fun, or exercise with a friend, so any discomfort is eased by laughter or conversation.

Identity over outcomes

Lasting change happens from the inside out and the habits we keep tend to be the ones we associate with our *identity*. So it's also helpful to focus on the kind of person you want to become. For instance, rather than thinking *I want to lose 5kg*, shift your mindset to *I'm a healthy person* – and make choices that align with that. Or instead of *I want to run a marathon*, try *I'm a runner* – the kind of person who goes out even when it's raining.

This identity-led approach works particularly well when it taps into your deeper values. For example, *I want to be a good dad for my children* makes it easier to leave work earlier or make time for self-care.

Aristotle observed that 'We are what we repeatedly do', so when you build that habit of daily meditation you begin to see yourself as 'a meditator'. However, we also need to be careful not to repeatedly do things that undermine who we want to be. For example, if spending time on social media tends to make you angry, you can recognise this and spend more time doing things that help you feel calm or enthusiastic.

Above all, the most important identity-shift is seeing yourself as someone who makes changes that can last. Charles Duhigg highlights the idea of 'keystone habits', which are behaviours that influence our other habits and motivate us to keep going. They can set off a chain reaction that builds momentum.

For example, the habit of a morning walk may lead us to having a more productive day and sleeping better. Or the habit of eating meals with loved ones may lead to healthier food choices or closer relationships. And so on. Over time, these keystone habits change how you see yourself. You start living more intentionally, with reliable habits that feel like part of who you are. You feel more in control of daily life.

Every day can be a fresh start

When people try to create a new routine, they often envision big results — waking up earlier, writing daily or exercising regularly. The classic example is making those New Year's resolutions each January. There's often a rush of early enthusiasm, but as days and weeks pass, motivation tends to dwindle.

Why does this happen? It's partly the expectation of immediate, sweeping change. We're creatures of habit — and change is hard. Our culture prizes instant gratification, celebrating quick fixes and overnight success stories. But true change is incremental. When the frustration of slow progress sets in, the new routine often gets abandoned.

This struggle isn't unique to you. Our brains are wired to resist change and they favour existing routines, because they're efficient and require less cognitive effort. Building new habits means disrupting established patterns and that takes time, patience and realistic expectations.

If we take an all-or-nothing approach it can lead to unrealistic goals — like 'I'll meditate for 30 minutes every morning' or 'I'll cut out all sugar.' But then we feel like a failure if we can't maintain perfection. A single missed day or slip-up can feel like proof that the entire effort wasn't worth it.

Thankfully, every moment is a chance to begin again. Katy Milkman's research highlights the 'fresh start effect' – moments when we feel a chance to reset, whether it's a new week, a birthday or even the morning after a difficult day. These moments give us permission to try again, without judgement.

Missed a day? That's okay. Progress comes from persistence, not perfection. Don't dwell on what went wrong – celebrate the choice to begin again.

> ### ➔ Learn from others
> I asked members of the Action for Happiness community for tips they'd found helpful in building their own habits. Here are some examples they shared:
> - 'I'm no athlete. But I do the thing of wearing my gym stuff during the day so I'm more likely to go in the evening.'
> - 'I like to stack habits by linking a new habit to an existing one. For example, when I'm brushing my teeth I think about things I'm grateful for.'
> - 'I use reminders on my calendar so I get prompts on my phone. I usually set them to repeat for a while, hoping over time the habit will stick.'
> - 'I remind myself of a deeply important reason for the habit – like greater fitness so I can spend more quality time with my daughter.'
> - 'I try to be my own encouraging voice saying things like "come on, this may feel hard but you'll feel better afterwards."'

- 'I like commitment in a group. We built a shared list of goals with friends – like reading or working out – and this motivated us to keep going.'
- 'I schedule five-minute pauses between appointments in my calendar to stop, breathe and stretch throughout the day.'
- 'For me it's leaving posters and Post-its around my house which I will see multiple times each day to motivate me.'

Build happier habits

Habits are like compound interest for wellbeing. Little actions accumulate day by day, leading to bigger benefits over time. It's not about adding more to an already packed schedule, it's about building-in small, meaningful, repeatable actions that align with the person you aspire to be. Here are some practical steps to build habits that stick:

💡 Start small

Begin with a 'one-minute version' of your habit. If you want to write every day, start with one sentence. If you'd like to meditate, try focusing on your breath for just a minute. Small steps create momentum – over time they grow into something bigger.

💡 Link to existing routines

Build your new habits into the rhythms of your day. Think of three things you're grateful for while brushing your teeth, or take deep breaths while making your morning coffee. By linking habits to familiar cues you make them easier to remember and repeat.

💡 Focus on feelings

Habits stick when they feel good. Celebrate small wins to create a positive emotional connection. This could be as simple as mentally saying 'I did it!' or smiling after doing your action. Reinforcing success with good feelings turns effort into reward.

💡 Create reminders

Visual or auditory cues can keep your new habits front of mind. A sticky note on your mirror, a phone reminder or even a small object placed in a visible spot can act as a gentle nudge. Cues help us remember, especially on the busy days.

💡 Make it more enjoyable

Pair your new habit with something you already love doing. For example, listen to a favourite playlist while getting active, or enjoy your favourite drink while journaling. This turns the new action into something you look forward to.

💡 Find a habit buddy

Share your goals with a friend and invite them to join you; for example, as a walking companion. Doing it together makes habits more enjoyable and adds a gentle sense of accountability, helping you stay motivated to show up and keep going.

💡 Reframe setbacks

Missed a day? Don't give up. Every moment can be a fresh start. Instead of focusing on what went wrong, use it as an opportunity to reset. Habit-building is about persistence, not perfection. Just take the next step forwards.

💡 Adapt to what works for you

Think of a habit that has stuck with you – what helped make it last? Notice what tends to suit your personality and lifestyle, then apply that to your new habit. Plan to do things at times when your willpower tends to be highest.

Let go of perfection

If we want habits to last, we need to accept that life is messy and plans often get disrupted. Flexibility is vital. The paradox of routines is that if they get too rigid or complex they can become a source of stress rather than strength.

The best routine is one you can bend without breaking. So if you're trying to do something every day, aim for 'daily-ish'. Then, when your day doesn't go to plan, you can adjust as needed and give it a miss. So with a daily-ish mindset, you can aim not to miss two days in a row. You might be ruthless about keeping your habit going, but gentle about how much to do.

On an ideal day, I might meditate for 20 minutes in the morning, get out on my bike, read some interesting articles, spend time with loved ones, eat healthily, reflect on what I'm grateful for and get to bed in good time. But, if something comes up – like an urgent deadline or someone needing help – I can adjust. Maybe I'll only manage a five-minute pause and try to remember to stay hydrated as I rush along. Then the next day I can get back to my daily-ish routines.

Remember that self-compassion is also an important habit to practise, which means recognising your needs and adapting to them. Don't have much energy? Do the easy version. Don't have much time? Scale it down. Find different ways to show up depending on the circumstances. The best habits are the ones that feel natural and sustainable, not forced. So let your actions adapt to the demands of the day.

It's important to remember that, however good our intentions and routines, we can never do it all. The day will never come when we have everything under control – and that's okay. So we have to be willing to let things go, disappoint some people and say no. In fact, this is essential so we can make time for the stuff that matters most.

There's also a risk that if we get so focused on 'optimising' our life we forget to actually live it. Remember, the aim is to make life happier, not harder!

Building happier habits isn't about willpower or discipline, it's about noticing what brings a sense of joy or purpose, then finding simple ways to repeat those actions until they become as automatic as brushing our teeth.

You won't get everything done, and life won't suddenly be perfect. But, over time, these habits will help you align your daily life with your deeper aspirations and move towards the person you want to be – one small, consistent step at a time.

BUILD HABITS: CHAPTER SUMMARY

Ask yourself:

❓ **How can I make my most important habits non-negotiable?**

Don't just:
✗ Fail to turn your helpful actions into lasting habits.

Try this out:
✔ Make the actions you find helpful part of your everyday life.

Chapter Ten:

Cultivate Calm

How can I be less anxious?

As a child, I remember feeling scared when my parents went out and left us with a babysitter. I'd lie in bed, unable to sleep, my mind spinning with anxious thoughts: *What if they don't come home? What if something bad happens?* Thankfully they always came back, but that didn't stop my young brain from conjuring up worst-case scenarios. Anxiety hijacked my thoughts, escalating ordinary situations into overblown fears.

Those anxieties changed shape in adulthood. I remember watching our daughter whizzing on her scooter alongside a busy road, worrying she might swerve off into the traffic. Or later seeing her cycle off on her own for the first time, feeling a knot in my stomach as I wondered if she'd be safe. Years later, it was the idea of her navigating crowded concerts or staying out late in London that kept me awake. I trusted her abilities, but my mind couldn't resist imagining every possible 'what if' or danger.

This same pattern shows up for me on a larger scale, as I

consider the state of the world. As someone who has worked on environmental issues, I've seen first-hand the daunting challenges we face. Becoming a parent only magnified those concerns, leaving me awake at night worrying about the kind of future our kids will inherit.

These moments – whether personal, parental or societal – taught me something important: anxiety is natural. It's our mind's way of trying to keep us safe in the face of uncertainty. But while anxiety can be protective, it can also become unhelpful and overwhelming. If left unchecked it can spiral, stealing our enjoyment of the present and making life feel like an endless battle with those 'what if' worries.

Through my own experiences – and my work with mental-health experts – I've found the key isn't to eliminate anxiety but to understand it. To work with it rather than against it. Anxiety is a messenger, not a master. It signals our desire to stay safe and protect what we love, but it doesn't always tell the whole story.

I've learned to soothe that anxious part of myself with a simple reminder: *It will be okay.* Not because life is free of challenges or comes with guarantees, but because we have the capacity to adapt – and most of our worst fears don't come true. Anxiety often comes from overestimating the threat and underestimating our ability to cope with it. When I feel the familiar rush of worry, I remind myself of all the times my fears didn't tell the whole truth: my parents came home; my daughter made it back safely. And when things did go wrong, it often wasn't as bad as I worried it would be. I found ways to adjust and respond. Yes, the world is uncertain and bad things do happen – but life carries on and, more often than not, we can find a way through.

Understanding anxiety

Anxiety arises from a mix of fear and uncertainty. It is our mind and body's response to perceived threats and unwanted outcomes. It's not necessarily about being in danger, but rather anticipating possible danger, especially when the situation is unclear or we feel unprepared. We get physical sensations like tension or a rapid heart rate, mental patterns such as worry or fear, and behaviours like avoidance.

Everyone feels anxiety at times. It's a natural human response related to our primal drive to survive. We have a built-in desire to reduce uncertainty, because everything we don't know may be a potential risk. When our brain faces an uncertain situation, anxiety emerges as a kind of warning signal, trying to regain control.

> **🧠 Your internal alarm system**
>
> The amygdala is a small, almond-shaped part of the brain responsible for detecting threats and triggering fear. Think of it as your internal alarm system – fast, reactive and designed to keep you safe. But in modern life, it can go into overdrive, responding to social stress or uncertainty as if it were life-or-death.
>
> When the amygdala is overactive, it fuels anxiety, making it harder to feel calm, connected or joyful. But we can also learn ways to calm this fear centre. Many of the practices we've learned already – like mindfulness and reframing – can help us tell the amygdala that 'It's okay. You're safe now.'

Anxiety arises from various sources. Often it's a completely appropriate response to an uncertain or worrying situation.

For example if we're facing insecurity, major changes or potential danger, anxiety is a vital signal to pay attention to.

However, it can also be triggered by lifestyle factors, such as poor sleep, stressful work, physical inactivity and social isolation. Or by things we consume, such as caffeine, ultra-processed foods, alcohol or news media. So even when we can't control an uncertain situation, making wise lifestyle choices can potentially help us stay calmer.

The big challenge is when anxiety gets stuck. For example, we may develop a 'learned habit' of feeling anxious – often as an attempt to regain a sense of control, solve problems or help ourselves to feel safer. Psychiatrist Judson Brewer explains that anxiety can become self-reinforcing, like a habit loop: worrying briefly reduces uncertainty, which trains the brain to repeat that response even when it causes distress. Over time, we unconsciously train ourselves to respond to certain situations with anxiety, even when there's no real danger. In particular, past experiences – especially traumatic ones – can sensitise our nervous system, making us more prone to anxiety.

> ### You deserve support
> We all have worries. But if anxiety becomes more pervasive, we may need extra help. There's a big difference between everyday anxiety and clinical anxiety. Generalised anxiety disorder (GAD) is a common mental-health condition where someone experiences persistent, excessive worry about a range of things – such as work, health, money, relationships or future events. The worries feel difficult to control, even when the person knows they may be exaggerated or irrational.

> Common symptoms include feeling restless or on edge, problems sleeping, irritability, fatigue and difficulty concentrating. In some cases, people can also experience intense physical symptoms, like racing heart, tightness in the chest, breathlessness or a sense of dread, like something terrible is about to happen.
>
> If you're feeling anxious all the time, or experiencing some of those physical symptoms, it's important to reach out to your doctor or a mental-health professional. The knowledge and tips in this chapter may prove helpful, but you deserve professional support that is tailored to you.

What's behind rising anxiety?

Reported levels of anxiety are significantly higher now than a decade ago — and experts continue to debate what's behind this general rise. Although it's a complex picture, there are three main factors at play in my view.

Firstly, there are some serious global forces causing a lot of very understandable worry and uncertainty. I'm writing this five years on from a global pandemic that killed millions, kept us locked indoors and profoundly shook our sense of certainty. Since then we've seen new wars and global conflicts, major financial shocks and growing political instability. And all of this is set against a backdrop of existential threats such as climate change and the rapid development of AI. It's no wonder life feels uncertain.

Secondly, recent social trends have been making us more anxious, too, with constant screen time and 24-hour news. Online algorithms feed us clickbait stories of outrage and other people's perfectly curated lives. Political instability and polarisation leave us afraid of our fellow citizens. Convenience culture nudges us towards fast, cheap and easy options – whether that's our food, information or entertainment. Unfortunately, the 'instant everything' life isn't as calm or rewarding as we may have hoped.

Although it's hard to prove causation, studies suggest that increases in screen time, social media use and social isolation may have all contributed to us feeling more anxious and less happy. Thankfully there's a growing awareness of these risks and I'm hopeful that in the coming years we'll shift towards healthier relationships with our devices and with what we choose to consume and pay attention to.

Finally, there has also been a positive cultural shift to more openness about anxiety and other mental-health challenges. People are more willing to share their feelings and seek support when they're struggling. This is a welcome change, which may also be contributing to increases in levels of diagnosis. Anxiety that was previously bottled up is now being talked about and treated – and that's generally encouraging.

In summary, it's understandable we're anxious. Much of this is outside our direct control – like global events – but we can also cultivate a greater sense of calm by making wise choices and being willing to open up about how we're feeling.

When it comes to deciding how to respond to life's uncertainty, I love the words of the *Serenity Prayer*, attributed to the Lutheran theologian Reinhold Niebuhr, which reads:

> ⭐ 'Grant me the serenity to accept the things I cannot change, the courage to change the things I can, and the wisdom to know the difference.'

As a former engineer, I like to think of this in terms of a flow chart:

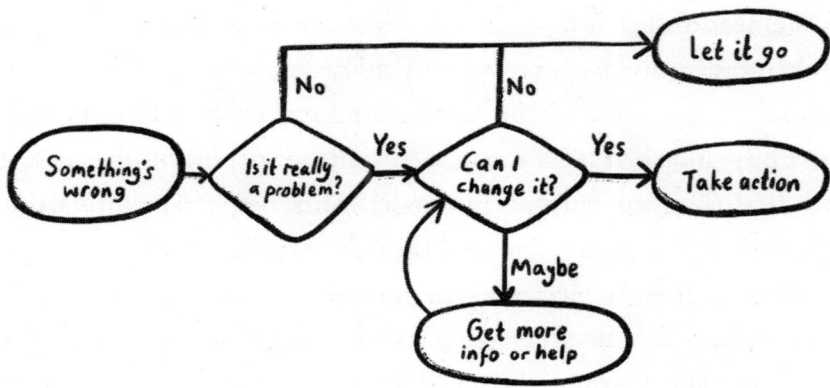

So let's now look at some practical ways to disarm our anxiety and feel calmer.

Reversing the downwards spiral

Anxiety often builds as a sort of 'downwards spiral' where our worries escalate, feeding into each other and causing progressively worse anxiety. We get stuck in a loop of thoughts about what could go wrong or what we need to do – or avoid – to prevent a catastrophe. This not only feels unpleasant, but it can also lead to us doing things that make the situation worse – or avoiding things that might help.

It's important to remember that although we're feeling anxious, *our anxiety is a story, not a fact*. And it may not be an accurate story. Sometimes it's an appropriate response to an uncertain situation. But often it's an unnecessary overreaction based on distorted facts or unlikely events.

So what are your options? Do you try to bottle it up, ignore those anxious feelings and push on through? Or do you let the worries take over until you feel like everything is out of control? Neither of these extremes are healthy ways to cope.

We need to learn how to process our worries more effectively. With mindful awareness, we can allow ourselves to notice that we're feeling anxious, take steps to reduce its effect on our mind and body and then gently investigate the story behind the feelings and find a more helpful response. This helps us cultivate an 'upwards spiral', where hopeful thoughts and helpful actions build on each other to reduce our worries and feel calmer. We then feel more equipped to weather what's going on around us.

Even small actions can help to reverse the downwards spiral. When feeling a sense of panic, we might pause to take a few deep breaths. Then we're in a better place to start an upwards spiral. After some calm breaths we may decide to share how we're feeling with a friend who can help us to keep things in perspective.

Write down what you're worried about

Bottling it up usually doesn't work, because the parts of us that are frightened or anxious need to feel heard. Research by psychologist James Pennebaker found that writing about our emotions, even just for a few minutes over a few consecutive days, can really help to reduce levels of anxiety and stress. He even found that people who do this tend to make fewer doctor visits and have stronger immune responses.

How does this work? By 'offloading' our worries and letting go of intrusive thoughts, this frees up our mental resources. The act of writing also helps us to process our inner experiences, giving us new insights and reducing the intensity of our feelings.

> **Write out your worries**

When you're feeling anxious, try this simple exercise to reduce stress, clear your mind and bring a sense of calm.

Get a notebook or open a blank document and set a timer for 10 minutes. Then just write freely about what's worrying you, without filtering or editing. Ask yourself what's on your mind and why it feels stressful or uncertain. This is just for you – no one else will see it. Spelling and grammar aren't important!

Then when the time is up, just pause and notice how you feel. You're not aiming to solve the problems. Just getting the thoughts out of your head and onto the page can bring a surprising sense of relief. Try repeating this exercise for a few days in a row or whenever anxiety builds up. Think of it as a way to clear your mental clutter and release anxious thoughts.

Dr Rangan Chatterjee has a version of this he calls the 'Brain Tap', where you set aside five minutes to transfer all those whirring thoughts, worries and to-dos out of your head and write them down on a piece of paper, like it's a rubbish dump.

Having acknowledged our anxious thoughts, we can also then use some helpful ideas from cognitive behavioural therapy (CBT) to question them. Rather than treating them as facts, CBT helps us examine our worries with questions like:
- Is this thought really true?
- What's the evidence for and against it?
- Am I catastrophising, or jumping to conclusions?
- If the worst did happen, how could I cope?
- How would I encourage a friend in this situation?

Use your body to calm your mind

Anxiety isn't just a mental experience, it's a full-body response. So when anxious feelings arise, you can enlist the help of your body to calm the nervous system and bring you back to the present.

Anxiety triggers our 'fight or flight' mode, leading to elevated heart rate, muscle tension and breathing which is faster and more shallow. Simple practices like slow, deep breathing activate the parasympathetic nervous system – our 'rest and digest' mode. Just a few conscious breaths can help to lower heart rate, relax muscles and help you feel calmer.

You could also do a gentle 'body scan' to identify any areas of tension and consciously relax them. Physical relaxation signals safety to the brain, which lowers anxiety. When the body relaxes, it tells your mind, 'We're safe, there's no need to panic.'

> **→ Box breathing**
>
> This is a proven breathing technique to bring your body and mind back into balance and help you feel calmer. It is used regularly by everyone from mindfulness teachers to elite athletes.
>
> Sit quietly for a few moments and repeat these four steps. Visualise going along the edges of a box, or even draw a box shape with your hands as you do each step:
>
> - (Up) **Breathe in** through your nose for a count of four
> - (Along) **Hold** your breath for a count of four
> - (Down) **Breathe out** through your mouth for a count of four
> - (Along) **Hold** your breath for a count of four.

Repeat this slowly and calmly for a few minutes, or as long as feels helpful.

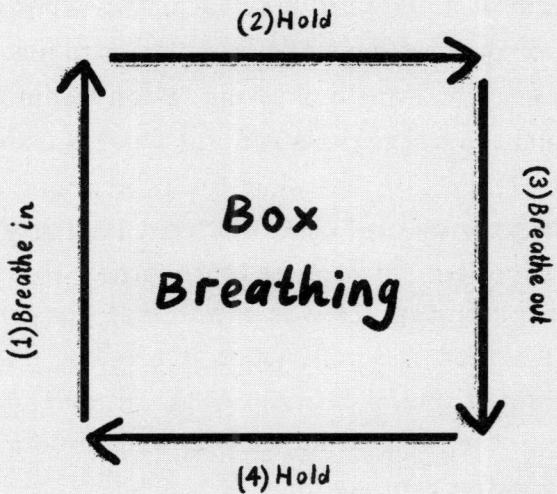

This simple rhythm slows your heart rate, activates your calming system and gives your busy mind something steady to focus on. You can do it any time when your thoughts are racing, or just as a daily reset.

From avoidance to acceptance

When we feel anxious, our instinct is often to escape or control. So we may avoid a worrying situation or try to distract ourselves. Or we might try to regain a sense of control through overthinking, believing that if we just keep thinking enough about what's making us anxious this will somehow protect us.

These strategies might bring short-term relief, but over time they tend to shrink our world and reinforce unhelpful beliefs and behaviours. If we keep trying to avoid or control our anxiety, it tends to grow. But by shifting our mindset from avoidance to *acceptance*, we can reduce the grip anxiety has over us.

This means you can allow the anxiety to be there, without trying to get rid of it. You can notice it with a sense of curiosity and then still carry on with your day. You're not giving up – you're dropping the struggle. Instead of saying, 'I don't want to feel this,' you're saying, 'I can feel anxious and still do what matters.'

> ### 🧠 Acceptance and commitment therapy (ACT)
>
> ACT is a modern form of psychotherapy that blends mindfulness with action. It was developed by psychologist Steven C. Hayes and colleagues. It teaches us how to accept difficult thoughts and feelings rather than trying to eliminate them – and to then commit to action, even when discomfort is present.
>
> Unlike CBT, which usually focuses on changing our thoughts, ACT focuses on changing our relationship to them. We can learn to notice anxious thoughts, 'defuse' them and get on with life while experiencing them.
>
> 'Defusion' is about unhooking from our anxious thoughts – seeing them as passing mental events rather than truths. A great way to do this is using the phrase, 'I'm having the thought that...' which reminds us thoughts are not facts.
>
> Instead of 'I can't cope' we say 'I'm having the thought that... I can't cope.'
>
> This small shift creates space. It's like being the observer watching clouds pass in the sky, rather than being swept up in the storm. Clinical evidence shows that acceptance-based approaches reduce anxiety more effectively than control-based ones. People report feeling

> more empowered, having fewer panic episodes and being able to live more fully even when anxiety shows up.

We can keep moving forwards, even when life is uncertain and messy. And it's never too late to start. Here's a lovely example of acceptance in action which I heard from one of our Action for Happiness volunteers called Laura, who said:

> ⭐ 'I am thriving ... sometimes. It feels good to say this. Things can be both challenging and easy, both happy and sad, both simple and complicated for me all at the same time! I used to think happiness would be reached when I was a certain age, or weight, when I had a particular job, but this meant I missed so many opportunities. Changing my perspective gave me back a million chances to access these things daily, even when things are challenging.'

Simple lifestyle changes to feel calmer

Techniques like breathing and acceptance are great, especially for things which we can't control. But our lifestyle choices also contribute to our anxiety, so a few conscious changes can often help us feel much calmer. Firstly, this means making time for the basics we covered in chapter four. Let's briefly revisit them again now:

• **Movement**: Regular physical activity, even just a short walk outside, releases endorphins, helps to calm the nervous system and regulates stress hormones like adrenaline and cortisol, which are released when we're anxious.

- **Sleep**: Lack of sleep amplifies anxiety, so it helps to establish regular sleep routines, avoid screens before bedtime and practise calming activities like reading or meditation to improve sleep quality.
- **Nutrition**: Healthy food choices and regular mealtimes tend to support a calmer state of mind than sugary, processed foods and constant snacking. We can also be mindful about how we consume things like caffeine and alcohol.
- **Tech use**: Social media, 24-hour news and online outrage all contribute to us feeling anxious. We can be more mindful about what we consume by reducing screen time and minimising exposure to distressing or enraging content.

Beyond the basics, we also need to break free from our culture of busyness. Too many of us push ourselves relentlessly, day after day. We find ourselves working late in the evening or prioritising deadlines over time with our loved ones. I know I've often done this myself and not made time to recover and reconnect.

I love my job and I work really hard. But I also want to prioritise family time and make time for my passions, like cycling tours and playing music. My wife Kate has helped a lot here too. In fact, just before we launched Action for Happiness, she said to me:

'Now listen, if you're going to be Director of Happiness, whatever that is, you obviously can't come home late and stressed every night.'

She was so right. And the sign she put by our side door, which reads HAPPY WIFE, HAPPY LIFE, is a helpful daily reminder too!

When we stretch a rubber band and let it go, it rebounds to its original shape. But if we keep stretching it beyond its capability it eventually deforms and breaks. This is like our stress response.

A little bit of stress is no problem – and in fact often helps us to perform at our best. But if we push ourselves too hard for too long this starts to change us. We may become more short-tempered or reactive, less able to make wise choices or care for those around us.

When we keep pushing we put our health and relationships at serious risk of breakdown. But when we give ourselves space to recover from stress we can still rebound back to normal, like that resilient rubber band.

Reach out to others

Anxiety often feels isolating, but talking to loved ones or connecting with supportive communities can really help. Sharing your experiences reduces the burden, and feeling cared for sends a powerful message to your nervous system: 'You're not alone.'

Talking to someone who listens and cares helps us gain perspective and stop spiralling in our own head. Also, when we're with someone who feels safe and grounded, our bodies naturally begin to mirror their calm. This is called 'co-regulation' – a biological process where nervous systems synchronise. Their warm voice, kind body language, or even just their presence, can help shift us from fight-or-flight into a calmer state.

It also helps to avoid spending time with people who tend to make you feel more anxious. And likewise, by using the ideas here to stay calmer, you can also help to prevent your own anxiety from spreading to others around you.

If anxiety becomes chronic or 'stuck' then it's vital to seek out professional help too. Approaches like CBT (see chapter seven) and ACT can really help. There are also various apps and programs designed for anxiety which can guide you through evidence-based techniques, such as mindfulness and habit-shifting exercises.

Putting it all together

In this chapter we've covered various ways to cultivate calm and let go of anxiety. Now we're going to bring them all together into a simple framework I've developed called the SAFER model. Because when we feel anxious, what we often really want is just to feel safer in an uncertain world. It has five parts:

💡 S – Sense what's going on.
Start by recognising that you feel anxious. You can use 'defusion' by saying, 'I'm having the thought that . . . I'm anxious.'

💡 A – Acknowledge the deeper worry.
Next, look behind that feeling with a sense of acceptance and curiosity. You can take a few minutes to write down what you're worried about.

💡 F – Frame it differently.
Having accepted what's going on, you can recognise that things may not be as bad as they seem and put your anxiety into perspective.

💡 E – Ease your body and mind.
You can use physical techniques – like box breathing or simple movement – to help calm your body, which in turn helps calm your mind too.

💡 R – Respond with one small step.
Now you're ready to take a small action to help the situation. This might be turning off your phone or reaching out to a friend for support.

> **➔ SAFER worrying**
> Five prompts to help you feel SAFER when you're worrying:
> - **Sense**. What thought am I having right now? (Defuse it)
> - **Acknowledge**. What am I worried might happen? (Write it down)
> - **Frame**. How can I look at this differently, or cope if it happens?
> - **Ease**. What can I do right now to calm my body? (E.g. box breathing)
> - **Respond**. What's a small step I can take next to support myself?

We live in a world where there's no shortage of problems to worry about. As the podcaster Chris Williamson reminded me, 'Problems are a feature of life, not a bug.' There will never be a time when all our worries are gone. The details will change, but dealing with problems and uncertainty is part of being human, not a personal curse.

By practising mindful living and doing what we can to create calm in the body and mind, we can change the way we relate to our worries and shift away from anxiety and towards meaningful action.

CULTIVATE CALM: CHAPTER SUMMARY

Ask yourself:
❓ **What behaviours help me to feel calm and safe?**

Don't just:
✗ Allow anxiety to leave you feeling unable to do the things you want.

Try this out:
✔ Learn ways to lower anxiety in your body, mind and environment.

Chapter Eleven:

Finding Meaning

Where am I really heading?

I felt embarrassed. Had I really been fooling myself so badly?

Having recently left corporate life, I was backpacking in India with Kate and taking some time to reflect on my future direction. The book I was reading had suggested a helpful thought experiment to get clearer about my values and priorities. This sounded good and I felt hopeful about what might emerge. But I was in for a surprise!

The idea was simple enough. I was given a list of 18 items that many people consider important in life, ranging from your income or relationships to where you live. I simply had to rank them in priority from 1–18, with the essentials at the top and things I could live without at the bottom. It forced me to think: *What really matters to me? What would I make sure to protect, no matter what?*

After some back-and-forth, I landed on my top six: personal growth, my partner, family, positive impact on society, friends and health. I was pleased with my list. These were the foundations that matter most in my life . . . or so I thought.

The next step was where things got uncomfortable: *Imagine a private detective had been hired to watch your daily life over recent years. What would their report say your top priorities were?*

Oh dear. I sat down and mapped it out – and the results were humbling.

Here was the truth: a detective reviewing my life wouldn't have found someone prioritising personal growth, family or wellbeing. They would have seen a stressed-out consultant working long hours, chasing status, salary and professional success. The things I claimed were 'non-negotiable' were nowhere near the top when it came to where I'd actually been investing my time and energy.

It was another big wake-up call. I'd always thought of myself as someone who cared about making a difference and who valued relationships over career ambition. But my actions told a different story. Perhaps it was no wonder my life had been feeling a bit meaningless.

So this became the next step in my Good Life Crisis and led to a conscious decision to refocus on loved ones and meaningful projects. I've also tried to go back to this exercise every few years, revisiting my priorities and checking to see how well my current actions match them. Time and again, this has helped me to course-correct.

What matters most to you?

When our priorities reflect our values, life feels more meaningful. But how often do you actually stop to think about what matters most? And even when you know your priorities, are you living in a way that's consistent with them?

→ Figure out what's important

This is your chance to work out what matters most to you right now. Below is an alphabetical list of 18 items people often consider to be important in life.

- Family
- Friends
- Health and fitness
- Income
- Independence
- Influence and power
- Making use of talents
- Personal growth
- Positive impact on society
- Prestige and status
- Professional growth
- Security
- Spirituality/faith
- Spouse/partner
- Stimulating/rewarding work
- Time for leisure and relaxation
- Wealth/savings
- Where you live

Now, find a quiet place where you can think, free from distractions. Your challenge is to put these items in order, based on your priorities at this point in your life. No ties or mergers allowed! Remember, choosing priorities involves making trade-offs and deciding which things you're willing to compromise on in order to make the important stuff happen.

> Once you've done your ranking, you might like to go one step further and imagine you're a detective that's been monitoring your life recently. Redo the list through their eyes. Are there any inconsistencies between your priorities and how you've actually been living?
>
> [Note: adapted from *In Transition* (1991) by Burton and Wedemeyer.]

Making time for what matters

Deep down we all want to feel purposeful, but we're often so busy getting through each day that we don't make time to focus on where we're heading and why. As a result, we can end up feeling lost or lacking a sense of direction.

Some of us have been busy rushing up the 'ladder' of other people's expectations, but without pausing to check whether our ladder is leaning against the right building. That was certainly true of me. What was I climbing towards? Or away from?

In an unpredictable world it's natural to feel unsure about what will happen in the years ahead. If we feel the social and economic systems around us are a bit broken we may actually want to preserve our mental wellbeing by trying to avoid thinking too much about the future. That's an understandable response.

But when we discover a gap between our values and how we're actually living, this is not a failure – it's an opportunity. It's our chance to recalibrate and make the most of this unique and precious life we have. In her book *Top Five Regrets of the Dying*, the nurse Bronnie Ware identified five common regrets expressed by people in her care during their final weeks of life. These are a great reminder of what really matters:

1. 'I wish I'd lived a life true to myself, not the life others expected of me.'
2. 'I wish I hadn't worked so hard.'
3. 'I wish I'd had the courage to express my feelings.'
4. 'I wish I'd stayed in touch with my friends.'
5. 'I wish I'd let myself be happier.'

None of us want to get towards the end of our lives regretting how we've spent our time. And I imagine no one ever says, 'I wish I'd spent more time *at the office*'! Thankfully, you still have the chance now to remind yourself what really matters and find a greater sense of meaning and purpose.

> 'Happiness is the meaning and purpose of life, the whole aim and end of human existence.'
> – Aristotle

The meaningful life

Research shows that having a sense of meaning is a major contributor to our long-term happiness and wellbeing. The psychologist and researcher Professor Michael F. Steger describes meaning in terms of three components:

- **Purpose**: having goals and aspirations that guide your life. So you have a reason to get out of bed in the morning.
- **Significance**: having the sense that your life has some value. So you feel that what you do matters, even if only in small ways.
- **Coherence**: having a sense of your overall life story. So all your ups and downs fit together in a way that makes sense.

We've all heard 'the meaning of life' referred to as some mystical quest — especially if, like me, you're a fan of Monty Python or the *Hitchhiker's Guide to the Galaxy*. However, Professor Steger brings a very helpful insight here. Rather than searching for this elusive meaning *of* life, he suggests we try to find meaning *in* life. We can all live in a way that makes life meaningful right here and now, through our actions and choices.

Steger's research shows that people who have a sense of meaning tend to feel happier overall, less depressed and more satisfied with their jobs. Meaning also acts as a buffer against stress, helping us navigate challenges with resilience and optimism. Feeling happy in the moment can be part of this, but meaning goes much deeper than just positive feelings. In fact, meaningful things often don't feel good at the time.

When Aristotle talked about happiness as the 'meaning and purpose of life', he wasn't talking about the pursuit of pleasure. He was referring to the fulfilment we get from a virtuous life — something he called *eudaimonia*.

> ### 🧠 Purpose beyond pleasure
> The ancient Greeks had two words for happiness — *hedonia* and *eudaimonia* — and they meant very different things.
>
> **Hedonia** is the happiness of pleasurable experiences. It's about feeling good in the moment . . . like enjoying a delicious meal, a relaxing afternoon or the thrill of something new. It's comfort, ease and quick bursts of joy.
>
> **Eudaimonia** goes deeper and is about human flourishing. The word comes from *eu* (good) and *daimōn* (spirit or true self). It's about living a virtuous life . . . one

> guided by purpose, integrity and personal growth. It's not always comfortable, but it's fulfilling. It's more than just feeling good, it's doing good too.

Meaningful activities often involve hardship along the way. For example, many parents of young children find their day-to-day wellbeing goes down due to lack of sleep and the new challenges of raising a family. Yet alongside this, they also often report that their lives feel more meaningful than before they had children.

This was definitely my experience when our children came along. I was exhausted, and I'll confess I totally lost the plot at times, especially when sleep-deprived! But having kids has made life infinitely richer. It's hard to put into words just how much they mean to me. I love them so much.

Lots of different things can bring this meaning *in* life. It might be our relationships and family roles, or it could be our religious faith, spiritual practice or sense of connection to the natural world. It might be the projects we care about, our hobbies and achievements, helping those in need or contributing to wider society.

Meaning can also emerge – and help us cope – in dark times. A really powerful example of this is Viktor Frankl's book *Man's Search for Meaning*, his harrowing but hopeful account of survival in Nazi concentration camps.

> ⭐ 'Those who have a "why" to live, can bear with almost any "how".'
>
> – **Viktor Frankl**

One key aspect of meaning is feeling part of something bigger than yourself – whether through family, community or a higher cause. Meaning often emerges from altruism and contribution, with studies showing that helping others provides a profound sense of purpose and activates reward pathways in the brain. We'll look more at this in part two.

Our crisis of meaning

Sadly, I feel our modern society is facing a crisis of meaning. Although more connected than ever, many of us feel strangely adrift, asking ourselves, 'What's the point of it all?' This may not feel as urgent as other crises, like geopolitics or the environment, but it is a profound and existential challenge. Millions of us feel like we don't belong or don't matter – and this really matters.

For much of human history, religious traditions offered a shared sense of purpose, morality and community. But across much of the Western world, participation in these traditions has declined. Churches, mosques, synagogues and temples are now less central to our culture than they once were. This isn't a critique of religion – it's an acknowledgement of the deep value it's given people for thousands of years.

In place of collective traditions, many of us have embraced new forms of identity built around status and personal achievement. But although these may bring greater freedom and self-expression, individualism and materialism can't satisfy our deeper human need to be part of something bigger. Seeking significance through possessions or social status rarely satisfies. Even when we're secure in terms of our material needs, many of us end up feeling lost or empty.

Deep down, we all want to feel valued and to be of value –

this desire to 'matter' is universal. While religion and spirituality continue to fulfil this need for many, meaning can also be cultivated in a secular world. But we need to discover how.

Should you follow your passion?

You often hear the advice to 'follow your passion' as a compass for guiding your life. Finding work you love has become a sort of secular stand-in for traditional ideas of divine purpose. But without a clear moral framework we're left to look within ourselves for meaning, using passion as our guide. Although this sounds uplifting, it can be unrealistic.

Firstly, many of us don't have a clear calling from an early age. Being told to follow your passion can feel daunting and create pressure to love what you do all the time. Then, when the inevitable hard or boring days come along, this can lead to disillusionment, burnout or constant career-hopping in search of a deeper purpose.

Rather than expecting to find work we feel passionate about, it's often better to find ways to 'craft' meaning into the work we're doing – like the hospital cleaner who sees their role as helping to save lives rather than just tidying rooms. In fact, research shows that passion often follows effort and develops through mastery, not the other way around. We become passionate about the things we invest our time in, especially when we feel competent and see that we're making a difference.

Finding your purpose

So if passion alone isn't sufficient, how can we live a more purposeful life? During my Good Life Crisis I came across another great tool to help with this. Initially it felt a bit simplistic, but to my surprise it completely changed the direction of my life. Without it, this book certainly wouldn't exist.

I had the good fortune to meet an author and coach called Neil Crofts who had a 'formula' to help people find their purpose. It uses the insight that we're most motivated if we can combine our passion with our talents to focus on something we want to change. His approach starts by asking yourself three simple questions.

Firstly, **what are your talents?** In my case, what came to mind was my experience as an engineer and consultant – I'm quite good at understanding and organising things.

Secondly, **what are you passionate about?** By this point I'd already seen the impact of small changes to make life happier – it had become my favourite topic!

Thirdly, **what change do you want to see in the world?** Ah, so many! But all the things I wished were different, from our fractured society to our warming planet, seemed to link to one core idea: I wanted to see a shift towards prioritising wellbeing.

The final step was then to bring all these answers together to reveal your own unique purpose in life. Here's what I wrote:

> *'My purpose is ... to use my talent for organising things and my passion for authentic happiness to change priorities in our society and help people focus on what really matters.'*

Wow! As I stared down at the scrap of paper in front of me, I couldn't quite believe I'd managed to draft my own personal purpose. Okay, the wording was a bit clumsy and maybe these ideas had been right in front of me all along. But I'd never seen this so clearly before. It felt really motivating.

Yet despite feeling energised, I had no idea how I'd put this into practice. So I tucked the piece of paper back in my drawer. Then a few months later I happened to read an article by Professor Richard Layard in a newspaper. His book *Happiness: Lessons from a New Science* had already had a big influence on me. Now here he was writing about the need for a new social movement focused on happiness.

Suddenly I could feel my heart pounding. This was it. In other circumstances I would have just put the article away and got on with my day job. At this stage I was working on clean-tech solutions for climate change – and enjoying it. Yet because I'd written down my life's purpose on that piece of paper, I just knew I had to act.

So I connected with Richard and, as they say, the rest is history. That exercise gave me the confidence and clarity to quit what I was doing and get together with him and others to co-found Action for Happiness. We've been working together ever since, promoting happier living – not just for individuals but across society. It's been hard work and at times the most challenging thing I've ever done. But the motivation that comes from doing something I really believe in has been extraordinary.

I've also seen that same 'coming alive' in many others who have changed direction to pursue causes they really care about – from teachers and community workers, to engineers and entrepreneurs.

Your purpose may be related to your work and career. But it could also be alongside or outside of your work-life – for example, through volunteering, family projects, running a club or being part of a local group.

> **What's your purpose in life?**
> Try coming up with your own answers to these questions:
> - **What are your talents?** Write down a list of things you're really good at. Things that come naturally to you. Don't be modest – be honest.
> - **What are you passionate about?** Write a list of things that make you feel motivated. Things you love to talk about, think about and do.
> - **What do you want to change in the world?** Write down things in society you wish were different. What makes you angry, or feels wrong?
>
> Now see if you can find a way to combine your talents, passion and anger in a positive and coherent way. This could be the foundation for your future direction:
>
> 'My life's purpose is to use my (**talents**) and (**passion**) to (**change**).'

Having a clearer sense of purpose helps you to organise your life around what matters most. This brings a greater sense of fulfilment as well as contributing to wider social good. But making a big shift to follow your purpose may not always be practical immediately. So, rather than a fixed endpoint, it helps to think of this more as an evolving guide for your path ahead. Also, as you pursue activities that really light you up, others will tend to be drawn to this too. You'll start to form new connections and communities with like-minded people who share similar values and interests.

'Ask what makes you come alive, and go do it. Because what the world needs is people who have come alive.'

– Howard Thurman

The power of goals

Once we're clearer on what matters to us, we need ways to put our good intentions into action. One of the most effective ways to do this is by breaking longer-term goals into more achievable next steps.

Long-term goals set your direction, like where you want to be in five or ten years, the kind of person you want to become or the change you want to contribute to. They act as a guiding force, shaping your everyday choices and priorities. But big goals can also feel overwhelming, so you need to break them down into bite-size actions and build confidence along the way.

Short-term goals provide the small, achievable next steps you can do this week or month to head in that direction. They give a sense of momentum, keeping you engaged and moving forwards.

Think of your long-term and short-term goals as different gears in the same engine, working together to move you forwards. The key is making sure they're connected, so your small daily or weekly efforts are helping you move towards the bigger picture you care about. In a world of distractions and competing demands, long-term goals act as a filter, helping you decide which short-term tasks are truly worth your time.

> ### → Get clear on your goals
> Now it's time to turn the thoughts you've had about your priorities and purpose into something tangible.
> 1. **Start with the big picture**. What's a long-term goal that matters to you?
>   For example: 'I want to contribute to my community in a meaningful way.'

> 2. **Break it down**. What are three short-term goals to move you in that direction?
> For example:
> - Chat to neighbours about what's going on locally.
> - Research nearby volunteering opportunities.
> - Attend one community group or event this month.
> 3. **Take the first step**. What's the smallest action I can take today to begin?

Your long-term goals can be aspirational, or even unachievable. In my case, cycling is something I love, not just for fitness but because it does wonders for my mental wellbeing. So to make sure I keep at it, I've set myself a truly ridiculous long-term life goal to 'cycle to the moon before I die!'

I'm not actually cycling in space, I mean the distance – which is a huge 384,400km. As I write this, I'm in my early 50s and only about 40 per cent of the way there. Even if I keep going at my current pace, I'm unlikely to reach my goal until I'm in my 80s. My kids think I'm daft and Kate isn't looking forward to the idea of me still in Lycra at that age!

But whether I actually make it isn't the point. The real value of this goal is that it gets me out on my bike, even on cold or rainy days when I don't feel like it. It turns a simple daily habit of cycling to work into something bigger and more motivating.

Whatever your passion, setting a big-picture goal can bring more purpose to your daily life. Whether your own 'moonshot' project is to write a book, learn a new skill or play a part in an important cause, having this longer-term vision will make every small contributing action feel more significant.

Importantly, you don't need to wait for the perfect time to start.

Life's other duties will never be out of the way and we can't assume we'll find time for the things that matter at some point in the future. Much better to start doing a bit of what you care about now.

> ⭐ 'So if you really mean it when you say you'd like to write a novel or spend more time with your ageing parents, or fighting climate change, or having fun, at some point you're just going to have to start doing it.'
> – **Oliver Burkeman**

Finding meaning isn't about having everything figured out, it's about the goals we set and the actions we take – one step, one choice, one ride at a time.

Everyday meaning matters too

If this all feels a bit overwhelming, don't worry. Meaning isn't just found in big goals or major life decisions. Often, it's in the everyday moments – like a conversation with a friend, a walk in nature or just the satisfaction of getting something done.

Making time for mindfulness can help us to notice and appreciate these moments, reconnecting us with things we often take for granted. Pause for a moment to look around you now. What everyday things can you see that are meaningful? Perhaps something in nature outside, a reminder of a loved one or even just an awareness of how precious it is to be alive today.

And if the work you're doing right now doesn't feel meaningful, that's okay too. Remember, meaning comes outside of work as well – hobbies, creative projects, helping others, playing an instrument, joining a club or singing in a choir.

> **Simple tips for everyday meaning**
> - Notice the extraordinary in the ordinary
> - Appreciate the good things, even on difficult days
> - Do something creative – write, draw, cook, build or play
> - Spend time outside and reconnect with nature
> - Help someone, anyone (more on this in part two)

The bigger picture

Did you know our solar system is orbiting the centre of our galaxy at around 230km per second? Each year we collectively travel over 7 billion kilometres across the Milky Way. So once in a while it's worth pausing to appreciate how far you've already come.

Although I'm no longer religious I still feel a sense of awe and wonder at the mysteries of our universe and the miracle of life. I also realise now that the Christian values that underpinned my childhood have continued to shape my journey. When we set up Action for Happiness, this wasn't just about helping people take action to feel happier themselves, it was also about helping people to be part of something bigger and to rediscover the sense of meaning that comes through community and contribution.

My mum likes to joke that although I may have lost my faith, I still have a 'missionary zeal'. But now I try to encourage people to discover the meaning that comes from helping to make our precious world a happier and kinder place.

Action for Happiness isn't about trying to replace religion, or create a new cult. It builds on timeless truths which I passionately wish everyone could discover, regardless of their background or faith. Above all, we thrive when we live for something beyond ourselves and contribute to the happiness of others.

FINDING MEANING | 187

 'Only a life lived for others is a life worthwhile.'
— **Albert Einstein**

If we just aim to make our own life happier, we miss something vital. The real secret is looking beyond yourself to help others live better lives too. The topics and skills we've covered here in part one have hopefully helped you to build self-awareness, try out some helpful actions and find ways to cope better in difficult times. With these building blocks, you're now better placed to look outwards, build connections with others and do more to help make the world around you happier too.

We've done the *inner* work, and now, as we move into part two, we'll explore the additional benefits from doing the *outer* work: looking beyond yourself and trying to be a force for good in the world. You can make life happier in a way that benefits you and contributes to something bigger too.

FINDING MEANING: CHAPTER SUMMARY

Ask yourself:
? **What are the greatest sources of meaning in my life?**

Don't just:
✗ Spend your whole time trying to meet others' expectations.

Try this out:
✔ Find and pursue meaningful goals that give you a sense of purpose.

PART 2:
HAPPIER TOGETHER

Looking outwards and connecting with others

Chapter Twelve:

Prioritise People

Am I focusing enough on my relationships?

I felt terrible. *What kind of friend was I?*

Two weeks before, I'd heard that a close friend was really unwell and going through a tough time. I was worried about them and had every intention of checking in a few days later and being there for them. But somehow I completely forgot – and only remembered when someone else mentioned it.

I felt so guilty, like I'd really let them and myself down. Neglecting a friend in need is not the sort of person I want to be. Yes, life was busy with work commitments and family distractions, but this was no excuse.

This also wasn't the first time. There were other recent occasions where I'd realised it felt far too long since I'd spoken to certain people. They really mattered to me, but I wasn't making time to stay in touch. Something had to change.

Rather than drowning in guilt, I asked myself: How can I be better at this in future? So I started setting little reminders to check in with people. At first it felt slightly forced – wasn't friendship supposed to be spontaneous? Would scheduling it take away its sincerity or feel a bit fake?

I discovered the opposite was true. The simple act of remembering to reach out began to enhance and rekindle my relationships, especially with old friends. I made a habit of scrolling through old photos and sending a happy memory to someone out of the blue. I noted meaningful dates – not just birthdays, but anniversaries of shared moments – and used these as prompts to get back in touch.

Now, whenever I find myself thinking about a friend or loved one, I try to make time to send them a quick message *there and then*, just to say 'Hi'. And when a friend is ill or having a tough time, I set a reminder to check in with them again soon, ensuring I don't let their struggles slip into the background of a busy life.

Between work, family and everything else, friendships can easily fall by the wayside. I had to accept that I wouldn't always remember to be a good friend, despite my best intentions. I certainly haven't cracked this yet – I still miss plenty of chances for connection. But by making time more consciously to stay in touch, lots of my relationships have become stronger. I feel happier, too, and for good reason.

Relationships are the foundation for a good life

A growing body of research confirms what most of us intuitively know: relationships are central to our happiness and wellbeing. In fact, the renowned Harvard study (see next page) has found that close relationships are the strongest predictor of a long, healthy and fulfilling life. Not money. Not fame. Not success. Just the quality of our connections with others. As the study's director, Professor Robert Waldinger, told me:

'The strength of people's relationships with others was the strongest factor in keeping them not just happier emotionally, but physically healthier.'

> ### What predicts a long and happy life?
> The *Harvard Study of Adult Development* began in 1938 and is the longest-running research project ever conducted into human life and health. Of the many findings from the study, the most consistent – and perhaps surprising – conclusion is that strong relationships are the most reliable predictor of long-term health and happiness.
>
> Strong relationships don't just enhance emotional and mental wellbeing, they also significantly affect physical health and even lifespan. People with strong social ties tend to live longer, experience less stress and be more resilient. Compared to factors such as wealth or education, strong social connections contribute more to overall wellbeing and predict better long-term health outcomes, including reduced risk of coronary artery disease, Type 2 diabetes and arthritis. Remarkably, the strength of your relationships at age 50 turns out to be a stronger predictor of health at age 80 than your cholesterol levels.

Yet, even though we know relationships matter, we often overlook just how important they are. I certainly had been. Many of us put more energy into other areas of our lives, like our career, hobbies or fitness.

We tend to assume that relationships sort of take care of

themselves. But in practice, they require ongoing attention – just like plants need watering or homes need cleaning. If we don't make time to regularly renew and deepen our relationships, we risk missing out on something vitally important. Putting real effort into our relationships is one of our biggest and most rewarding opportunities to make life happier.

> **➜ Connect right now**
> Bring to mind someone you care about and haven't spoken to in a while. Take a moment right now to send them a friendly message and let them know you're thinking of them.

How to keep relationships in good shape

One helpful way to think about relationships is the idea of 'social fitness'. Just like with physical health, our relationship health depends on ongoing effort. Relationships usually fade, not because of conflict but because of neglect. Friendship withers without attention. So little actions like checking in and expressing appreciation help to keep our relationships fit and healthy.

To build our social fitness we can use our own 'relationship gym'. Like working out for physical fitness, this involves identifying and repeating habits that help to maintain and improve the relationships that matter to us – from partners and family members to old friends and colleagues. Small, regular actions keep us from drifting apart.

We talked earlier about mindfulness being the 'bicep curl' for our mind. This is more like gentle circuit training for our relationships, over months and years. And unlike the gym, this has the potential to be an ongoing source of joy rather than a chore. People who engage in relationship-strengthening activities tend to report higher life satisfaction.

Just as we adapt our physical exercise to suit our age and situation, we can do the same with our social exercise too. Whether you're young or in later life, the opportunity to build relationships is always there. The important thing is to make it a priority rather than taking it for granted.

> ➜ **Improve your social fitness**
> - **Check in regularly**: A quick text or call to see how someone is doing can make a big difference.
> - **Be fully present**: Put down your phone and give people your full attention when you're with them.
> - **Celebrate milestones**: Acknowledge birthdays, anniversaries and achievements to show you care.
> - **Express gratitude**: Let people know you appreciate them. Send a simple thank you to let them know how much they helped.
> - **Make time for in-person**: Whenever possible, prioritise face-to-face time. Physical presence builds stronger connections.
> - **Share positive experiences**: Plan enjoyable activities together, whether it's a shared meal, a hobby or a walk.
> - **Catch people doing good**. When someone does something thoughtful, take a moment to acknowledge their kindness.
> - **Accept people as they are**. No one's perfect, so value them as they are (and let them see you as you are).

Nurturing different relationships

Our relationships come in different shapes and it helps to notice the different roles they each play in our lives. Most important are the core relationships with people we feel closest to, like our partners, best friends, family members or anyone who deeply understands us. We can think of these people as our 'inner circle'. Here we want to really build trust and be willing to show vulnerability (more on this in chapter fifteen).

These are the people we want to depend on – and be there for – during tough times. But sometimes we take them for granted or assume they'll always be around. So it's important that we make time for meaningful interactions and be willing to both seek and provide emotional intimacy and support.

When life gets busy, it's especially important we don't accidentally neglect our close friends. Unlike our family ties, our friendships are voluntary. This is their great strength – as they say, 'friends are the family we choose'. But being optional also makes our friendships vulnerable and precious. They need intentional care to keep thriving.

> 'Of all the things that wisdom provides to help live one's life in happiness the greatest by far is the possession of friendship.'
>
> – **Epicurus**

Then there's our 'outer circle' – colleagues, neighbours, extended family and friends we don't know so well. We may interact with these people fairly regularly but we aren't deeply connected to them. And that's perfectly okay.

Here our focus may be on shared activities, interests or even just the fact that we're in close proximity, for example at work. These relationships help us stay socially engaged and bring a sense of belonging. So although we may not reveal our innermost feelings to them, it's still helpful to make an effort to talk, check in on how they're doing and get together socially.

There may also be people who feel somewhere between inner or outer for you – that's fine. The key point is we can nurture our close bonds while also maintaining wider acquaintances. A healthy balance involves recognising that both deeper and wider relationships add richness to our lives – and making time for both.

Then, beyond our inner and outer circles, there are the people all around us who we see but don't necessarily interact with or feel a connection to. We call these people strangers, but as the Irish poet William Butler Yeats once said: 'There are no strangers here. Only friends you haven't met yet.' I love that sentiment.

So why do we shy away from talking to strangers? Often it's not that we're antisocial – we just assume it will feel awkward. We fear we'll be judged or not know what to say. This is compounded by our social norms, especially in big cities, which reinforce the idea that we should keep to ourselves. And with our devices, headphones and busy schedules, it becomes all too easy to retreat into our own little world.

But most of those worries are imagined. Studies show that we consistently underestimate how rewarding it will be to strike up a conversation with someone we don't know. We think we'll be bothering them, but they usually appreciate it. We worry it will feel weird, but more often than not it feels great.

Humans are wired for connection and, once we take that small step, we rediscover that even a brief exchange can brighten someone's day, including our own. Talking to strangers makes both parties happier and helps us feel more human. It reminds us that we're all in this together. In a world with more loneliness and division, these tiny acts of everyday connection have an outsized impact.

> **→ Try this: say hello to strangers**
> Next time you catch someone's eye or stand together in a queue, give them a smile and consider saying hello. It's likely to be easier and more rewarding than you imagine. By making a point of sharing a friendly greeting with people you see along the way, you're helping to spread happiness and maybe reduce loneliness.
>
> Then if you're comfortable – and they seem open to it – why not start a brief chat? You could ask them what they're up to today or share something good about your day. Or perhaps take a moment to notice something you have in common or appreciate something about them, like their colourful clothing.

What if I feel alone?

We all feel lonely at times. This can be true even when we're surrounded by others. Many younger people now report feeling lonely, despite lots of online friends. This matters because evidence suggests that prolonged loneliness can harm our health. It can keep the body in fight-or-flight mode, increasing stress hormones and inflammation. Of course, some of us really enjoy being by ourselves. But loneliness is different to solitude – it's the feeling of lacking connection, rather than choosing to be alone.

If you're feeling lonely at the moment, don't worry. As this chapter shows, there are practical ways we can increase our sense of connection to others. In the words of an old saying, 'The best way to have a friend is to be a friend', so a good starting point is to find a way to reach out and help someone you know. Or just let them know you appreciate them. It's also good to actively seek out opportunities to connect, such as volunteering or joining an interest group.

> **➔ Create a micro-connection**
> We tend to underappreciate the power of micro-moments of connection. Even tiny interactions — like greeting a neighbour with a friendly smile or chatting with someone at the supermarket — can boost wellbeing and help to reduce loneliness. These moments create a sense of belonging and help us feel more connected to the people around us in our everyday lives.

And if you see, or think of, someone who may be more alone than they want to be, reach out to them. If the thought crosses your mind, act on it.

How we communicate really matters

The health of our relationships is often determined less by what we say and more by how we say it. Maya Angelou put it beautifully:

'People will forget what you said, people will forget what you did, but people will never forget how you made them feel.'

It's important that we avoid negative communication patterns, which have been found to be major predictors of relationship breakdown, for example:

- **Contempt**: Mocking, sarcasm or disrespect, which conveys superiority (e.g. rolling eyes, sighing or saying 'I'm surprised you even bothered').

- **Criticism**: Attacking the other person's character rather than specific behaviours ('You're so selfish. You never think of others').
- **Defensiveness**: Playing the victim or deflecting responsibility ('You're too sensitive. It's not *my* fault if you're upset').
- **Withdrawing**: Shutting down emotionally or refusing to engage (e.g. giving the silent treatment or walking away).

Dr John Gottman, a renowned psychologist, spent decades studying relationships and discovered that the ratio of positive to negative interactions is a strong predictor. He found that thriving relationships have at least five positive interactions for every negative, whereas struggling ones often have a ratio more like 1:1 or worse.

Gottman also noticed that strong relationships are built on how we respond to each other's 'bids for connection' – our small attempts to seek attention, validation or closeness. When we regularly acknowledge and engage with these bids, our connection remains strong, helping to build the 'emotional bank account' needed to get through difficult times. However, when we dismiss or ignore these bids, our account gets depleted and the relationship deteriorates.

Being there in hard times matters – but studies show that how we respond in good times also shapes our relationships. So when someone shares something they've achieved or something they're excited about, instead of just saying 'well done', ask follow-up questions. Be curious. Celebrate with them. This deepens connections and strengthens bonds, whether at home, at work or beyond.

> 🧠 **Active constructive responding**
>
> Active constructive responding (ACR) is a communication style that strengthens relationships by showing genuine interest and enthusiasm when someone shares good news or positive experiences. Instead of offering a dismissive or passive response, ACR involves being fully present, asking questions and celebrating the other person's achievement or joy.
>
> For example, if a friend shares that they got a promotion, an ACR might be: 'That's such great news, tell me more about how it happened.' This response not only validates their feelings but also deepens the emotional connection by reinforcing that their success is valued and appreciated. It's a great way to increase trust and closeness.

Myths about love and connection

One of the most important relationships is with our partner or spouse, if we have one. This ideally involves deep emotional intimacy, shared goals and daily interdependence. Having a strong and secure partnership can be a major contributor to lifelong wellbeing – and research shows that high-quality romantic relationships are linked to greater happiness and lifelong health.

But popular culture often promotes misleading myths about love and relationships. One of the most pervasive is the idea that once we find 'the one' everything will effortlessly fall into place. The truth is that all meaningful relationships require significant and ongoing effort, no matter how well-matched two people may appear to be.

Another related myth is the 'soulmate' concept – the belief that there is one perfect person out there who will complete us. While this sounds romantic, it can actually be limiting. Healthy relationships are based on interdependence, not dependence. The best partnerships allow both partners to grow, evolve and complement each other rather than expecting one person to fulfil our every need.

The experience of 'falling in love' at the start of a romantic relationship is a wonderful feeling. We're often drawn to our partners for subconscious reasons we're not fully aware of and that feels novel and electrifying at first. This is real and meaningful, but in the longer term these romantic feelings alone aren't enough.

What contributes most to lasting happiness for a couple is what Professor Arthur Brooks calls 'companionate love'. This goes beyond the emotional highs and lows of passion and attraction. It's based on real affection and mutual understanding – a deeper sense of friendship and acceptance. In fact, research shows that people who see their spouse as their best friend tend to have greater wellbeing than those who don't.

Prioritise people, not devices

Technology can bring big benefits for our relationships – especially by helping us stay connected. These days tech and social media provide countless ways for us to share, chat and stay close to people we care about. We now do this digital connecting all the time, including with people we see in real life – and even those we live with! But these online connections still aren't the same as actually being together. Our relationships are built not just on what we say but also our non-verbal communication.

In person, we use body language – like facial expressions and gestures – to convey emotion, but these cues are often lost in text or video. Also our physical presence matters. Human touch triggers the release of oxytocin, sometimes known as the 'cuddle hormone', which builds trust and closeness. And it's not just about hugs – even subtle cues like hand gestures and eye contact help us feel seen and connected.

When we're with someone in person we share moments together. We're also less likely to multitask or be distracted by notifications, leading to more uninterrupted attention. And there's usually less chance of miscommunication when we're together.

> ➜ **Tips for healthier tech use**
> - **Have device-free time**: Set specific times during the day or week to disconnect from tech and focus on face-to-face interactions. For example 'no screens after 9pm' or 'tech-free Sunday'.
> - **Create no-tech zones**: Designate spaces in your life where phones and other devices are kept out, such as the dining table or bedroom.
> - **Listen without multitasking**: When someone is talking to you, put your device down and really listen. (More on this in the next chapter!)
> - **Stay in the room**. Turn off non-essential notifications (or use 'do not disturb' mode) so you stay present when you're with loved ones.
> - **Model healthy habits**. If you're trying to encourage less tech use, lead by example. Show others that you prioritise people over devices.

Small efforts, lifelong rewards

In this chapter we've seen how relationships are vital for our happiness, health and even longevity. But good relationships take ongoing effort and it's important that we maintain our 'social fitness'. In the next chapter we'll dive into the most important building block of all for deepening our connections with others – listening! And later we'll also look at how to deal more effectively with challenges in our relationships too.

Ultimately, we all want to feel loved and that we matter. Often the greatest thing we can do for others is to simply let them know they're loved and they matter.

> **PRIORITISE PEOPLE: CHAPTER SUMMARY**
> Ask yourself:
> ❓ **Which relationships do I need to give more priority to?**
>
> Don't just:
> ✗ Assume your relationships will stay strong without working on them.
>
> Try this out:
> ✔ Focus on your 'social fitness' and invest time in your relationships.

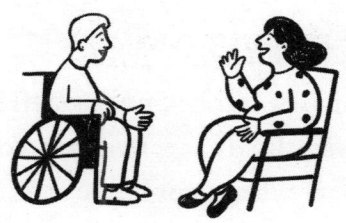

Chapter Thirteen:

Listen Actively

Do I really hear what people are saying?

'Dad, can't you just let me be ANGRY!?'

Oh dear, she'd absolutely nailed it. And I'd missed an opportunity.

My daughter had been opening up about an infuriating experience she'd had at school. She was understandably upset and clearly wanted to vent her frustration. I didn't like seeing her so distressed and my 'engineer dad' brain naturally kicked in. Before I knew it, I was offering well-intentioned solutions ('why don't you try . . .') and trying to cheer her up ('don't worry about it, darling . . .').

What she needed from me in that moment wasn't advice, or even encouragement. It was to feel heard and to have her difficult feelings validated. She didn't need someone to suggest fixes or tell her it was no big deal. With hindsight, a much better response would have been something like: 'I'm sorry, darling, that sounds really difficult. You're feeling upset and angry – and that's understandable.'

I should have known better because I'd already learned this lesson. Many years back I came across research on the power of active listening – and the importance of 'reflecting back' what the other person is saying. I was sceptical but decided to give it a try that evening with Kate when I got home after work. As she told me about her day – and what was on her mind – I tried to just repeat back what she'd said in my own words.

No added opinions or advice. Just echoing what she was saying.

It felt really clumsy, and frankly a bit embarrassing. I felt sure she was about to ask me what the hell I was doing! Instead, after this had gone on for a while, Kate turned to me and said: 'Thanks, it's been really good talking this evening.'

This blew my mind. She'd never said that before. I found myself wondering just how many conversations I'd had with people without really helping them feel heard. Ever since, I've been trying to do better. Yet here I was, years later, trying to solve my daughter's problems rather than just listen. And she'd rightly called me out.

As we've already noted, building our relationship skills takes ongoing effort.

What's wrong with how we normally listen?

Most of us think we're good listeners. I spent years assuming I was the sort of friendly person that people liked to talk to. But, as I learned the hard way, we often fail to listen deeply to each other. Most of us have huge potential for improvement, and I'm certainly still a work in progress.

Research shows that active listening improves relationships, increases trust and even enhances our own ability to process information. We know this intuitively too. When someone is truly present with us, we feel seen, valued and understood.

> 💬 'The most precious gift we can offer others is our presence.'
>
> **– Thich Nhat Hanh**

Each time we fail to offer someone our attention, we miss an opportunity. In fact, active listening is a vital life skill I believe everyone should be taught in school – just like reading or writing. But in practice it's usually left to chance. Many of us grow up in environments where listening is the exception rather than the norm. Where emotions are managed rather than met. Where quick fixes are prioritised over deeper connection.

So in this chapter we're going back to basics – let's start with what we get wrong.

Not listening takes various different forms. We're distracted, trying to multitask or focusing on what we want to say in reply. We may rush the other person by interrupting or guessing what they're going to say. We get caught up in our own feelings or we assume we know how they're feeling without checking. We may try to relate what they're saying to our own experiences, bringing it back to us. Or we just keep watching TV or staring at our phone while our loved one is talking, so we fail to hear their request or notice when something is up.

But perhaps the most common and problematic failure is when we jump to giving advice or problem-solving. This may come from a good place, where we genuinely want to help, yet there's often something going on underneath this too. Perhaps we feel uncomfortable with their discomfort and want to brush these difficult feelings aside.

That upsetting moment with my daughter helped me see this in myself. Having often found emotions like anger or sadness uncomfortable, my instinct was that it was 'better' to keep them under control rather than allowing them out. When I was growing up, our family tended to value solutions over emotions. Finding a positive response usually mattered more than sitting with difficult feelings.

Although this approach can be a form of resilience, I was carrying this belief that fixing problems was the best way to show I care. But when my daughter was upset she wanted to be heard, not fixed. She needed me to sit with her in her anger and to acknowledge her frustration, without trying to smooth it over.

Hearing vs listening

In a world full of noise, busyness and distraction, it's easier than ever to slip into surface-level interactions where we hear words yet don't really absorb them. But deep listening requires something different. It requires our presence. We need to pay attention, avoid assumptions and create space for the other person.

There's a big difference between hearing and listening. Hearing is passive – it happens automatically when sound reaches our ears. But listening, real listening, is an active process. It requires more than just taking in words, it means absorbing their meaning, tuning into the emotion behind them and resisting the urge to mentally prepare our own response while they're still speaking.

All too often, we listen just enough to form a reply. Instead of being fully present, we're already thinking ahead: *What advice should I give? How does this relate to my own experience? What should I say next?*

Real listening begins with simply being quiet while the other person is speaking, turning our full attention to them and showing with our eye contact and body language that we're ready to listen. That we're in 'receive' mode, rather than 'broadcast' mode.

Then comes the core listening skill which so many of us miss – reflecting back what the other person is saying. This involves checking in with them to make sure we've understood. The best way to do this is by paraphrasing elements of what they've said, using simple phrases like 'It sounds like what you're saying is . . .' and then briefly trying to summarise their point in our own words.

Importantly, we also need to check that they feel understood and we've not missed the point. We can do this by asking: 'Is that what you meant?' If our listening has gone well, the other person will let us know ('Yes, that's it'). Or if not, they may correct our summary ('No, what I meant was . . .'). Either way they feel heard.

Above all, you're trying to get to the core of what they've said – and how they feel – to check you've got this clear. This helps you understand them and it helps them feel understood by you. It's a genuine win–win.

> **→ Try this: reflecting back**
> Practise simple reflection in a conversation today. After someone has finished speaking, simply offer them a shorter summary of what they've just said using your own words to check you've got them.
>
> There are two key things going on here. Firstly, you really need to listen in order to be able to reflect back the most meaningful part of what they said. Secondly, it signals that you're listening, which may also lead them to either sharing more or clarifying something which you might otherwise have missed or misunderstood.
>
> Tip for reflecting: 'It sounds like what you're saying is (. . . summarise here).'

> Tip to check after reflecting: 'Did I get that right?'
> Reflecting back may feel uncomfortable at first. That's okay, these things take time. There's no one right way and, as with other actions in this book, it's about experimenting to discover what works best for you.

When someone is really listening, they're not distracted, not glancing at their phone, not waiting for their turn to talk. Their attention is fully on the other person. In those moments, we feel truly heard – and it makes a big difference. When we offer this gift of full attention to others it can take our relationships to the next level.

> ⭐ 'The ultimate touchstone of friendship is not improvement, neither of the other nor of the self. The ultimate touchstone is witness, the privilege of having been seen by someone.'
>
> **– David Whyte**

Barriers to connection

If listening is so powerful, why don't we do it more often? The truth is, many of us were never taught how to respond wisely when difficult feelings come up. From a young age we pick up – either explicitly or subtly – that certain emotions are problematic. Anger, sadness and frustration are often seen as things to manage or avoid, not express. Whether through family expectations or social norms, we absorb the message that talking about difficult feelings makes people feel uncomfortable. Instead we're encouraged to 'move on' or 'look on the bright side'.

So when someone shares their struggles, our instinct is often to lighten the mood, shift the conversation or offer encouragement. We may downplay the significance of their emotions, saying things like 'It's not that bad', or offering reassurance, like 'You'll be fine.' Although well meaning, these responses suggest their feelings aren't valid or acceptable. It may even leave them feeling worse.

We often jump to problem-solving: hear the issue, find the solution, fix it. This is especially true at work, where efficiency is valued. But most people aren't looking for an easy solution – they're looking for understanding or someone to share the burden with. Once understood, they'll often go on to solve the problem for themselves.

> **The psychology of listening**
>
> Psychologist Carl Rogers was a pioneer in person-centred therapy and believed active listening is essential for building trust and understanding. He identified three core principles for this:
> - **Empathy**: Put yourself in their shoes and try to understand their emotions and experience from their perspective.
> - **Unconditional positive regard**: Avoid judgement, show acceptance and respect regardless of what they say.
> - **Authenticity**: Be genuine in your listening – don't fake interest or understanding.
>
> Rogers also laid the groundwork for the concept of 'psychological safety', which has rightly had more focus in recent years, including in workplaces. He highlighted

> the importance of people feeling safe to be themselves without fear of judgement or negative repercussions. We can provide this psychological safety by making it clear to others that it's safe for them to speak up and share their feelings.

Imagine you told a loved one: 'I had a dreadful day, my boss criticised our project and I'm so annoyed.' How would it feel if they replied with: 'You shouldn't let it get to you,' or 'Maybe you could change your approach?' These responses may seem comforting or practical, but they don't acknowledge how you're feeling. They jump past the emotions to the fix. Instead, we'd prefer them to say something like: 'I'm so sorry you had a tough day; that sounds really frustrating. Want to tell me about it?'

True listening means allowing difficult emotions to be present without trying to shrink or reshape them. It means saying 'I hear you' and trusting that just being fully present is enough. When we resist the urge to fix, we open the door for something more valuable: *validation*. Rather than advice, they need acceptance and space to process. We rarely have the right solutions anyway, whereas by listening we give them time and space to find their own helpful ways forwards.

> **→ Build your listening skills**
> Once you've got the basics of reflecting back, here are some helpful next steps to further enhance your listening:
> - **Validate what they're saying**: People often worry they aren't making sense or they might be judged, so let them know that how they're feeling is

understandable. A great way to do this is simply to say something like 'that makes complete sense'.
- **Use clarifying questions**: If you're unsure what they mean, ask a question to check, or make a guess to learn more about their feelings or needs (e.g. 'Are you upset because you think it's unfair?')
- **Be curious**: If someone says something you find uncomfortable or you disagree with, bring a sense of curiosity rather than judgement. For example: 'I wonder what's behind why they feel this way?'
- **Be *interested* (rather than interesting)**: We tend to think people want us to be interesting or charismatic, but our favourite people tend to be those who help *us* feel interesting. So focus more on being interested rather than trying to be interesting by responding enthusiastically to them.

Active listening takes practice

As with any important skill, listening well takes repeated effort. Over time we can get better at letting the other person speak, being more present, resisting the urge to jump in and accepting feelings without rushing to smooth them over. This skill is especially important in moments of heightened emotion. When someone is overwhelmed, they need a calm presence – someone who can hold space for their discomfort without trying to change them. The way they talk will adapt to the quality of listening we offer.

Like many themes throughout this book, what we're really talking about here is a form of mindfulness. 'Mindful listening' requires patience and self-awareness. Staying mindful also helps us to recognise our own emotions during a conversation and, if need be, to regulate them so we can remain present, even if a conversation feels triggering.

The more we develop this skill, the more it ripples both inwards and outwards. We get better at recognising our own emotions instead of pushing them aside. And we build stronger connections – not by fixing people, but by really being there for them.

> ### ➜ Deep Listening
>
> Listening expert Emily Kasriel has an eight-step approach for what she calls 'Deep Listening', which builds on what we've covered so far:
>
> 1. **Create space**. Provide psychological safety by choosing a place and time to speak where conversation feels easy and possible.
> 2. **Listen to yourself**. Start with self-reflection to recognise how you're feeling and what you're bringing to the conversation.
> 3. **Be present**. Put aside the internal and external distractions that get in the way of listening, so you can be fully present for the other person.
> 4. **Be curious**. Bring curiosity to the conversation, recognising that you don't already know what's in the other person's mind.
> 5. **Hold the gaze**. Use eye contact – and also welcoming body language and tone – to let them know they're being heard and accepted.
> 6. **Hold the silence**. Rather than rushing to fill moments of silence, show respect through stillness, giving them space to process and think.

> 7. **Reflect back**. Check your understanding of what they've said and how they're feeling using paraphrasing and clarifying questions.
> 8. **Go deeper**. Help bring to light the deeper stories or needs that may be hidden beneath what's being said.

Conversations that matter

We all have everyday conversations at surface-level – the 'How are you?' on the street, the chat about the weather with a neighbour, the quick coffee with a colleague. These everyday moments keep us connected to a broader web of people and remind us we're part of a community. But we also need something deeper. We need people who we can talk more intimately to about things close to our hearts. Things we might not share in public or talk about more widely. Our deeper hopes, fears, needs or goals.

Studies show that engaging in more substantive conversations – and less small talk – is associated with higher wellbeing. These bigger conversations make space for us to drop the performance and speak honestly. They usually happen with the few people we trust enough to share our problems with, without worrying how they'll land. It's not about constant intensity – even with our closest friends and family, much of life is still small talk about meals, plans and daily mishaps. But it's vital to also have those deeper moments where connection moves from pleasant to profound. When we make time for conversations that matter we strengthen not just our relationships but also our own sense of meaning and belonging.

Are some of your friendships stuck in a comfortable but predictable routine where you tend to follow the same patterns and cover the same topics? To break out of this 'friendship autopilot' we need to be willing to venture into new territory. We may expect deeper conversations to be uncomfortable, but they can be refreshing and uplifting. I've often noticed how much happier I feel after a really honest and authentic conversation compared to one where the topics feel more shallow or superficial.

> **→ Have more conversations that matter**
>
> Over the coming days, notice your balance between small talk and more meaningful topics. Who do you feel most comfortable opening up to?
>
> Here are a few questions you could try. Asking just one of them, with genuine interest, can gently shift a conversation from polite to meaningful:
> - What's been on your mind recently?
> - What are you most looking forward to at the moment?
> - What do you find helpful when life gets stressful?
> - What are your biggest sources of joy right now?
> - What's been the highlight of your week so far?
> - What are you hoping the next few months will bring?

As mentioned earlier, one of the most important relationships is with our partner or spouse. But with the busyness of daily life it can be surprisingly rare for couples to pause and truly listen to each other without interrupting, offering solutions or bringing up other things. Also, we may find ourselves in a relationship which is a bit lopsided in terms of who does most of the speaking or how we communicate.

For relationships to stay close it's vital to make time for talking openly about the things that matter. One helpful practice is to agree with your loved one that you want to make time to really listen to each other without interruption.

> **→ Uninterrupted five minutes each**
> Set aside 10 minutes at a convenient time – for example while having a meal together, chatting on the sofa or in bed with your partner. The idea is that you each get five *completely uninterrupted* minutes to share your thoughts and feelings while the other just listens. Then, repeat the other way around so that both of you feel fully heard. You may well learn a lot more about what's going on for the other person and feel that they've understood you more.
>
> Remember: this is *not* about responding with your views, or agreeing or disagreeing, it's about letting them speak and hearing what they say.

Can we bridge our divides?

So far we've mainly focused on people we want good relationships with. What about those we don't get on with or even want nothing to do with? Understanding these people is also important, even when we disagree.

In recent years it feels as if society is more polarised and people are less willing to listen to each other or hear views they disagree with. As we've seen, it's hard enough listening deeply to our own loved ones. At a societal level this gets amplified because we tend to be even less good at listening to people who are different to us. If we feel people are against us – or part of a group with very different views or values – we may even try to silence them or call for their opinions to be 'cancelled'.

On top of our own listening flaws we have the added fuel of online sharing and social media, which further stoke divisions. Algorithms prioritise posts that cause anger and outrage, as this leads to more attention. So we get bombarded with content that lacks nuance and amplifies disagreement. All of this reduces our ability to understand what people are really trying to say and why.

Professor Paul Dolan describes the underlying problem as 'beliefism' – our tendency to dismiss people who hold different beliefs to us. Although tribal allegiances may be part of human nature, if we surround ourselves with like-minded voices we can get trapped in echo chambers. Paul believes we need to encourage tolerance through deliberate listening. It's easier said than done, but I agree. We need to find the courage to have more constructive dialogue across ideological divides.

> 'You can reduce the annoyance of someone's stupid belief by increasing your understanding of why they believe it.'
>
> – Kevin Kelly

To overcome my own beliefism, I've spent the last few years intentionally exposing myself to opposing viewpoints. For example, I listen to podcasts from both the left and right of the political spectrum on divisive topics like migration, inequality or free speech. This has not only helped me to clarify my own views but also to understand why the people I disagree with feel the way they do.

The sad thing is that when we take up tribal positions we jump quickly to assuming bad intent – for example, believing someone is malicious, evil or intentionally doing the wrong thing. This erodes trust and leads to more fragmentation and hostility. But it doesn't have to be this way, even when we disagree.

If we shift from certainty towards curiosity and empathy, this increases our chance of finding ways to bridge divides. We can suspend our pre-judgements and approach interactions with the humility of 'not knowing', again by asking thoughtful questions to deepen our understanding and reflecting back to validate what we hear.

By taking a mindful approach we can also recognise that people who see the world differently are in fact still 'like us' insofar as they're trying to live their lives in the way they feel is best. Even when we don't like their behaviour — or strongly disagree with their views — they may still be acting from a place of sincerity and good intent. For example, older people may have a life history we're not aware of, while younger people may be responding to new pressures we don't understand.

Rather than binary thinking, we need something more nuanced. So instead of, 'That person is bad and should be cancelled', we might find the courage to say, 'I strongly disagree, but I have a sense of what's behind it and where they're coming from.'

Let me be clear. This isn't about tolerating injustice or accepting things that are wrong. It's about finding more helpful ways to navigate our most challenging disagreements. Working to avoid misunderstanding, build trust and reduce conflict. Imagine a world where we all took this approach, especially our leaders. Just think how much more collaborative and constructive everything could be!

> **→ Curb your beliefism**
> Start by recognising areas where you may exhibit 'beliefism' — not just having strong views, but dismissing people who don't agree with you. Next, set an intention to consciously listen to viewpoints that are different to yours, taking a curious and open-minded approach.

> For example, this could be by engaging with a more diverse range of videos, news sources or influencers.
>
> This is *not* about changing your views. It's about recognising that people who don't share the same perspective can still have understandable – and even legitimate – views. Even when you don't agree you can still respect their right to hold that opinion. And you can allow yourself to see that they may in fact hold this view sincerely – and for what they feel are valid reasons – even if you think they're completely wrong or misguided.

Listening even when we disagree

The vital point is that validation doesn't mean agreement. We don't have to see eye to eye with someone's perspective to acknowledge their feelings as valid. Saying, 'I hear you,' doesn't mean, 'You're right.' It simply means, 'I understand that this is your reality right now.' That small shift can make a big difference.

One powerful example comes from the world of conflict resolution. Experienced negotiators sometimes introduce a simple but transformative rule for both sides: you can't respond until you've summarised the other side's view in your own words – and they confirm you've got it right. This isn't about grudgingly repeating a few phrases – it's about demonstrating that you've genuinely grasped their perspective. This forces people to slow down, set aside rehearsed rebuttals and really think about what the other side is trying to say. In doing so, they often discover parts of the argument they can relate to or at least respect, even if they still disagree.

This technique can be remarkably effective at breaking

deadlock. Many heated debates are fuelled less by the issues themselves and more by the feeling of being misunderstood or ignored. When someone hears their own position reflected back accurately it lowers their guard and creates space for dialogue. It also humanises the opponent. Once you've articulated someone's viewpoint well enough that they feel heard it becomes harder to dismiss or dehumanise them. In polarised times, we need this now more than ever.

> **→ Listen to someone you disagree with**
>
> Next time you're talking with someone you don't see eye to eye with, treat this as an opportunity to build your skills. When they say something you disagree with, steady your natural reaction and instead pause and listen. Then, as calmly as possible, reflect back the message of what they said.
>
> 'So what you're saying is . . .'
>
> This doesn't mean you agree, it means you're listening. And when they feel heard they'll be more likely to listen to you too.

Listening as a form of love

Having established that good relationships are vital for our happiness we've now seen how listening is the core skill we need. Listening well can make a difference in almost every situation – whether socialising or supporting someone in tough times. Good conversation is less about getting our point across and more about the extent to which we help the other person feel understood. Not agreed with – understood.

When we give someone our full attention, we're saying, 'You

matter. Your thoughts and feelings are worth my time.' In this sense, listening is a form of love. It builds trust and helps us feel psychologically safe. It is a profound act of care and affection. Wise listening also helps us feel happier in ourselves. We have more meaningful connections and we begin to notice the power of small moments of just *being there*.

Finally, listening is a foundation we need to build on for the big challenge in our next chapter – how to share our needs and resolve problems in our relationships.

LISTEN ACTIVELY: CHAPTER SUMMARY

Ask yourself:

❓ **Can I reflect back what people are saying so they feel heard?**

Don't just:

✗ Give unwanted advice or make your own points when someone's talking.

Try this out:

✔ Help people feel heard and understood by really listening to them.

Chapter Fourteen:

Understand Needs

Can I help resolve our difficulties?

Have you ever had an argument where you left feeling worse, not because of the issue itself but because of the way you spoke to each other?

I never expected an iceberg lettuce to send Kate and me spiralling into one of our worst ever quarrels. But early one evening that's exactly what happened. She'd asked me to pick up some salad on the way home, but when I arrived and started unloading the bag, she frowned. 'I can't believe you bought this!' she said, clearly upset.

We'd recently started living together and I honestly had no idea she didn't like iceberg. Perhaps I should have known. Maybe it was obvious? All she'd really meant was 'This isn't the lettuce I wanted.' But in that moment of rejection all I heard was, 'You got it wrong. Again.' Suddenly, it wasn't about lettuce at all. It was about me feeling criticised – like I'd tried to be helpful and now I was being told off. And before I knew it, we weren't talking about salad anymore – we were in a full-blown, absurd shouting match.

Embarrassingly, this isn't the only time a simple household disagreement has escalated into a blazing row. We once ended up in a tug-of-war over damp laundry. Literally. I'd hung my cycling gear up inside but Kate wanted the washing to dry outside in the sun. A normal conversation could have solved it in seconds. But instead we ended up yanking on opposite ends of a pair of damp shorts, our mutual frustration ridiculously bubbling over into something much bigger – and completely unnecessary.

It wasn't until later, after the shouting, after we'd both calmed down, that I asked myself 'What was really going on there?' Because it was never really about laundry or lettuce. It was about what those moments represented, the unspoken feelings underneath.

Conflict in relationships is inevitable

Before we begin unpacking the subtleties of unmet needs, let's start by simply recognising that all relationships involve misunderstandings and conflict – it's part of being human. Having a good relationship is definitely *not* about avoiding disagreements or difficult conversations – in fact these can often be the signs of an unhealthy relationship, where resentments or misunderstandings go unsaid.

Instead, the key point here is learning to *respond* to our inevitable disagreements with skill and compassion, and ideally with some humility and warmth too. Crucially this includes avoiding blame or accusation and focusing instead on trying to really understand the other's needs and to communicate our own needs clearly.

This can be incredibly hard, though, especially in our closest relationships where we often find ourselves feeling triggered or rehashing the same old conflicts.

> ⭐ *'If you think you're enlightened, go spend a week with your family.'*
>
> **– Ram Dass**

In the last chapter, we explored the importance of reflecting back what the other person has said to confirm our understanding and help them feel heard. This is also the starting point for working through tense situations and conflict.

When we disagree with someone, our instinct is usually to defend our position or argue our case, especially when we feel we've been misrepresented. Yet arguing tends to put up a wall between us and the other person and stops communication in its tracks.

Using active listening in a disagreement helps to keep the conversation moving forwards. By staying curious we can try to really understand what's behind the other person's words. This turns out to be a much better way of resolving issues and lays the foundation for them to hear our perspective and avoid misunderstandings.

Stay on your side of the net

One of the most common mistakes we make is commenting on the other person's motivations or feelings rather than our own. In reality we almost never have all the information about what's going on for them. Let's look at this more closely.

In any interaction between two people, there are three different components:
- **Intent**: the internal motivations or intentions behind one person's actions.
- **Behaviour**: the observable actions or words that can be seen or heard by both.

- **Impact**: how the other person perceives and is affected by the behaviour.

Crucially, each person only knows the reality for two out of three of these components – neither has the full picture! When you behave in a certain way, you're aware of your intent and behaviour but you can only guess the impact it has on the other person. You don't know this, only they do.

Likewise, when someone else says or does something, you observe their behaviour and you know the impact it has on *you* – but you can only guess what their underlying intention was. Again you don't know this, only they do.

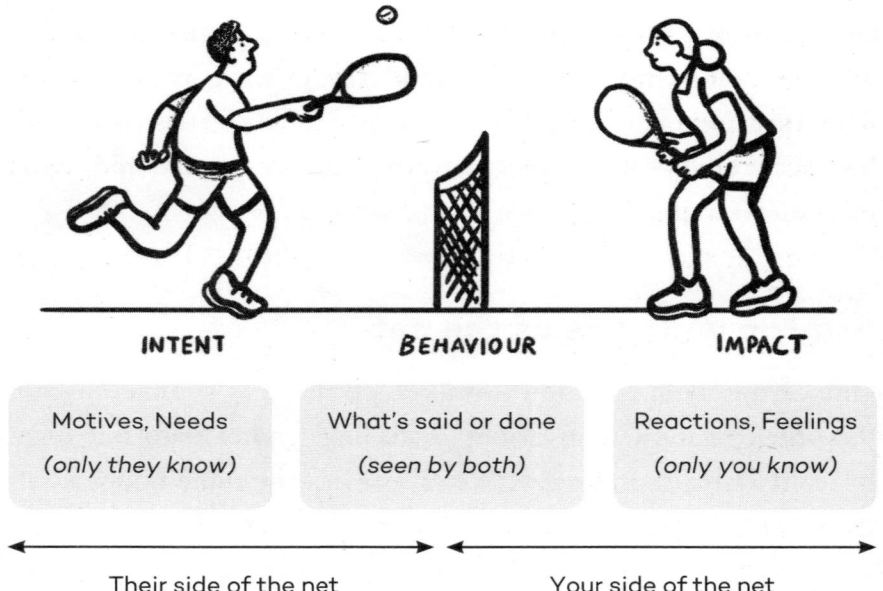

In their popular Stanford course on 'Building Exceptional Relationships', David Bradford and Carole Robin use the metaphor of needing to 'stay on your side of the net', where the net is the boundary between your experience and the other person's.

Each of us is responsible for our side of the interaction. But when we 'cross the net' – by describing the other person's intentions or feelings – this significantly increases the chance of misunderstanding and conflict. It's much more effective to share your own experience rather than leaping to assumptions about the other person's experience.

Many arguments escalate because we default to blame. We feel hurt or frustrated, and before we know it we're saying things like:
- 'You never listen to me.'
- 'You don't even care how I feel.'
- 'You're always so dismissive.'
- 'You did that on purpose.'

Even if there's some truth in what we're saying, phrasing it this way puts the other person on the defensive. Accusation triggers resistance and over-generalising feels like character assassination. Instead of hearing what we need them to hear, the other person is more likely to push back, argue or shut down.

You can stay on your side of the net by using 'I' rather than 'You' statements:
- **Describing** behaviour without guessing motives ('I noticed you interrupted').
- **Sharing** the impact on *you* ('I felt like I wasn't being heard').
- **Avoiding** assumptions or judgements ('You don't care', 'You're selfish', etc.)

Staying on your side respects boundaries, making space for your reality and their autonomy. Your feedback highlights the impact of their behaviour on you rather than assuming their intent. This reduces defensiveness and makes it much less likely the conversation will become a confrontation.

For example, instead of saying, 'You don't care about this project', which assumes the other person's feelings, you might say, 'When you were late, I felt concerned about our project.' This focuses on the observable behaviour and how it affected you. Referring to a specific example like this also tends to be more helpful than overgeneralising.

Arguments as a clash of needs

Most conflicts aren't really about the surface-level disagreement, like buying the wrong lettuce. They're about underlying needs: like our need to feel appreciated, or to feel safe, or to avoid feeling out of control. Yet, in the heat of the moment, it's easy to miss what's really going on.

If we fail to recognise and share our deeper needs, seemingly small disagreements can feel like vicious personal attacks or rapidly spiral into something much bigger. We often find ourselves surprised by the strength of our reactions and how quickly we're overcome with feelings of anger, fear or sadness. I was once so overcome with frustration at my request being repeatedly ignored that I suddenly threw my cup of coffee, breaking the mug, staining the wall and shocking my daughter who was watching. I was surprised by my anger and it was definitely not a proud moment!

That said, anger can actually be clarifying. It often covers up an underlying fear or need, relating to something important that's under threat. So, when you notice yourself feeling angry, ask: 'What could this be showing me?' Then try to express it with words (rather than throwing your coffee!), while maintaining eye contact and staying present.

We assume that if someone really cares about us they should

know what we need and naturally act in ways that meet our expectations. When they don't, we often take it personally. We feel frustrated, hurt or dismissed. But most of the time, the other person isn't intentionally ignoring our needs – they just don't see the full picture.

Why was I so bothered about Kate wanting to hang my cycling gear outside? Well, at a rational level it was because I thought things might get lost – this had happened before. But our fight wasn't rational. It got heated because I'd made a specific request for my clothes to stay put and she'd started moving them anyway. My need to have my wishes respected was ignored. My preferences seemed daft to Kate – after all, it was a sunny day outside and she was right, they would dry more quickly. She was being thoughtful, yet I couldn't see her perspective. At an emotional level, I felt disrespected and that my requests didn't matter. As a result I became unreasonably angry – again!

In my case, a better response would have been: 'I'm angry you just went ahead and did that anyway, even after I asked you not to. Respecting each other's wishes is really important to me.'

In moments of tension, we instinctively focus on why we're right and why they're wrong. We dig our heels in, often convinced that if we could just explain it clearly enough they'd come around. But conflict is better solved by trying to recognise underlying needs, rather than trying to prove a point. Unmet needs lead to misunderstandings, overreactions and hurt feelings.

So when there's a difference of views, one helpful shift we can introduce is simply pausing to reflect on the needs at play rather than escalating the disagreement. Before reacting, try asking:

- What need of mine isn't being met here?
- What need of theirs might be driving this?

Even if the other person isn't able to do this too, shifting our perspective helps to de-escalate the situation. Instead of seeing them as wrong or unreasonable we can recognise that they are simply trying to meet their own needs, just like we are.

This doesn't mean ignoring our own needs or excusing harmful behaviour. It means approaching conflict with curiosity rather than defensiveness. Often, that shift is enough to change the tone and outcome of a tense conversation.

> 'Behind every criticism there is a wish: tune in to the wish not the criticism.'
>
> **– Esther Perel**

By recognising that arguments stem from underlying needs, we can move from blame and reactivity towards understanding and resolution. The idea of 'winning' an argument is no longer the most important thing. This also puts the onus on us to communicate our own needs clearly to avoid misunderstanding. As the author Neil Strauss wrote:

'Unspoken expectations are premeditated resentments.'

How to communicate better

Thankfully, there's a powerful and proven way of speaking that can help us resolve our conflicts far more constructively, even when we're angry or frustrated. It's called 'nonviolent communication' (NVC) and was developed by psychologist Marshall Rosenberg, who grew up in Detroit during times of racial tension and violence.

NVC can be helpful for our close relationships and also more widely too, for example at work. It shifts the focus from blame to clarity using four steps:

1. **Observation**: Describe what happened, factually. Say what you see, not your judgement – no exaggeration, no interpretation, just the facts.
2. **Feeling**: Share how it made *you* feel, not what you think is going on for them.
3. **Need**: Express the deeper need or value behind your feelings.
4. **Request**: Ask clearly for what you need going forwards, without demanding.

These steps may sound a bit formal, but they can really help us to choose words that encourage understanding rather than defensiveness. Our tone of voice matters, too, so it helps to speak calmly rather than conveying irritation.

> **→ Avoiding accusations: NVC example**
> Instead of saying: 'You're so dismissive. You don't care about what I say.'
>
> Try: 'When I shared that idea and you moved on quickly [observation], I felt dismissed [feeling]. I need to feel like my input is valued [need]. Could we take a moment to revisit it? [request]'
>
> The difference is subtle but powerful. The first statement is an accusation – it tells the other person who they *are* (dismissive, uncaring). The second keeps the focus on your own experience and offers a clear path forwards.

NVC encourages us to say what we see, share how we feel, explain what we need and ask clearly for what might help. This doesn't guarantee that the other person will agree or change their behaviour, but it removes blame or criticism, making it much easier for them to listen and respond constructively. This approach doesn't just help us avoid arguments – it helps us build stronger and happier relationships.

> **→ WARNING: Healthy boundaries**
> Using NVC does *not* mean that we should tolerate abusive behaviour or try to maintain all our relationships at all costs. We need to recognise our limits and be willing to step away from unhealthy relationships when necessary. This is vital for self-care, especially in 'toxic' relationships where boundaries are crucial. Abusive relationships are never acceptable.

Setting difficult conversations up for success

Whenever possible, it's helpful to consider the timing of tough conversations. Even the best-phrased request won't land if the other person feels ambushed, defensive or too tired to engage. If people aren't in the right headspace to listen or talk openly, a conversation that could be productive one day might not go so well another.

Addressing a problem in the heat of frustration – when emotions are high and patience is low – rarely leads to resolution. Likewise, bringing something up when either of you is distracted or overwhelmed is more likely to lead to difficulties. So you can increase the chance of a difficult conversation going well by finding a good time. For example:

'I'd love to talk about something that's on my mind. Can we find a good time?'

This simple invitation does two things. Firstly, it signals that the conversation topic really matters to you, so it won't feel like an offhand complaint. Secondly, it gives the other person the chance to come to the conversation ready to engage, rather than feeling caught off-guard.

It can also be helpful to admit that you're feeling unsure how the conversation will go. Psychologist Dr Joan Rosenberg suggests that we can pre-empt difficult or emotionally charged conversations by acknowledging the discomfort up front and helping to disarm it in advance. For example, try saying:

'I'm a bit worried about talking about this and how you'll respond to it.'

We can also use our mindfulness skills to stay calmer – both before and during a difficult conversation – for example, by taking some deep breaths and trying to notice what's going on for us and for the other person, without judgement.

> **Mindful moment: 'Just like me'**

This is a short mindful exercise to help you recognise the similarities between you and someone who you may be having difficulties with.

Start with a few calm deep breaths. Then, with the other person in mind, think to yourself:
- They experience ups and downs in life, just like me.
- They have an inner world of thoughts and feelings, just like me.
- They have hopes and fears that matter to them, just like me.
- They are carrying old wounds and assumptions, just like me.
- They want to love and be loved, just like me.

Deep down we all share this basic yearning to be happy

> and free from suffering. On this level, there is no real difference between us.

Disagreeing agreeably

No meaningful relationship can stay intact without running into differences of opinion or priorities. Disagreements are inevitable. The trouble isn't that we disagree – it's how we do it. And across society, it feels like our disagreements have been getting bigger and harsher. We've developed an unhealthy reliance on always being right.

Let's zoom out again for a moment. As more of us use social media to engage with ideas – and each other – we run into algorithms that reward outrage over empathy. Valid debates quickly descend into nasty name-calling or point-scoring. And the skills we've been looking at here are usually nowhere to be seen. Listening to our opponents and wanting to understand them is becoming a lost art. Yet demanding that everyone shares our beliefs is unrealistic. The wisest people don't have all the answers – they have the courage to say, 'I don't know.'

Dropping our reliance on being right can also leave us calmer and more in control. Dr Rangan Chatterjee has some great advice here. In a world of disagreement, he encourages us to stay curious and take offence less.

> ⭐ 'When we are curious, we naturally act with more compassion and integrity. If our default approach is always to find out more, we're automatically more empathetic towards other people and viewpoints.'
>
> **– Dr Rangan Chatterjee**

With this attitude, we may learn something new that shifts our perspective or even discover that they're right and we're wrong! Or we may learn that they're misguided, uninformed or prejudiced. Here again, Rangan has a brilliantly helpful five-word phrase to show our disagreement, but in a less confrontational way:

'I have a different perspective.'

This is what we need for healthier relationships and a less polarised society – the ability to say 'I see it differently' without implying 'You're wrong' or 'You're a bad person.' We're staying true to what we believe while respecting their right to an opinion. Disagreeing agreeably helps us stay connected while recognising our differences. So disputes then become less about 'winning' or 'losing' and more about learning.

This skill is as vital around the kitchen table as it is in the public square. You can use this approach with your family, friends, colleagues, in online conversations – whenever you come across someone with a different opinion to you.

In these heated conversations, mirroring the other person is especially important – but also hard! So when someone shares their perspective, instead of jumping straight in with your own views, try to ensure you reflect back their feelings first:

'It sounds like you felt ignored when that happened. Is that right?'

Remember, reflecting back means you're listening, *not* that you agree. When the other person feels heard, they're far more likely to be open to your perspective in return. Mirroring slows an argument down in a good way. It shifts the dynamic from a heated back-and-forth to more of a dialogue where both sets of feelings are acknowledged.

Post-match analysis

Sometimes conversations just don't go well. Maybe we didn't handle it as skilfully as we could have done, by making an accusation or taking things personally. Or perhaps the other person was in a difficult state of mind or didn't really hear our needs or requests, despite our best efforts.

The truth is, you can't change the other person, but you can change and adapt what you do. So, rather than dwelling on their behaviour, do your own 'post-match analysis' and reflect on how you might handle it differently next time. Ask yourself:

- What did I learn about what's going on for them?
- What triggered me?
- What was my actual need?
- How could I have shared my perspective differently?

Sometimes our own needs affect how we respond to others. For example, my need to feel appreciated gets in the way of hearing when Kate is upset and needs support. I have a tendency to take things personally rather than staying present for her and helping with what she's dealing with. When I'm able to remember this, I'm less likely to get defensive and more likely to respond helpfully.

If we have particularly strong emotional reactions in a relationship – like shame, anger or anxiety – this is often linked to foundational needs or experiences from our childhood. Although we can't change our past, recognising how our current feelings are linked to earlier experiences can help us to *respond rather than react* in difficult situations.

If possible, try to recognise when your reaction is bigger than necessary for the situation. You can also be open about this, for example by saying, 'I realise I got very upset just now and I think it was bringing up some old issues for me. Can we come back to this later?' Having this self-awareness helps to reduce reactive fights and increases the other person's awareness of what's going on for us. We'll dive more deeply into healing past wounds in chapter sixteen.

Making apologies that actually heal

When conflict happens, what really determines whether a relationship strengthens or weakens isn't the argument itself — it's what happens after. This includes being willing to take responsibility and apologise when we've let ourselves or the other person down.

A real apology isn't just a reflexive 'I'm sorry' thrown out to smooth things over. It's a genuine step towards repair, acknowledging the impact of our actions. A genuine apology includes three things:

1. **Regret**: showing genuine empathy for the impact of your actions.
2. **Responsibility**: owning your role, without excuses or deflection.
3. **Remedy**: expressing a willingness to help put things right.

Weak apologies often try to deflect the blame and can leave the hurt person feeling dismissed rather than understood. If you say, 'I'm sorry you felt that way', this implies the issue is their perception, not your actions.

By contrast, a strong apology takes ownership and acknowledges the other person's experience. Instead of defending ourselves we focus on the impact our words or actions had, whether or not they were intentional. For example, we might say, 'I'm sorry. I realise what I said came across as dismissive. That wasn't my intention, but I can see that it hurt you. I'll try to avoid doing that in future.'

> ⭐ 'In toxic relationships, people give blame but don't take responsibility. They're always wronged, never wrong. In healthy relationships, people are slow to take offense and quick to admit fault.'
>
> **– Adam Grant**

Our apology is also just the first step. What really rebuilds trust is follow-through: showing, over time, that we're aware of past hurts and making an effort to do better. Instead of rushing to fix everything immediately, it helps to ask:

'What would you find helpful to make things better?'

This signals that you're not just trying to end the conversation but you're hoping to make things right in a way that matters for them. It's turning the situation into something you can work through together, rather than something that drives you apart.

Appreciating each other

This chapter has focused mainly on problems in relationships, but it's also vital we keep doing positive things to nurture the good aspects of our relationship too.

> ### ➡ Share nice thoughts out loud
> When you think a nice thought about the other person, make a point to tell them. For example, if they do something you really appreciate, or you see a characteristic you admire in them, or you've really enjoyed spending time with them, just let them know. Thinking something nice about someone else but not telling them is like wrapping a beautiful present but then never giving it.

True connection isn't just about supporting each other through struggles – it's about actively sharing in each other's joy. Yet, we often miss opportunities to do this. Think about how we typically respond when someone shares good news. We react passively – 'That's great!' – and quickly move on. Or, without meaning to we turn the conversation back to ourselves: 'Oh yeah, I had a similar experience when . . .' While well-intentioned, these responses are a missed opportunity. Active-constructive responding is much more helpful (see chapter twelve).

Confelicity is a lovely word which means taking joy in another person's happiness – it's sort of the opposite of envy. When we do this it can strengthen relationships in a way that few other things do. Instead of simply acknowledging someone's good news we can amplify it by expressing genuine enthusiasm. Psychologist Shelly Gable has shown that this is one of the most reliable ways to strengthen connection. For example:

'That's amazing! What was that like for you?'

'Tell me more – I want to hear all about it!'

This validates that the other person's happiness matters – that their wins aren't just individual but something worth celebrating together. By making a habit of fully engaging with their good news we remind people that their happiness is important to us too.

Conflict as opportunity

These skills we've covered – recognising needs, communicating with care, repairing conflict and celebrating each other – build the foundation for meaningful, resilient relationships. We become closer not by avoiding conflict but by learning to disagree in ways that strengthen connection rather than eroding trust.

→ **Top tips for dealing with conflict**
- **Pause before reacting**: instead of reacting instinctively or going straight on the defensive, pause and reflect on underlying needs (yours and theirs).
- **Assume positive intent**: when we see others' actions as attempts to meet their needs (rather than attacks) we're more likely to empathise with where they're coming from.
- **Focus on understanding**: when someone is behaving in a way you find difficult or disagree with, build a clearer understanding of what's behind this by listening first.
- **Use specific language**: make factual observations and actionable requests rather than generalised complaints or accusations, e.g. 'When I find plates left in the sink ...' rather than 'You always leave a mess.' Or, 'I would really appreciate you getting home a bit earlier,' rather than, 'You're never around to help!'
- **Describe your feelings (not theirs)**: share the impact this situation has on you and how you feel rather than accusing them or assuming you know how they feel or what's behind how they're behaving. Aim to always use 'I ...' statements rather than 'You ...' statements.
- **Lean into discomfort**: rather than avoiding conflict (especially as a people-pleaser) remember that your needs are valid and being willing to have difficult conversations often leads to greater understanding.

- **Keep safe boundaries**: don't over-compromise, and be willing to walk away if needed.

Every moment of tension is an opportunity: to pause instead of reacting, to express rather than accuse, to listen instead of defending. Every moment of joy is a chance to deepen bonds, to engage with enthusiasm rather than just move on. Over time these small daily choices build lasting relationships that are much happier.

UNDERSTAND NEEDS: CHAPTER SUMMARY

Ask yourself:
❓ **What is my underlying need and how can I express this clearly?**

Don't just:
✘ Assume you know what someone needs or they know what you need.

Try this out:
✔ Aim to understand people's needs and be clear about your own needs.

Chapter Fifteen:

Remove the Mask

Can vulnerability be my source of strength?

I still remember the day Vicky disappeared.

Vicky was one of the most talented, impressive people I'd ever worked with. She was hard-working, creative and full of energy. I looked up to her. When you wanted a complicated project to go well, you asked Vicky to run it – she was reliable and a natural leader. But during the years we worked together I noticed she put herself under immense pressure, prioritising keeping clients happy over her own wellbeing.

To be honest, I'd been doing this myself too. Long hours, high-pressure situations – it was the culture we worked in. No one wanted to show signs of struggling. We all wore our professional masks and kept striving towards the next big milestone.

Then one day, she was gone. No warning, no explanation – just never came back. I later learned that she'd experienced a 'breakdown'. The relentless hours and stress had become too much. Yet in our workplace there had been no space for her to share how she was really feeling, no room to ask for help.

When I finally realised what had happened I felt guilty that I hadn't been there for her. I was in the middle of my own struggles with stress-induced back pain, so I could have shared how I was feeling and offered space for her to do the same. But just like Vicky, I'd been hiding what was really going on.

Years later we reconnected and thankfully she was much happier, having shifted her priorities and focused more on wellbeing alongside work. It seemed to me that she'd gone through her own form of Good Life Crisis, where a big wake-up call ultimately led to a helpful change of direction. But it had been a painful journey.

The underlying problem was that, in our macho work culture, showing vulnerability felt like a weakness. Even outside of work our loved ones and friends mostly didn't realise what we were going through. We appeared to be doing well, but the reality inside was much darker. We just didn't let it show.

These days I'm in an organisation with a very different ethos, one that intentionally encourages vulnerability and emotional honesty. We still work hard and deliver important work under pressure, but the sense of connection and support we're able to give each other is like nothing else I've come across in a workplace.

All Action for Happiness meetings start with a 'check-in' where we go around the circle of attendees – whether in person or online – and each share how we're doing that day and something we're grateful for. The depth of these conversations can be surprising. Sometimes people share simple stories from everyday life, like a morning walk or a family moment. But on difficult days we also share the tough stuff, too – from losing loved ones to major health issues or personal crises.

We don't try to solve each other's problems and no one is under any obligation to say anything if they don't want to. We simply make space for people to talk openly about their feelings in that moment, before moving on. As a result, we all start each meeting feeling heard and more connected to each other. Interestingly, we also tend to work better together and get more done too.

The power of vulnerability

Many of us believe that sharing our struggles is a sign of weakness. We worry that revealing our fears or problems will damage our relationships – or that people will think less of us. However, vulnerability is a surprising superpower in our mission to make life happier. It's a form of courage that allows for more authentic connections. And it gives others around us permission to relax and be themselves too. Most importantly it frees us from the exhausting weight of pretending we have it all together.

Brené Brown is a researcher who has spent decades studying vulnerability and shame. She says vulnerability 'sounds like truth and feels like courage', noting that it may not feel comfortable but it's never a sign of weakness.

Think about the people you feel closest to. They're most likely the ones who don't just know about your triumphs, but also your doubts, fears and struggles. Vulnerability turns acquaintances into friends and colleagues into allies. It allows us to feel accepted and valued for who we are, not just for what we achieve. Yet if it's so powerful, why do we resist it and keep our struggles inside?

Why we hide how we feel

Exposing ourselves emotionally can feel uncomfortable – and that's understandable. We're taking a risk in revealing things others may not know about us and we feel uncertain about how they might respond. But when we allow ourselves to be seen – truly seen – we create the conditions for trust and intimacy.

One of the biggest barriers to vulnerability is shame. We fear being judged or rejected. We tell ourselves that no one else would understand, that our struggles are ours alone. But in truth, many people around us are experiencing similar feelings. When we suppress our emotions, we don't protect ourselves – we isolate ourselves.

> 'Shame needs three things to grow exponentially in our lives: secrecy, silence and judgement.'
> **– Brené Brown**

Another reason we avoid vulnerability is perfectionism. Many of us feel pressure to always appear competent, to never let others see us struggle. We think we need to be strong, self-sufficient, in control. But real connection doesn't come from pretending to be perfect – it comes from being real. Hiding our struggles also fuels 'imposter syndrome'. We feel like we're pretending to be capable while secretly doubting ourselves. And the more we hide those doubts, the more they grow.

I can relate. Writing this book has brought up my own fears: What if people judge me? Who am I to think people want to read this? What if it's awful and no one likes it? Even after years of working with experts and learning so much, I don't just have moments of self-doubt – I get full imposter syndrome. But gradually I've learned that being open about my feelings doesn't weaken me – it does the opposite. Things are better when we stop trying to prove ourselves and start showing up as our real selves. I'm just another flawed, imperfect and struggling human. I'm still learning and I make plenty of mistakes – as my loved ones would be more than happy to tell you if you asked them!

Encouragingly, we've seen a recent cultural shift towards people being more willing to talk about their inner lives. One inspiring example is Meg Zeenat Wamithi, who had major mental-health struggles from a young age, including depression, social anxiety, anorexia and suicide attempts. When I interviewed Meg she shared her experiences openly and described how hard it had been experiencing such intense emotions. She explained to me how vulnerability had been a vital part of her recovery, helping her reclaim her story and be at peace with it instead of bottling it up or letting it define her. Over time she'd found ways to overcome many of her struggles and it was really moving to hear about her journey.

Vulnerability (with boundaries) is strength

When we allow ourselves to be open and honest we discover that we don't have to be perfect to be enough. Avoiding discomfort doesn't make pain disappear – it buries it more deeply. But when we acknowledge our emotions and share them with people we trust, we build our resilience and discover ways to move forwards.

You may have noticed that when people seem perfect, or never let their guard down, it can be harder to relate to them. Most of us are more drawn to people who are quirky and comfortable in their own skin. We want them to be honest about how things are rather than to pretend everything's fine, so we need to be willing to do this too.

Vulnerability actually strengthens our relationships. Whether in families, friendships or at work, creating a culture of openness increases trust and collaboration. Leaders who acknowledge challenges inspire loyalty. Friends who share struggles grow closer.

Parents who admit their own uncertainty show their children it's okay to be human.

Being willing to open up requires courage. However, practising vulnerability doesn't mean we should share everything with everyone. So we also need to be intentional in choosing when to be open, who with and how much we reveal. We want to choose people we trust and who will respect and support us, rather than those who might exploit us or refuse to hear what we share. We also need to set our own boundaries and be willing to step back from a deeper conversation if it's not the right situation.

So before sharing, pause and ask yourself: Is this a safe space for me to be vulnerable? And is now a helpful time to do this?

> **→ Thoughtful honesty**
>
> Being vulnerable doesn't mean spilling your deepest fears to everyone you meet. It's about sharing in appropriate ways that build connection and with people you trust. Here are some ways to do that:
>
> - **Choose your audience wisely.** Confide in those you trust or people who seem likely to respond with empathy rather than judgement.
> - **Acknowledge discomfort.** If sharing feels difficult, say so. Expressing your uncertainty can be a powerful form of honesty.
> - **Set healthy boundaries.** Vulnerability isn't about oversharing or tolerating harmful behaviour – you can choose what to share and when.
> - **Avoid performative sharing.** Vulnerability isn't about seeking attention or validation – it's about real conversations that build connection.

The cost of numbing our feelings

When we experience difficult emotions, many of us try to escape discomfort by numbing it. We turn to distractions like social media, shopping, alcohol, overeating or overworking. But the problem is, numbing our pain doesn't work selectively. We end up numbing all our feelings, including enjoyment, hope, love and curiosity. Distracting ourselves from difficulties may offer temporary relief but it ultimately disconnects us from ourselves and from others.

If we avoid vulnerability we also lose the deeper human experiences that give life more meaning. We miss out on authentic relationships, creative breakthroughs or the satisfaction of overcoming our fears. The truth is, emotions demand to be felt. If we don't acknowledge them they find other ways to surface, through stress, anxiety, burnout or physical pain. By choosing to face our emotions and share them, rather than numb them, we give ourselves the chance to grow and live more fully.

Creating safe spaces for vulnerability

We're often our own harshest critics, replaying self-limiting beliefs that may not be true. So, talking to someone – whether a friend, loved one or therapist – can help us process our emotions, gain perspective and challenge the negative stories we tell ourselves. We all need spaces where we can be real and speak openly about our challenges without fear of judgement.

Talking therapy is one great way to safely explore our worries. The therapist can validate our difficult feelings and help us see our own role in situations and where change might be possible. As the renowned author and therapist Lori Gottlieb explained to me, therapy is about more than venting – it's an active process where we gain insight and learn tools for change. By offering a non-judgemental ear, but also an objective perspective, therapy can help us challenge our unhelpful stories and move forwards. It also helps us recognise when past wounds are shaping our present reactions, allowing us to break free from old patterns.

However, therapy may not be available or affordable, so we can look for safe spaces in other areas too. They might be found in close friendships, where mutual trust allows for honest conversations. They might emerge in structured groups, such as the Action for Happiness community, where people share their struggles and support each other.

Even workplaces can foster psychological safety by encouraging open conversation and prioritising mental wellbeing. If your workplace doesn't offer this, seeking out trusted colleagues, mentors or support networks can help. I'm pretty sure that if we'd had a boss or mentor who modelled vulnerability, Vicky and I could both have responded to our work stress in much healthier ways.

Creating space for vulnerability isn't just about what we share, it's also about helping others to be more open. When we practise deep listening, express empathy and show up with honesty, we invite others to do the same. So vulnerability is contagious – when we lower our own mask we give others permission to lower theirs too.

It's important to get the right balance. When we use our listening skills to help someone feel really heard it creates more space for them to emerge from their shell and be authentic. Likewise, when we're brave enough to share how we feel, they get to know us better and feel encouraged to do the same. But some relationships are imbalanced, with one person doing more of the sharing while the other usually listens. So notice which role you normally play and look for opportunities to create more balance.

We also need to respect other people's boundaries. They may be ready to open up and share what's really going on inside, or they may prefer not to lower their mask at this point. That's fine. We can check what sort of support they'd prefer by asking something like, 'Do you need an ear or a hand?' And if they're not ready to share, we can still support them in other ways.

> ➡ **Connecting the dots**
> Vulnerability ties into many of the ideas we've explored in this book:
> - **Keep it Real**: avoiding forced positivity means being authentic with ourselves and others.
> - **Tame That Critic**: self-compassion includes allowing ourselves to be vulnerable without self-judgement.
> - **Prioritise People**: deep, meaningful relationships grow when we reveal more of ourselves.
> - **Listen Actively**: truly hearing others encourages them to open up too.
> - **Understand Needs**: acknowledging our deeper emotional needs helps us connect more authentically.

Authenticity over perfection

Deep down we all want to feel that we matter and that we belong. Unfortunately we've been taught that staying strong and appearing successful are the best ways to show the world that we're important and to feel appreciated by others. As a result, we often put lots of effort into building up our image and reputation – for example, by buying the right brands or working tirelessly to build a career that seems impressive.

However, true success and self-worth come from inner fulfilment rather than external validation. When we remove our mask, we don't just feel lighter, we create a ripple effect, inspiring others to be more honest and authentic. This is where deeper connection and real growth happen. If more of us could learn to show our true selves this would make a massive difference to our collective happiness. We'd spend less time chasing wealth and outwards signs of success, and more time focusing on the things that really matter – like healthy relationships and projects we really care about.

> **REMOVE THE MASK: CHAPTER SUMMARY**
> Ask yourself:
> ❓ **What mask am I wearing and who can I reveal my feelings to?**
>
> Don't just:
> ✗ Keep things bottled up inside, worrying that people will judge you.
>
> Try this out:
> ✔ Have more conversations that matter and share your inner feelings.

Chapter Sixteen:

Heal Those Wounds

How do my past relationships shape me?

'That makes perfect sense.'

I could see the emotion in Kate's face as she heard the therapist say this. I felt it too. Twenty years into our marriage, we were sitting in a room for a 'couples therapy' session, trying to work through some recent challenges we'd been having.

The therapist had started with obvious stuff, asking us about why we'd come and what we hoped to get out of it. But she then invited both of us to talk in surprising depth about our pasts, asking about our early memories, family history and significant moments.

Despite having spent nearly half our lives together, this conversation was remarkable. Within half an hour we both revealed things we'd never really spoken about previously. It wasn't that we'd been hiding things, just that we'd never looked back like this before.

As Kate revisited key moments in her life I suddenly saw more clearly the impact of her earlier years: the profound effect of her dad's stroke, going away to boarding school and the pressures she faced as a teenage girl. With those simple words – 'that makes perfect sense' – the therapist reassured Kate that her behaviour and feelings were a totally understandable response to what she'd been through. And I realised that I'd probably never helped her feel heard like that before.

Then, as I opened up about my past, I started to piece together how my childhood shaped me: growing up in a home where we rarely expressed difficult emotions. I felt very loved but also developed a discomfort with conflict and an eagerness to always please or impress people.

As the therapy sessions continued, we both began to see how our pasts remain present today. Those formative experiences still shape our expectations, our reactions to each other and the ways we communicate. It was surprising to discover how much our present-day problems were rooted in things that happened decades ago.

Let's take an example. A few years previously I had adopted a more conscious approach to my food choices and eating patterns. Kate hadn't liked this and I couldn't understand why. She was hurt by my changes and I felt she was overreacting. We both got upset and it became a source of real tension.

As we opened up to each other in therapy, the deeper reasons behind this tension became clearer. I'd grown up with a family expectation that we always had to finish our food, so as an adult I often end up overeating, even finishing up other people's leftovers! My recent diagnosis of high cholesterol had been a shock and it motivated me to set healthier boundaries around what and when I eat. Meanwhile, in Kate's earlier years she'd been surrounded by teenage girls with strict food rules and disordered eating. So when I started being less flexible with food choices it brought back memories of controlling behaviours which left her feeling uncomfortable and less safe. Suddenly the upset caused by my new habits made much more sense to both of us.

By seeing these patterns more clearly, Kate and I could bring more flexibility and understanding into our relationship. We started to feel closer again and better able to navigate our challenges. Rather than seeing each other as unreasonable, we felt more empathy for each other's younger selves and what was behind our behaviour.

Because, let's face it, all of us are 'weird' in our own unique ways.

> ⭐ 'Intimacy is the capacity to be rather weird with someone and finding that that's okay with them.'
> **– Alain de Botton**

We all face struggles, and all of our close relationships will run into problems at some point. This is just a natural and inevitable part of us all being complex and messy humans. Yet we often fail to recognise how much our behaviour has been shaped by our earlier years. We can't change our past but we can learn to recognise how our prior experiences continue to affect us. And we can learn to move forwards with greater compassion for why we – and others around us – are the way we are.

How early life shapes us

The way we grow up profoundly affects how we see the world and how we relate to others. Our childhood experiences influence our emotional regulation, stress response and coping mechanisms. Some people are raised in ways that help them build healthy coping skills, while others develop avoidance strategies due to difficult environments.

The roots of how we relate to others actually go back to our very earliest days. As babies we're born with underdeveloped brains that get shaped by early interactions with our caregivers. A baby's brain is wired through its emotional experiences. In particular, the right hemisphere, which plays a key role in our emotions and relationships, is shaped by the caregiving we receive in infancy.

If this care is consistent, loving and responsive, this helps the baby regulate their emotions. But if a baby experiences neglect or emotional deprivation, the stress-response system becomes overactive. According to renowned physician and trauma expert Gabor Maté, experiencing neglect, stress or trauma in early life leaves people more prone to anxiety, depression or emotional dysregulation. On the other hand, consistent love and care helps them develop emotional resilience.

As we grow up, our experiences in family life influence our relationships as well as our coping mechanisms. Families tend to pass down both strengths and struggles, often without consciously being aware of these. Problems often stem from silence, secrecy or lack of communication. If our caregivers were open about emotions and processed them healthily, we're more likely to do the same. But if we grew up in an environment where feelings were suppressed, dismissed or punished, we may struggle to process difficult emotions effectively as adults.

When a family avoids talking about their feelings, this may lead a child to internalise distress rather than talk about it or seek help.

> ✩ 'Pain is passed down in families until someone is willing to feel it.'
>
> **– John Richards**

Historical patterns repeating

There's a wonderfully insightful phrase that I first heard when interviewing the author and therapist Lori Gottlieb: 'If it's hysterical, it's usually historical.'

She's right – our strongest emotional reactions in the present often have roots in our past. So whenever we experience an unexpectedly strong feeling or reaction, this can be a helpful opportunity to recognise how our past is still affecting us now.

> **➜ What's my history here?**
> Next time you have a strong emotional reaction, pause and ask yourself:
> 'How old am I feeling right now?'
> This can help to uncover prior experiences that are driving current emotions and reactions. This self-awareness is the starting point for change, helping us see how our early years continue to shape our coping mechanisms.
> Remember: you coped the best way you could at the time, so go easy on yourself.

One of the strongest influences on how we handle emotions and relate to others is the 'attachment style' we develop in childhood. When a child has a secure and loving start they learn to trust others and develop empathy. But when a child experiences an insecure or neglectful upbringing they may find it harder to trust others or believe they're worthy of love and care. Without emotional attunement, a child may develop attachment issues, leading to relationship difficulties and emotional instability.

🧠 Attachment styles

Attachment styles explain how we emotionally bond and relate to others in our close relationships. This psychological framework comes from the work of John Bowlby in the 1940s and 1950s, refined later by clinicians such as Mary Ainsworth.

- **Secure attachment.** Generally feels comfortable with both closeness and independence – often linked to early experiences of being emotionally supported and responded to. Tends to trust others and themselves, making it easier to develop stable and satisfying relationships.
- **Anxious (or preoccupied) attachment.** Tends to worry about rejection or abandonment – often linked to early care being inconsistent or unpredictable. May seek reassurance, feel dependent or experience emotional ups and downs in relationships.
- **Avoidant (or dismissive) attachment.** Tends to value self-reliance and keep emotional distance – often linked to closeness not feeling available or safe in early life. May downplay their need for connection or feel uncomfortable with emotional intimacy.
- **Fearful (or disorganised) attachment.** A mix of anxious and avoidant tendencies – often linked to early experiences of trauma or inconsistent caregiving. May long for closeness but find it overwhelming or hard to trust.

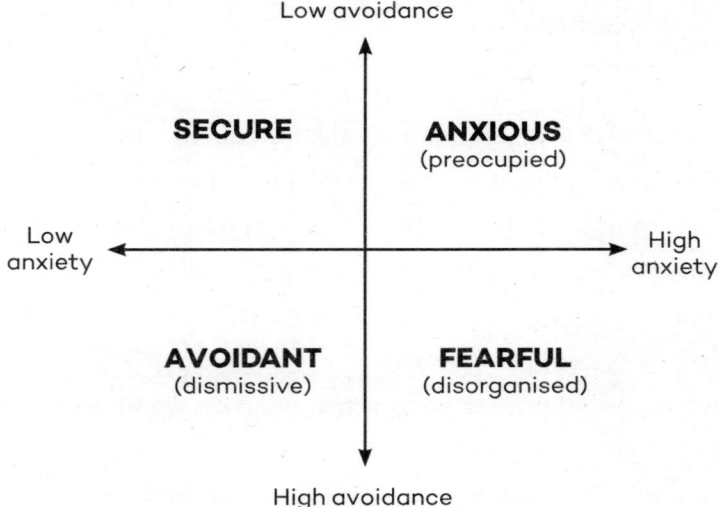

Thankfully, unhelpful family patterns can be overcome. Although we inherit emotional legacies, we're not doomed to repeat them. Through self-awareness, therapy and intentional changes, we can break destructive cycles and improve our relationships. Even small changes in how we respond to others – such as listening more, setting boundaries or showing warmth – can make a big difference.

Breaking the trauma cycle

Trauma is when an event overwhelms our mental and emotional capacity to deal with it. One way to think of this is as a time of 'perceived helplessness', when we were in a situation that we wanted to be different but felt outside of our control.

Trauma activates the brain's amygdala and threat system, leaving us on high alert. It can lead to heightened stress responses, ongoing distress and even flashbacks. Although we often associate trauma with life-threatening events such as accidents or violence, it's actually broader than this. It can include other distressing experiences, such as grief, burnout, job loss, miscarriage or infertility.

We may have a 'big-T' trauma, where life seems to be going one way until some terrible event happens and things are never quite the same again. Or it might be more like a thousand paper cuts; for example, a child experiencing repeated daily moments of uncertainty where their limbic system gets activated. Trauma isn't just about what happens, it's about how we experience it and how our nervous system processes it.

When we avoid processing our trauma it can remain unresolved. This may eventually lead to self-destructive behaviours, addiction, chronic illness and mental-health issues. But with self-awareness and support we have the power to break the cycle of trauma.

> *'It is not the pain of grief that damages individuals and even whole families, sometimes for generations, but the things they do to avoid that pain.'*
>
> **– Julia Samuel**

We can't change the stressful event, neglect, abuse or other tragedy that happened in the past. But we can look back and recognise the behaviours we adopted to cope in that situation. Some of these might have been healthy, such as asking for help. However, we may have adopted unhelpful survival strategies – including avoidance, co-dependency, self-harm or aggression.

By accepting what happened we can recognise it wasn't our fault and the behaviours we adopted were the best way we knew how to respond at the time. We can then identify patterns that aren't serving us now and replace them with healthier ways of coping. For more complex issues, it's important to reach out for help or professional support. In other cases we can find our own way forwards. For example, instead of avoidance, we can try a breathing exercise to calm our nervous system.

Remember, trauma, although painful, can also lead to transformation. People who experience post-traumatic growth (see chapter one) report stronger relationships, a renewed sense of purpose and greater appreciation for life.

Rewriting 'shit stories'

People who experienced childhood trauma often carry an invisible weight – the ingrained belief that something was wrong with them. Instead of recognising they were in a harmful environment, they internalised the blame. To heal and move on, we need to shift our perspective from 'What's wrong with me?' to 'What happened to me?' – not as an excuse, but as a way to understand our story.

One helpful way to look back at the impact of past experiences is to see the role played by the 'inner protector', a part of us that's been actively working all our lives to keep us safe. This developed as a survival mechanism in childhood, helping us navigate difficult situations. But in doing so, it may also have led to unhelpful beliefs.

As children, if our emotional needs aren't met, we face an impossible choice: blame the caregivers we depend on, or blame ourselves. Seeing our caregivers as unreliable or unsafe is too terrifying, so we take the blame instead. We internalise painful beliefs like 'I'm not good enough', 'I have to earn love', or 'If I show my feelings I'll be rejected.'

These beliefs aren't personal failings but natural adaptations, ways to create a sense of control in an unpredictable world. The inner protector has reinforced them, urging us to behave in ways that minimise risk: striving for perfection, avoiding vulnerability or keeping people at arm's length. Yet as adults, these strategies no longer serve us. Instead of protecting us they keep us stuck. By recognising this we can stop repeating unhelpful patterns or reinforcing inaccurate beliefs that helped us survive when we were younger.

> ### ➔ Thank your 'inner protector'
> Here is an exercise that you might like to try:
>
> **Step 1: Identify.** Think of an unhelpful belief you often say to yourself, for example: 'I'm no good', 'I can't trust anyone', 'I must be perfect', or 'I can't show my feelings.'
>
> **Step 2: Appreciate.** Recognise that this belief was a useful survival strategy at some time in your past. It's like an old friend that served you well but is no longer needed. Take a moment to thank the 'inner protector' for taking care of you in the past.
>
> **Step 3: Move on.** Having thanked your protector, you can now consciously challenge this limiting belief. Try to bring to mind an example when this belief has not been true in recent years. For example, if your belief is 'I'm not good enough', remember an achievement you're proud of. Then next time this thought reappears you can calmly thank the protector again and let it go.

Beneath the protector's defences is a deeper part of us that still holds the traces of our early emotional experiences – sometimes referred to as our 'inner child'. This includes our original childhood curiosity and joy but also the unmet needs and longings we pushed aside. When we experience overwhelming feelings – like self-doubt or fear of abandonment – it's often this younger part of us still seeking acknowledgment.

If we're able to validate the emotions we felt as a child, rather than repressing them, this can be very powerful. So we might say, 'It's understandable you felt this way, but you're safe now', or 'It wasn't your fault.' The aim here is to help our inner child feel accepted and loved. By comforting our inner child we can move on rather than staying stuck.

We can't change what happened in our earliest years but we can choose to take responsibility for how we treat ourselves and others now. However, revisiting painful childhood memories can sometimes bring up other issues, so this is often best done with the help of a trained therapist or counsellor.

> **➔ Comfort your inner child**
>
> If revisiting your childhood feels manageable right now, these steps can help. But if not, that's okay – perhaps you could talk to a therapist about this instead?
>
> **Step 1: Reconnect.** Take a moment to reconnect with your childhood self and what they needed more of. Perhaps it was to feel safe? Or to have more consistent care?
>
> **Step 2: Comfort.** Come up with a phrase that your inner child needed to hear. Then try saying this to yourself and really meaning it. For example: 'I am enough as I am', 'I am worthy of love', 'I'm safe right now', 'I don't need to be perfect', or 'I'm allowed to feel all of my feelings.'
>
> **Step 3: Repeat.** Once you've found a phrase that helps you feel comforted, keep this in mind to repeat to yourself when difficult feelings arise.

By reconnecting with these deeper parts of ourselves, we can begin to rewrite the patterns that have shaped us, allowing us to break free from inaccurate beliefs, let go of old wounds and create healthier ways of relating to ourselves and the world.

The unconscious patterns of love

Have you ever wondered what draws us to our partners?

I'd always been intrigued about how I instinctively felt more attracted to some people than others, and how this seemed to go deeper than just looks or shared interests. People talk about feeling a 'chemistry' with someone, but is that real or imagined? And why is it that two people who seem very different often end up together?

When I came across the work of relationship therapist Harville Hendrix, this all suddenly made more sense. In his many years of work with couples, Hendrix discovered the deeper reasons we're attracted to our partners but are usually not aware of. According to his 'Imago' theory, we unconsciously carry an inner image of love, shaped by our earliest caregivers. We do this in three main ways.

Firstly, we're drawn to people who *feel familiar* because they echo some of the positive traits or warmth we experienced as children. This feels safe and comforting, even if we don't realise why.

But familiarity cuts both ways. So secondly, we often find ourselves attracted to people who *recreate difficulties* from our early years, like a parent who was harsh, absent or unpredictable. Hendrix argues that we're hoping to heal old wounds by 'getting it right this time' with someone who reminds us of the original hurt. So if you often felt rejected as a child you may be unconsciously drawn to a partner who triggers that same feeling, hoping to finally 'fix' this problem.

Thirdly, we also feel pulled towards people who show *qualities we learned to hide* in ourselves while growing up. So an introvert may feel drawn to an extrovert, or someone who's cautious may get together with a free spirit. These are the disowned parts of ourselves that we secretly long to reclaim.

Incidentally, this is also why modern dating apps tend to be flawed. We think we're looking for people with certain looks or interests, but we're really not! So people find themselves on endless dates with others who seem nice and have things in common, but there's a frustrating lack of chemistry. No app can yet capture the deeper, often unexpected attraction we feel when we're with someone who helps us feel whole.

These subconscious drives also help to explain the familiar stages of our intimate relationships. It starts with that 'falling in love' phase where we feel an overwhelming attraction to the other person. In this early period we're drawn to their sense of familiarity and complementary qualities – and it feels exhilarating.

Yet sooner or later the initial euphoria wears off and the relationship starts to feel more difficult. This is a phase of disillusionment, when the very things that drew us together begin to frustrate us. The differences that once felt exciting are now annoying, and the familiarity that felt safe now triggers old wounds. Many couples give up at this stage, which is sadly why so many relationships break down and marriages fail.

But here's the part I find really hopeful and inspiring. These difficulties don't mean that our relationship is doomed – they're simply inevitable given our pasts. And if both partners can learn to recognise these patterns, they find opportunities to grow rather than reasons to separate. By working through our discomfort together we can help each other heal our pasts.

> ⭐ *'Your love relationship has a hidden purpose – to help you overcome the limitations of your childhood'*
>
> **– Harville Hendrix**

Yes, it's painful to realise that the very traits that frustrate us in our partner are the same ones that drew us in. But instead of being a fatal flaw, this pain can be a guide to the hidden parts of us that need attention. Instead of pushing each other away, partners can grow together and begin to reclaim lost parts of themselves.

Hendrix says 'conflict is growth trying to happen', so the purpose of long-term love isn't just togetherness or stability, but transformation. Our partner can become the person who helps us heal our past – and we can be that person for them. The key is to become aware of these unconscious wounds and create a conscious, loving relationship.

Based on these ideas, Hendrix developed 'Imago Relationship Therapy' (IRT) and, when Kate and I were looking for some help, we found a therapist trained in this approach. A key part of IRT is the 'Imago Dialogue', which builds on the active listening we covered earlier but involves a couple taking turns to share their feelings and feel heard. Kate and I found this really helpful in our therapy. It can also be used in other relationships, including with friends, family members or close colleagues.

> ### The Imago Dialogue

The Imago Dialogue is a structured way for two people to communicate with deeper understanding and without defensiveness. It has three steps:

1. Mirroring: The receiver (listener) repeats back what the sender (speaker) has said without adding their own interpretation. For example:

- Sender: 'I feel hurt when you cancel plans last minute.'
- Receiver: 'What I hear you saying is that you feel

hurt when I cancel plans last minute. Did I get that right?'

The receiver asks 'Did I get that right?' to make sure they've understood.

2. Validation: The receiver acknowledges that what the sender is saying makes sense, even if they don't necessarily agree (this is crucial!). For example:
- Receiver: 'That makes sense because you value reliability and feel disappointed when plans change.'

This reassures the speaker their thoughts and feelings are valid.

3. Empathy: The receiver tries to connect with how the sender really feels and expresses understanding.
- Receiver: 'I can imagine that when I cancel plans you might feel unimportant or let down and that must be painful.'

The receiver can also ask 'Is there more?' to encourage more to be said.

Then Swap Roles. Once the sender feels fully heard, they switch roles and the receiver becomes the new speaker.

Toxic Relationships

We often hear talk about 'toxic relationships', but what does this mean? This is when unhealthy dynamics create instability, emotional pain and dysfunction in a relationship. These patterns can occur in various areas of our lives, including romantic, friendship, family and workplace relationships.

> **→ Unhealthy relationship dynamics**
> Here are 10 examples of unhealthy behaviour in relationships, which can often be traced back to our families or formative years:
> 1. **Passive-aggressive behaviour**: expressing resentment indirectly rather than openly, e.g. using sarcasm or subtle digs.
> 2. **Blaming**: refusing to take personal responsibility and instead blaming the other person. e.g. 'I only shouted because you made me cross.'
> 3. **Keeping score**: bringing up past mistakes to gain the upper hand, e.g. 'Well, you forgot last time so why should I care now?'
> 4. **Silent treatment**: ignoring or refusing to engage in conversation as a form of punishment without explaining why they're upset.
> 5. **Gaslighting**: making the other person question their memory, perception or sanity, e.g. 'You're imagining things, I never said that.'
> 6. **Withholding**: deliberately withholding love or support as a form of punishment, e.g. not showing affection until the other person 'earns' it.
> 7. **Guilt-tripping**: making the other person feel guilty to manipulate their actions, e.g. 'If you really cared about me, you'd do it for me.'
> 8. **Possessiveness**: jealousy or controlling behaviour masked as caring, e.g. 'I don't like it when you go out – let's just stay in together.'

> 9. **Constant criticism**: repeatedly showing contempt or making them feel small, e.g. 'You're useless. I don't know why I put up with you.'
> 10. **Walking on eggshells**: needing to constantly monitor what you say or do to avoid conflict, e.g. 'If I mention it they'll explode, so I won't bother.'
>
> Noticing these patterns isn't about blame, but rather to approach our relationships with more self-awareness, honesty and understanding.

If we recognise that we're experiencing or contributing to these toxic patterns, we can take steps to avoid them. The starting point is to acknowledge this is happening. Then we can try to communicate more carefully and take steps to set clear boundaries and adjust our behaviour. You can't control how someone else chooses to behave, but you can choose how you respond. It's also important to maintain safe boundaries.

Bringing it all together

This chapter has continued to build on earlier topics of listening, needs and vulnerability, to explore how your past shapes your present. You may be bringing hidden parts of yourself into your adult relationships without realising it. By taking time to reflect on your formative years you can identify how these shaped your beliefs about yourself and the world. Your coping mechanisms were a natural response to your situation, but they may no longer serve you well now. With self-care and support those unhelpful internalised stories like 'I'm not good enough' can be replaced with more supportive beliefs, and with this greater self-awareness and acceptance, you can continue to grow and strengthen your relationships.

In the next chapter we're going to move on to a topic that many of us find very challenging, but has huge potential to make life happier: forgiveness.

> **HEAL THOSE WOUNDS: CHAPTER SUMMARY**
>
> Ask yourself:
> ❓ **What wounds am I still carrying from past relationships?**
>
> Don't just:
> ✘ Continue replaying the same old relationship conflicts and traumas.
>
> Try this out:
> ✔ Acknowledge your 'inner child' to accept and let go of old wounds.

Chapter Seventeen:

Let it Go

How can I forgive and move on?

Meeting Jo Berry and hearing her story is one of the most powerful and humbling experiences I've had. We met at a conference on empathy, and her quiet courage has stayed with me and changed how I think about what's possible with forgiveness.

Jo's father had been a UK member of parliament, but in 1984 he was killed by the IRA bombing of a Brighton hotel. This devastated her family and changed the direction of her life. 'It felt as if a part of me died in that bomb,' she said later, 'but somehow I held on to a small hope that something positive would come out of the trauma.' After years of grief, Jo was determined to understand more about the motivations behind the violence. Her journey led her to Northern Ireland, where she had conversations with people who had been involved in the Troubles, including those she'd considered as 'the enemy'. Then after the Good Friday Agreement, the man responsible for the bombing, Patrick Magee, was released from prison.

Jo took the courageous step to reach out to him and express a desire to meet.

Jo and Patrick first met in 2000. She was terrified, and initially he just wanted to justify his actions politically. But as Jo talked about her father and shared what she'd been through, Patrick began to open up emotionally too. He was able to acknowledge her pain and then told her his backstory. This conversation marked the start of a profound transformation for both of them. Over time, they developed an unlikely friendship. Patrick later admitted that, instead of resorting to violence, he could have chosen to sit down for a conversation with Jo's father.

Jo then said something that astounded me: 'I realised if I'd gone through everything he'd been through, I may have even made the same choices.' Wow! That same choice to plant the bomb that killed her dad? It seemed hard to believe, but Jo explained her realisation that people's actions are shaped by their circumstances. Once she had a really clear understanding of his life, she said 'it felt like there's nothing to forgive'.

In the years since, Jo and Patrick have spoken together hundreds of times in different settings, including schools, prisons and conflict zones. They formed an organisation, Building Bridges for Peace, which works on breaking the cycle of violence and encouraging dialogue and mutual understanding. Patrick said later, 'The hope lies in the fact that we are prepared to carry on.' I find this such an incredible and hopeful story about the power of empathy.

Seeing humanity in others – even those who have caused harm – is essential for conflict resolution. Acts of violence diminish everyone involved, and lasting peace requires dignity, understanding and shared responsibility. Forgiveness is not about condoning past actions but about building a future free from ongoing retaliation or hatred. Our world needs this more than ever right now.

Being open to forgiveness

Forgiveness is a topic that brings up a lot of resistance whenever I mention it. We tend to find it really hard. Yet if we want to make life happier we must be open to forgiving. Not condoning or letting people off the hook, but letting go and moving on.

Life is inherently difficult, and so much of our suffering comes from disagreements and perceived injustices. When we're wronged – or see others treated badly – we feel hurt and angry. We want to see justice and hear apologies, but often these situations go unresolved. This leads to resentment and damages our relationships. Across society this perpetuates cycles of conflict and reprisals that last across generations.

Forgiveness is really about making peace with life being difficult. It's not about excusing harm or injustice but about releasing the personal burden of resentment. It does not erase our memory or invalidate our suffering. Instead, it reframes it, helping us move from anger to understanding and from pain to recovery.

 'Without forgiveness, there is no future.'
— **Desmond Tutu**

When we hold on to past harm it creates unhappiness. The forgiveness expert Dr Fred Luskin likens this to 'dragging a junk pile through life'. We often do this culturally and socially too. Families, groups and nations keep cycles of resentment going by continuing to blame each other for past wounds. If we continuously retell our stories of injustice, we stay trapped in our suffering instead of learning and moving forwards.

When I met Dr Luskin, he used a phrase which I keep coming back to:

'Forgiveness is giving up all hope for a better past.'

This insight shifts our focus from fixing the past to accepting reality as it is. Wishing the past had been different is unproductive because it keeps us emotionally stuck. Holding on to grievances removes peace of mind and can damage our mental and physical wellbeing. When we don't let things go, our nervous system stays on higher alert and continues to scan for threats. Our 'unforgiveness' keeps us trapped in our anger and victimhood, reinforcing our suffering rather than resolving it.

> **➜ What happens if you hold a grudge?**
> Here are some potential risks when we hold on to resentment:
> - Getting so wrapped up in the wrong that you can't enjoy the present
> - Becoming irritable, anxious or depressed
> - Bringing bitterness or anger into new relationships and experiences
> - Losing out on valuable connections with others
> - Passing on old resentments to the next generation

Forgiveness isn't only vital for our personal wellbeing but also for wider society. It can help to minimise acts of hate, revenge and retaliation. And it can bring healing for both victims and perpetrators. Even in the face of unimaginable suffering, those who choose forgiveness – like Jo Berry did – can reclaim their inner strength and move forwards.

This is about shifting focus from the injustice of the past to the reality of the present and the possibilities of the future. Healing comes from acknowledging our suffering, processing it and then consciously letting it go. So in this way forgiveness is as much for yourself as for others – it allows you to reclaim your inner peace.

> **→ Do a resentment audit**
>
> In order to forgive, you first need to recognise what you're holding on to. Try using this 4R process to 'audit' any historic resentments you're carrying. It may take some effort, so choose a time when you're feeling open-minded.
>
> - **Reflect**. Bring to mind a specific resentment towards a person or an old situation where you're still carrying grievance or anger.
> - **Recognise**. Think about how this resentment continues to shape you now, including its impact on your mental health, relationships and behaviours, perhaps including how you treat others who were involved.
> - **Review**. In light of these impacts, ask yourself honestly: Is holding on to this resentment helping me or hurting me (or others)?
> - **Repeat**. Continue to repeat the steps above for other people or situations until you feel you have a clear picture of the resentment you're carrying and the impact this continues to have on your life.
>
> This is not about revisiting the wrong to remind yourself how badly you were treated. It's also not about saying what happened was okay; it's noticing the impact this resentment is having on you and others now.

Why is forgiveness so hard?

One big obstacle to forgiveness is the belief that our own suffering is uniquely terrible, which isolates us and deepens our wounds. But if we can recognise that pain is universal, this helps shift our mindset away from resentment. Pain is an inevitable part of life, but resentment is a choice.

Forgiveness is hard because it can feel like we're letting someone who hurt us off the hook for their actions. But we're not freeing others from things they've done, we're freeing ourselves from their damage and releasing ourselves from anger.

Anger is a natural response to feeling wronged. Sometimes our anger is entirely appropriate, to ensure that we stay safe in a specific situation or stand up to injustice. But if we hold on to our anger, especially over long periods of time, it 'burns' inside us and can end up doing us more harm than the original problem it came from.

> ⭐ 'Holding on to anger is like grasping a hot coal with the intent of throwing it at someone else. You are the one who gets burned.'
>
> **– attributed to the Buddha**

Letting it go isn't saying that what happened was okay – your anger may well be justified. What forgiveness does is allow you to let go of the pain you're holding on to inside and move on. You can still take steps to stop dangerous situations in future, or stand up for causes you care about, but releasing that burning resentment is an act of self-care.

> **Steps towards forgiveness**
>
> Forgiveness takes patience and practice. Here are some practical steps to move towards forgiving and letting go:
> 1. **See the potential**. Start by recognising the value of forgiveness, why it's helpful and how doing this can make life happier.
> 2. **Identify the issue**. Bring to mind a specific issue or relationship that needs healing, including what happened and who or what you want to forgive.
> 3. **Feel your pain**. Acknowledge your feeling about the harm done to you and notice how those emotions affect your behaviour. (Note: you may find it helpful to talk about this with a trusted friend, support group or therapist.)
> 4. **Decide to forgive**. Make a conscious choice to forgive them. You are not condoning what happened, you are taking control.
> 5. **Let it go**. Release the power that the offending person or situation has had on your life. Just let it go and move on.

One place forgiveness seems particularly hard is online. Social media platforms amplify outrage and encourage resentment, hindering our ability to forgive. The public visibility of online actions can also make it more difficult for people to move past mistakes and let them go. We find ourselves wanting to 'cancel' or deplatform people, rather than to listen or give them a second chance.

Yet even as modern life feeds our rage and pain, the latest research on the power of forgiveness shows that it not only helps to improve the quality of our relationships, it can also increase our self-esteem, lower anxiety and stress levels, reduce blood pressure and even support our immune system.

Choosing your identity

Another barrier to forgiveness is the way in which our past hurts get tied up in how we see ourselves and the world around us. Whether consciously or not, we all adopt an identity – and the big danger comes when people define themselves by their past suffering. Adopting victimhood as an identity reinforces helplessness.

When our identity is 'I've been harmed', then our world view tends to be framed through resentment. This leads to anger, blame and a sense of powerlessness, all of which makes life unhappier. It may even lead us to wanting to hurt those who hurt us. But true strength is being able to cope with hardship without harming others.

Dr Fred Luskin therefore warns against over-identifying with being a victim. Although past harm is real, clinging to it prevents healing and growth. If we relive our suffering repeatedly, we carry old wounds into new situations and relationships.

Thankfully this identity we carry is malleable and we can break free from our victimhood. We can choose to shift our narrative and reclaim power over our lives. The key to personal freedom is to be able to acknowledge pain while also choosing to move on. Victimhood is a mental trap and reinforces our suffering. Forgiveness involves letting go of the desire for retribution against those who wronged us. Not for them, but for us.

If we try to forgive from a position of judgement we'll find this is almost impossible. Instead we need to start from a position of *acceptance* of how things are. Yes, people do bad things, but we can also recognise that they may have been responding to their unique circumstances – such as their childhood, upbringing or difficult life experiences. Just as Jo realised when she met Patrick.

> **➔ Forgiveness and boundaries**
>
> Despite its benefits, forgiveness is also complicated and deeply personal. So if forgiving someone feels impossible, we can start by going easy on ourselves and recognising this is hard. It may take some time and that's okay. Also, forgiveness can bring potential risks in certain situations, for example in the context of abusive behaviour or violence. In more extreme cases, forgiving without safe boundaries could lead to further harm or negative behaviour. So we also need to maintain healthy boundaries. Forgiveness is about letting go of the past, not tolerating abuse or mistreatment in the present.

Let go of the little things

While it's crucial to learn how to forgive serious and painful hurts, it's equally important to approach our daily conflicts from a place of open-mindedness. In everyday life, other people are constantly behaving in ways that can potentially upset us. They might express displeasure at something or they may ignore us, criticise us or leave us feeling small or rejected. This hurts!

Sometimes their behaviour or displeasure may be a direct response to us and be about us. They may even be raising a valid concern. For example, if Kate expresses frustration that I've left oily handprints on the door after cleaning my bike, I may feel criticised, but she's making a fair point!

But . . . and this is the important bit . . . often the way people treat us says much more about how *they* are feeling and what *they* are going through at that point than anything *you* have done.

A classic example of this is road rage. We've all seen a red-faced driver going over the top with their anger, which seems completely out of proportion to the situation. In reality this anger is less about the incident on the road and more a reflection of their underlying emotional state. They may be super-stressed at work or having a tough time caring for an ill loved-one at home. We can't see what's really going on for them, but in that case it's fairly obviously not about us.

Likewise in our everyday relationships, people who appear to be bringing displeasure or stress into situations are often showing us what's going on for them and what they need or how they're feeling. They may not actually be responding to us or intending to criticise us, so we don't need to take it personally.

I find this is particularly true with our 'nearest and dearest' where we often speak in harsh or direct ways we'd never think of doing with someone we know less well. But this is actually the sign of a close relationship, where someone feels able to speak their mind and let their emotions out. It may not feel nice, but it's often a healthy sign.

It can be hard to know what's really going on for the other person, so we can use our active listening skills and ask open questions like, 'Can you help me understand what's going on here?' or 'Okay, how can I help?' But if they're in an extreme emotional state and not open to talking, then it may be best to just walk away and reconnect later.

Once we understand more about what's going on for them we can respond more calmly and wisely rather than instinctively reacting or getting defensive. Unless it's clear that they're making a specific request of us – like me not leaving greasy marks on the door frame – then it's almost always best not to take their behaviour personally.

> **→ How to cope with their stress**
> - Don't take it personally – how they're behaving is not necessarily your fault.
> - Don't jump to fix things – you are not in charge of reducing their stress.
> - Don't get defensive – you don't need to fight back or to apologise for disappointing them (unless you actually did something wrong).
>
> Focus on responding calmly, rather than reacting defensively.

Another phrase I find helpful to remember here is, 'You don't need to attend every argument you're invited to.'

This reminds us that we have a choice. Sometimes it's important to get involved and stand up for what we believe, especially if it's needed to protect someone or something we care about. But this is a choice, and sometimes it's simply better – both for us and others – to choose inner peace over conflict. By using our emotional intelligence and self-control we can avoid engaging in every potential confrontation and protect our wellbeing.

What if I need forgiveness?

Sometimes we need to be forgiven ourselves. The first step is to acknowledge the wrong you've done and how this may have affected the other person. Be honest, but avoid judging yourself too harshly. If you're genuinely sorry for what you did and want forgiveness, you may want to reach out to the person. If so, be sure to share your regret honestly and sincerely. Use the skills from previous chapters to focus on your behaviour (not theirs) and ask open questions with active listening to understand their feelings.

It's important to ask for forgiveness without making excuses. You can't force someone to forgive you and they may not be ready to forgive yet. Forgiveness is a process and this may take time. Although you can't control how they respond, you can behave with integrity. By being honest and treating them with respect you'll have done what you can to help put things right and move on.

Finally, it's also vital that we learn to forgive ourselves too. We often beat ourselves up over things we did (or didn't do) and hold on to regrets about them. But through the lens of forgiveness we can recognise that this was an earlier version of ourselves who was doing the best they could at the time. Dr Rangan Chatterjee observes that 'regret is a form of perfectionism', which I find a helpful way of framing this.

The truth is that all of us are imperfect, and just because we got something wrong it doesn't mean we've somehow failed at everything. When you're able to forgive yourself you can avoid unnecessary guilt, learn from the past and make wiser decisions going forwards. As Rangan says: 'If we could have done better, we would have done.' And when you face similar challenges in future you'll be able to make different choices.

Now, having learned to forgive and move on, our next chapter shifts to one of the most life-changing and inspiring choices of all: to spread kindness.

LET IT GO: CHAPTER SUMMARY

Ask yourself:
❓ **What anger am I holding on to that I can choose to let go of?**

Don't just:
✗ Keep carrying the burden and anger of seeing yourself as a victim.

Try this out:
✔ Forgive and let go, not to condone it but to set yourself free.

Chapter Eighteen:

Spread Kindness

How can I be helpful and inspire others too?

Conway Hall was packed, and in a rare moment of silence, everyone was leaning forwards in anticipation. We'd just spent a wonderful 45 minutes listening to a former monk, Thupten Jinpa. He'd been sharing his insights, not just as an expert in the science of compassion, but also as the Dalai Lama's longtime translator and close companion on his travels around the world. As the host, I'd turned to the audience and a young woman had just asked Jinpa a brilliant question:

'You've spent all these years working with the Dalai Lama, what's the most important lesson you've learned about happiness?'

I was genuinely intrigued to hear what he'd say and I could sense others in the room were too. Jinpa paused for a while, then eventually smiled and replied:

'Whenever anything happens, I simply ask myself, "What's the kindest way to respond to this situation right now?" – and then I just try to do that.'

This simple yet powerful idea has stayed with me ever since that moment. In fact, I've been trying – not always successfully – to put it into practice ever since. At work, at home, in the pub, at the shops, while commuting. As a parent, husband, son, colleague, friend and neighbour. Remembering to ask myself this question – and trying my best to act on it – has honestly been life-changing. It helps me to reflect more carefully on the impact of my actions and how they affect others around me.

I regularly find it hard to live up to Jinpa's ideal, especially in moments when I feel criticised, unappreciated, angry or let down. Yet I've found it to be a wonderful guide to almost any situation. Being kind isn't about taking the easy option – often kindness involves courage or upholding boundaries – but if we choose to respond in the kindest way possible, it almost always helps the situation. For everyone involved.

Kindness is part of our nature

Although kindness is often portrayed as something soft or optional, evidence tells a different story. Kindness is actually fundamental to who we are, and our capacity to care for each other has been vital for us as a species.

Historically, humans have always survived through cooperation. Charles Darwin is usually associated with the 'survival of the fittest' theory, but he also observed that our natural instinct was to care for others. In *The Descent of Man* (1871) he wrote: 'Those communities which included the greatest number of the most sympathetic members, would flourish best and rear the greatest number of offspring.'

Although humans obviously do have strong instincts for self-preservation, we also evolved to care about each other, and this is wired-in biologically. Unfortunately our current culture tends to amplify competition and selfishness. So to make life happier, we need to actively cultivate our compassionate instincts, not just our self-centred ones.

> **➜ Being kind is not the same as being nice**
> In this chapter we'll use the everyday word 'kindness', but what we're really focusing on is 'compassion'. This is about more than just being aware of other people's feelings or being superficially 'nice'. Being nice can lead to avoiding difficult truths or staying passive, whereas being truly kind involves honesty, courage and not avoiding hard things.
>
> Crucially, compassion is about *taking action* to help. This instinct can arise naturally when we see someone suffering, but it's also something that needs to be nurtured. By actively encouraging the kinder side of our nature we can turn good intentions into action.

Being kind helps others

The fundamental motivation for kindness is *to help*. Although we will discover in this chapter how much kindness helps us, too, that's *not* the main reason we do kind things. By being kind to others we can:
- Lift their mood
- Help them feel seen and valued
- Show them we care and they're not alone
- Create a sense of safety or reassurance
- Help them get through difficult moments
- Reduce levels of anxiety or worry
- Support their healing or recovery.

As we saw in part one, we're often wearing a mask and hiding our inner selves from others. So it helps to remember that everyone around is wearing their own mask too. Many people may seem okay when they're not. Showing empathy and kindness can help us to connect on a deeper level and encourage people to open up.

> **The Rabbit Effect**
>
> At one Action for Happiness event, Dr Kelli Harding told a remarkable story she calls the 'Rabbit Effect'. In a research study, two groups of genetically identical rabbits were fed the same high-fat diet, yet their health outcomes were dramatically different. The researchers were baffled. Eventually they discovered that the healthier group had been cared for by a particular research assistant who talked to the rabbits and showed them kindness and affection.
>
> When the study was repeated under controlled conditions, similar results emerged, suggesting that care and social interaction were influencing the rabbits' physiology. This challenged the usual biomedical model and prompted Dr Harding to delve deeper into this area of research. She found that social factors are far more influential than is often recognised. Medical care accounts for only around 10–20 per cent of health outcomes at a population level. Many of the strongest influences on our health relate to experiences of connection – like feeling heard, safe and supported. These factors can be as important as diet, exercise and medical treatment.

Being kind helps us too

Although our primary motivation is to help others, being kind also benefits us in a surprising range of ways. Most obviously, doing good feels good. Many of us have experienced that boost you get from being kind – sometimes called the 'helper's high'. This is because kindness activates the brain's reward system, releasing feel-good chemicals like dopamine, serotonin and oxytocin. Our generosity, even if imperfect, is naturally rewarding.

Acts of kindness also support our mental health, easing symptoms of stress, anxiety and depression. Kindness shifts our attention away from our own worries and towards a more outwards-looking mindset. People who regularly practise kindness tend to feel more confident, less reactive and better able to cope with everyday situations and relationships. Over time, kindness helps us cultivate a greater sense of inner peace and emotional balance.

> 'We've been told that achieving our own success will make us happy. But happiness comes from helping other people to live happier lives.'
>
> **– Stephanie Harrison**

Research also shows that being kind helps us become more resilient, enabling us to face life's bigger challenges with greater courage and calm. This fits with what we see in remarkable people like the Dalai Lama or Desmond Tutu, whose deep compassion goes hand-in-hand with steadiness and inner strength.

Perhaps most surprisingly, kindness can transform our physical health in profound ways. It has been linked to reduced inflammation, lower blood pressure and even slower ageing. It also supports the nervous system, contributes to heart health and helps us cope better with illness and recovery.

As the 'Rabbit Effect' study showed, our physical health is shaped by our social world. Acts of kindness and compassion trigger the release of oxytocin, sometimes called the 'love hormone'. But it may be better thought of as the 'kindness hormone' because its effects go beyond romantic love, enhancing cooperation, trust and social connection. Oxytocin also supports the cardiovascular system, providing anti-inflammatory benefits that can help reduce the chronic low-grade inflammation linked to heart disease and other metabolic issues.

> 'The science is clear: kindness improves your immune system, your heart health, even your longevity.'
> **– Dr Kelli Harding**

Dr David Hamilton, an expert on the health benefits of kindness, describes how people who regularly feel or express hostility tend to have stiffer arteries, while those who are more loving and kind have healthier, more flexible arteries. I find it fascinating that our emotional states can both affect and reflect what's happening in our blood vessels. As David said to me, 'kindness literally softens us from the inside out'.

> **Spending on others vs ourselves**
> Various scientific studies have shown that people tend to feel happier when they spend money on others rather than on themselves. Remarkably, these benefits go beyond just good feelings and might even be life-saving! In one study at Harvard Business School, researchers

examined the benefits of gift-giving for people previously diagnosed with hypertension. Participants were each given three payments of $40, contained in a sealed bottle (to mimic a medical treatment), over six weeks. Half were told to indulge themselves while the rest were encouraged to spend the money on someone else.

Amazingly, they found that participants in the 'generous' group saw a significant drop in blood pressure, beyond what would be expected from their usual treatment. They recorded average blood pressures of 114/67mmHg, compared with higher averages of 121/73mmHg in the 'self-spending' group. This difference is similar to starting a new blood pressure medication or adopting a new diet and exercise regime.

The wider benefits of kindness

As well as helping both the receiver and the giver, our acts of kindness contribute more widely. Kindness helps to build trust, warmth and reciprocity in our relationships, within families, workplaces and communities. It brings us together and strengthens feelings of belonging. Being kind also reinforces the belief that we can make a positive difference, creating a sense of agency and purpose, even in times of difficulty.

Evidence suggests that if we could design systems to encourage more kindness and compassion – in areas like education, healthcare and workplaces – this could lead to better outcomes, including lower burnout, improved morale and greater resilience.

> **Making time for kindness**
>
> When we're constantly rushing from one thing to the next it becomes all too easy to overlook the needs of others. One of the biggest sources of accidental *unkind* behaviour is busyness.
>
> In a well-known study at Princeton, theology students had to give a talk. Some of them were asked to use the story of the Good Samaritan and some were also told they were running late. On their way to giving the talk, they passed a man in distress, which had been set up as part of the study. Whether they stopped to help him had little to do with their beliefs or the topic they were about to preach on. What really mattered was how much of a hurry they were in.
>
> This experiment shows that when we're pressed for time, our capacity for compassion can shrink. It's not that we stop caring, but that urgency narrows our attention and gives us tunnel vision. Slowing down, even slightly, creates the space to notice others. So if we want to be the kind of person who'll stop to help when needed, we need our lives to allow room for it.

Kindness is also contagious, and each time we do something kind it creates a ripple. Every small act has the potential to lift someone's mood and inspire them to be kinder too. Even seemingly minor gestures – like a smile or a few kind words – can spark a chain reaction of positive influences, both online and in everyday life.

Seeing the effects of our kindness not only inspires us to keep going, it also motivates others to follow our example. This creates a ripple that gets amplified, because witnessing – or even hearing about – acts of kindness often inspires others to act similarly. In our interconnected world, when we intentionally share kind acts or stories of generosity these have the potential to 'go viral' and spark even more kindness.

Studies show that each act of kindness can ripple through 'three degrees of separation' – from the original person to those around them and onwards to others. Some researchers estimate that one act of kindness can indirectly affect over 100 people. This ripple can spread across families, workplaces, communities and society as a whole. In workplaces, kindness leads to more cooperation and higher morale. In schools it reduces bullying and boosts wellbeing. And in wider society it encourages inclusion, reduces polarisation and strengthens social ties. Kindness isn't a luxury in tough times – it's what we need to get through them.

How to be kind

This all sounds great, but how do we actually go about putting kindness into action?

For me the starting point is simply the intention to do more small everyday acts – like calling a friend, smiling at a stranger, or taking a moment to chat with a neighbour or colleague. It's about approaching our interactions with a spirit of generosity.

We can be generous without needing to give money. We can give our time, attention, hospitality, creativity, friendship or emotional support. For example, we may not have cash to help someone on the street, but we can still be friendly and kind in other ways. As we saw earlier, active listening is one of the greatest gifts we can offer. When we truly listen, without judgement, it helps people feel seen and valued.

> **Reflect on kindness**
> A great way to focus more on kindness is to notice examples of giving and receiving help in daily life. Take a moment now to ask yourself:
> - Where do I see others helping?
> - Who helped me recently?
> - What opportunities will I have to help today?

Although I love the idea of *random* acts of kindness, we can also be *intentional* with our kind acts. There are countless ways to be kind, and when we start looking out for opportunities to help we usually spot even more chances. Here are five of my favourite everyday ways to put kindness into practice:

Look out for small moments to help

Start by deciding to keep a conscious lookout for small moments where you can be helpful. Hold the door open, say thank you or let someone merge in traffic. Offer to carry a bag, check in on a colleague or give a genuine compliment. Look up from your phone and see who might need a hand. Kindness doesn't have to be big or dramatic.

Be more Ted!

Have you seen the show *Ted Lasso*? One of the reasons I love Ted is because he brings genuine warmth and optimism to every situation. He chooses to interpret ambiguity positively and doesn't take himself too seriously. You can be more Ted by looking for the good in people, encouraging togetherness rather than division and being willing to laugh at yourself rather than taking offence or getting defensive.

💡 Create ripples

Help rebalance constant negativity in the media by sharing stories of kindness rather than of fear. Celebrate good deeds, retell stories about kind things people have done and choose *not* to amplify negativity in your messaging or posts. Stories of kindness can trigger oxytocin and feelings of 'elevation', which deepen your sense of connection to the people around you.

💡 Show your appreciation

Make a point of showing genuine appreciation to those who help. Gratitude isn't just vital for our own wellbeing, it's a gift we can offer to others too. So try to 'catch' people doing something kind and let them know it's valued. Make time in meetings for people to acknowledge each other's contributions. Write grateful notes for loved ones, friends or colleagues, and encourage others to show their thanks too.

💡 Cheer people on wholeheartedly

In a world addicted to competition and comparison, choose to share the joy of other people's triumphs. Too often we see other people's success as a threat, but a rising tide lifts all boats. So rather than subtly qualifying your support, minimising what they're doing or feeling envious, cheer them on wholeheartedly. Show you care and truly want the best for them.

The Platinum Rule

When I was a child we'd often be reminded of the Golden Rule: 'Do unto others as you would have them do unto you.' In other words, treat people how *you'd* like to be treated. This is great, but we can take this one stage further by focusing on our impact, not just our intentions. This is sometimes called the Platinum Rule: 'Treat others how *they* want to be treated.' To do this, we need to use our listening skills and invest time in getting to know the other person. Then we can tailor our actions to their needs and preferences.

> **→ What would a kind person do?**
>
> One helpful way I've found to encourage myself to be more compassionate is to consider in advance what a 'kind person' might do in a given situation – even if I'm not feeling particularly kind myself at the time.
>
> You can try this now by bringing to mind some situations you regularly find yourself in. Then, plan in advance what you'd like to do, or be like, in each situation. You can use this format to link your action to a specific location, time or event so you remember it:
>
> **I will [DO THIS] in [LOCATION] at [EVENT].**
>
> Here are some personal examples:
> - I will make a point of saying something appreciative when I see a loved one at the start or end of each day.
> - I will behave considerately when riding my bike and be tolerant when drivers, pedestrians or other cyclists do unexpected things.
> - I will make eye contact and smile at people I pass when out walking.
> - I will take time to say hello and thank people doing helpful work that often goes unnoticed, like cleaners or shop assistants.

> - I will pause before criticising or judging, and only share my frustration if it's helpful to the situation.
>
> I certainly don't always remember these. And even when I do, I often fall short. But keeping them in mind – and reminding myself regularly – has made me far less likely to miss everyday opportunities to be kind.
> What will your list include?

Choose being kind over being right

The author Dr Richard Carlson once wrote: 'Choose being kind over being right and you'll be right every time.' Although the scientist in me wanted to dismiss this as naive, it's now one of the ideas I find most helpful (but also challenging!) in daily life.

When I think another person has got something wrong – or especially if I've been wronged – I usually feel a strong urge to put things right. I might want to correct them or perhaps even 'win the argument'. Although this is sometimes appropriate, I've learned the hard way that it's often more about my own ego and doesn't necessarily help. By continuing to make my point, I may actually make things worse.

This raises an important question: What does it really mean to be 'right'? Does it have to be about proving a point? Or could it be about reaching the right outcome for the situation, taking into account the other person's needs and the potential upside of just letting something go?

Choosing 'kind' over 'right' means we prioritise empathy and understanding, rather than insisting on proving our point. Why? Because sometimes maintaining a good relationship or avoiding unnecessary conflict is more important than factual accuracy. I might technically be right in a disagreement with a friend, but pushing my point could harm our friendship.

This doesn't mean abandoning my values or beliefs. But it might mean listening more carefully, acknowledging their feelings or even agreeing to disagree. Letting go of the need to 'win' often leads to a calmer and more constructive outcome.

Choosing kindness is not about giving up on truth or compromising values, it's about recognising that *how* we communicate matters as much as what we say. Relationships tend to thrive more on connection than precision. In the heat of disagreement, a gentle or vulnerable response can lower defences and open hearts in ways that cold correctness rarely does. Often what people need most isn't the 'right' answer but to feel heard and respected.

> **→ Helped, heard or hugged?**
> When a loved one comes to you with a problem, the author Sahil Bloom suggests asking, 'Do you want to be helped, heard or hugged?'
>
> This simple question gives them the chance to say whether they want advice, to be listened to or simply to feel cared for. It allows you to respond in the way they need most in that moment.

Kindness to ourselves

As we saw in chapter six, many of us are kinder to others than we are to ourselves. Yet, as the saying goes, 'You can't pour from an empty cup.' In an aircraft we're told to put our own oxygen mask on before helping others – and for good reason. Likewise, being kind to others starts with being kind to ourselves. This includes giving ourselves permission to say no when needed and making time for rest and recovery. Learning to show ourselves the same warmth and care we offer to others is what allows kindness to be sustained over time.

When I looked into the research on kindness, I realised something I'd never recognised before. Asking for help from others isn't selfish, or a sign of weakness or neediness – it's an act of kindness. When we ask for support, this gives others the opportunity to experience the 'helper's high'. When we battle on all by ourselves we're not 'being strong', we're actually missing the chance to give others a happiness boost by helping out. So next time you're keeping a problem to yourself because you don't want to be a burden, remember that asking for help is good for the helper as well as for you.

We also need to ensure our kindness is healthy and appropriate. Being kind doesn't mean being passive or allowing ourselves to be mistreated, and it doesn't mean saying yes to everything. True kindness can be firm, assertive and even disruptive when it challenges injustice or ignorance. We can uphold boundaries and say no while still showing empathy and compassion – in fact, this is essential. Kindness includes honesty, courage, firmness and clarity.

'Loving kindness'

When I first came across the idea of 'loving-kindness meditation', I'll confess I thought it sounded a bit cheesy. It conjured up images of those embarrassing cards covered in hearts and cuddly bears – not really my sort of thing.

But everything changed when I had the chance to meet and learn from Matthieu Ricard. Matthieu had been a scientist but chose to leave his career in molecular genetics to become a Buddhist monk, living in the Himalayas. He was the Dalai Lama's French translator for decades and is one of the wisest and most warm-hearted people I've ever had the privilege to spend time with.

Matthieu taught me that loving-kindness begins with a simple wish: that all beings, without exception, may find happiness and be free from suffering. Rather than being something vague or idealistic, loving-kindness is also a skill that can be strengthened through meditation. Regular daily practice can change the brain and deepen altruism and emotional resilience. Matthieu has helped demonstrate this in practice, working with leading neuroscientists who spent years studying him using MRI scanners. They observed the remarkable impact of this benevolent attitude on his brain.

Building this skill can also help us navigate challenges. For example, practising loving-kindness helps to protect caregivers from burnout. It also helps us respond to hostility with firm kindness – standing our ground but without animosity. This can help us to de-escalate conflict and preserve our inner peace.

> **→ Loving-kindness meditation**
>
> This is a form of mindfulness that involves sending warm thoughts to yourself and others. Think of it like giving yourself a mental hug and then extending that warmth outwards. Although it has roots in Buddhist tradition, it's a secular practice anyone can do, regardless of their beliefs. You can also do it anywhere – in bed, out walking, in the kitchen or even in a difficult meeting or while stuck in traffic!
>
> **Step 1: Breathe**. Take a few deep breaths to help you relax.

Step 2: Inner warmth. Begin by directing a feeling of warmth towards yourself. Quietly repeat kind phrases such as: 'May I be happy', 'May I be healthy' and 'May I be free from suffering.' Don't worry too much about the exact words, the important thing is sincerely wishing good things for yourself.

Step 3: Outer warmth. Bring to mind a loved one or someone you care about and send the same warm wishes towards them, repeating: 'May you be happy', 'May you be healthy' and 'May you be free from suffering.'

Step 4: Wider warmth. Now try expanding your compassion outwards to all beings. You might imagine warm light radiating from inside you and spreading in all directions. Repeat your phrases, this time for everyone: 'May they be happy', 'May they be healthy' and 'May they be free from suffering.'

Make life happier, for everyone

The real message of this book is that true fulfilment comes not just from seeking happiness for ourselves but from a genuine desire to bring happiness to others. This is the core idea the Dalai Lama shared when I had the honour of hosting him at a big event in London. In our self-centred, consumerist society, we often see compassion as burdensome or naive. But the Dalai Lama reminds us that compassion is deeply rewarding. Rather than being a sacrifice or a sign of weakness, it can be one of the most profound sources of emotional strength and meaning. This is how we make life happier, for everyone – including ourselves.

> *'If you want others to be happy, practise compassion. If you want to be happy, practise compassion.'*
>
> — **The Dalai Lama**

Unfortunately we've adopted systems and behaviours that often undermine our natural tendency for cooperation. This starts in schools, where the relentless focus on attainment teaches young people that success is about doing better than others. It continues in consumer culture, which encourages the accumulation of designer brands and luxury goods as markers of success. It's present in our workplaces, where employees are pitted against each other for performance-related rewards. And it underpins the self-serving perspectives that make it so hard to overcome major societal challenges such as climate change.

This 'get ahead or lose out' ethos not only fails to bring out the best in us, it's also deeply flawed. In schools, helping young people develop social and emotional skills doesn't just enhance wellbeing, it's also been shown to boost attainment. In organisations, research by Adam Grant, professor of management at Wharton, shows that 'givers' – people who help others without seeking anything in return – are more successful in the long term than 'takers', who focus on maximising benefits for themselves.

At a societal level, the World Happiness Report consistently finds that two of the strongest drivers of national wellbeing are social support and generosity. Our success as a society depends on whether we see each other as a source of help rather than a threat. That's why it matters that we take time to connect with and support those around us – at work, in the shops, on the train and in our neighbourhood. These small moments of friendliness and care aren't trivial and meaningless – they're the beating heart of a good society.

Kindness strengthens social bonds, reduces hostility and helps to create communities where people look out for each other. It can bridge divides, encourage conversations and open up space for collaboration – even across ideological or political lines. A culture of kindness softens 'us vs them' mentalities, replacing judgement with understanding and respect. As kindness becomes more visible it can even shift social norms, making compassion and generosity feel more like the norm than the exception.

Above all, happiness isn't an individual pursuit – it's something we create together.

SPREAD KINDNESS: CHAPTER SUMMARY

Ask yourself:
❓ **What's the most compassionate way I can respond to this?**

Don't just:
✘ Focus only on what's best for you rather than helping others.

Try this out:
✔ Discover the joy of helping and notice how kindness ripples out.

Chapter Nineteen:

Trust People

Do I see and encourage the good in others?

'We'd never let her go by herself, anything could happen! You can't trust people.'

I was really surprised when my friend said this. Despite living nearby and being similar in many ways, it suddenly hit me that our worldviews were different – and in ways that had big implications for our lives and our loved ones.

Kate and I had invited local friends over for dinner. We had young families at the time and the chat had inevitably turned to kids – including whether we allowed our 10-year-olds to go out by themselves. In this one short conversation it became clear we had very different ideas about parenting, especially in terms of risks and the messages we pass on to our children.

As a child growing up in the 1980s I vividly remember the TV adverts and school posters warning us about 'Stranger Danger'. Although well-intentioned, I've long wondered what the ripple effects of these campaigns have been for wider society. How many frightened children grew up to be frightened neighbours and frightened parents?

Thankfully, I never really bought into Stranger Danger. Although I appreciate how fortunate I was to grow up around trustworthy adults, I just don't think it's a message that reflects reality for most of us. Yes there are the occasional horrific stories, but statistically there are far more important things to worry about – like crossing roads safely. In fact, children are at a far higher risk of being struck by lightning than being abducted by strangers. It's scary, but extremely rare.

Moreover, I believe most people are basically good. So when they were young we told our kids that if they were ever in trouble it's okay to ask a nearby adult. This is far more likely to be helpful than dangerous. We did of course encourage them to be streetwise and use their intuition about who felt safe to approach, but we didn't want them to grow up scared of others. Most strangers are just people you haven't met yet.

So this is where that dinner party conversation revealed a disconnect with our friends, who seemed to have passed on the Stranger Danger message. I respect their choices and recognise that our differing approaches reflect our backgrounds. Yet I couldn't help feeling that, for their kids, seeing the world with a little more hope might have helped them grow up with a greater sense of confidence and possibility.

Am I too trusting? Well, you could certainly make a case for being more protective. And like everything in life, there are risks. But I'm with Satish Kumar on this. Let me explain.

Satish is an Indian-born activist and author, renowned for his work as a campaigner and environmentalist. In the 1960s he set off on a 'Peace Pilgrimage' that took him on a walk from India to the United States, passing through Afghanistan, the Soviet Union and Europe. His purpose was to deliver a message of nonviolence to leaders, including at the United Nations. As you can imagine he encountered a lot of unfamiliar people and risks along the way.

I've met Satish on various occasions, but the moment that really stays with me is when we were on stage together after the screening of a film he'd featured in. Satish was explaining how he chooses to trust people as much as possible and said:

'Yes, sometimes I get let down. Every now and then I have a wallet stolen or something goes wrong. But having these small problems occasionally is *so* much better than living every day in fear and assuming people are out to get me.'

I think he's right. And as we'll see, our approach to trust has profound implications, not just for our own wellbeing but for our ability to build a thriving society.

What is trust, really?

Trust is the belief that someone or something can be relied on. It's vital for relationships and a foundation for cooperation. And as our lives become ever more complex and uncertain, trust feels more essential and more at risk than ever. As author and trust expert Rachel Botsman puts it, 'Trust is a confident relationship with the unknown.' I like to think of it as the hidden glue that holds society together.

The sense that we can depend on each other lays the groundwork for all our social interactions, from our general feeling of safety to our moments of closest intimacy. We naturally develop trust with people who show up for us and can be relied on: family members, partners, friends or colleagues. But in many situations, we also trust strangers – like doctors, teachers, taxi drivers or first-time babysitters, who we expect to follow social norms and treat us fairly.

When people trust each other they're more willing to cooperate and tend to achieve more than they could alone. They also feel safer and can devote more energy to the greater good rather than self-protection. But when trust is missing or betrayed, relationships struggle to survive.

> **The science of trust**
>
> Research suggests that our brains are naturally wired for trust. In experiments, when people trust another player in a game to behave fairly, the parts of the brain linked to decision-making and positive emotions become more active. In other words, trusting someone can actually feel rewarding.
>
> Professor Paul J. Zak has studied this in depth, showing how brain chemistry shapes human connection. When someone trusts us – or acts in a trustworthy way – our brains release oxytocin, a hormone that increases our willingness to reciprocate and behave kindly. Zak argues that this provides a biological basis for morality, nudging us towards cooperation, fairness and empathy.

For decades, researchers have measured general levels of trust by asking a question like this:

'Generally speaking, would you say that most people can be trusted, or that you can't be too careful in dealing with people?'

How would you answer?

It turns out that levels of trust vary widely, not only between countries but also across different social contexts and over time. In many Western democracies, including the US and UK, social trust has declined since the mid-to-late 20th century. In contrast, trust has remained high and stable in many Nordic countries, such as Finland, Norway and Sweden. This is often linked to strong welfare systems, effective governance and relatively low levels of inequality. In low- and middle-income countries, trust levels vary more widely and are often shaped by factors such as economic instability, conflict and corruption.

To me, the decline of trust in many advanced economies is deeply concerning. But the real tragedy may be this: when it comes to trust, we're falling for fake news. Research consistently shows that people are far kinder and more trustworthy than we expect – and that misunderstanding has real consequences for our happiness.

A remarkable study published in *Science* illustrates this beautifully. Behavioural economist Alain Cohn and colleagues 'lost' over 17,000 wallets across 355 cities in 40 countries. Each wallet contained keys, contact details and varying amounts of cash. The aim was to see how honest people really are when no one's watching. The results were both surprising and hopeful. Contrary to predictions from traditional economic theory, the more money the wallet contained, the more likely it was to be returned.

In follow-up studies, researchers asked people how likely they thought it was that a lost wallet would be returned by a stranger. In every country studied, people significantly underestimated how honest others would be. For example, around two-thirds of wallets dropped across North American cities were returned – double what people predicted.

It seems we are far too pessimistic about one another – and this matters. Believing that people can be trusted turns out to be a powerful predictor of wellbeing. According to the World Happiness Report 2025, having confidence that a lost wallet would be returned is associated with higher life satisfaction – with an effect around seven times larger than that of doubling your income.

Why has trust been falling?

At Action for Happiness, we once commissioned a UK-wide study comparing the values people experience in their local communities with their perceptions of the UK as a whole. When people talked about their local lives they described many positive values: family, friendship, helpfulness, care for others and community services. They also mentioned some challenges – such as concerns about drug use or the future – but overall the picture was surprisingly upbeat. By contrast, when the same people were asked about wider society it was as if they were describing a completely different country. Responses were dominated by negative themes, including crime, violence, bureaucracy, corruption, wasted resources and apathy. Sound familiar?

But hang on a second. This was a nationally representative survey covering the whole country. So how could such a bleak national picture be made up of so many relatively positive local experiences? It just didn't add up. I've since seen similar patterns in various other studies. Put simply, we tend to have a far worse view of the places and people we *don't* know directly. Our perceptions of society as a whole are shaped less by our own experience and more by headline-driven news and attention-grabbing social media, which tend to amplify the negatives.

Although the media plays a big role, it also goes deeper than this. As Jon Yates notes in his insightful book *Fractured: Why Our Societies Are Coming Apart and How we put Them Back Together Again*, we all have a 'people like me' bias. We tend to spend most of our time with people who are similar to us in terms of background and beliefs. This is understandable, but it's also a missed opportunity.

Having more diverse social ties has been shown to increase

happiness, reduce stress and even to lower the risk of heart disease. So when it comes to building – or rebuilding – trust, a great place to start is what Yates calls our 'common life'. This means giving more priority to shared institutions and rituals – like clubs, community events or local groups – that bring us face to face with people who are different from us.

> ⭐ 'Trust is earned in the smallest of moments. It is earned not through heroic deeds, or even highly visible actions, but through paying attention, listening, and gestures of genuine care and connection.'
>
> **– Brené Brown**

Why trust helps and cynicism harms

The benefits of trust extend across society. Economies flourish when we believe agreements and contracts will be honoured. Neighbourhoods are safer when local residents trust each other. And studies show that people who live in high-trust societies tend to experience less stress, live longer and report greater wellbeing. This doesn't mean we should take unnecessary risks. For example, despite living in a safe neighbourhood I'm still aware of crime locally and we're careful to lock our doors.

So trust isn't naive optimism, it's more like an invisible web that holds our communities together. When we trust others we take a small leap of faith in their good intentions – and that leap often pays off. In high-trust environments people are more willing to share resources, cooperate and play their part. They're more likely to return lost wallets and help their neighbours. As Satish reminded me, trust frees us from the burden of constant suspicion and creates space for connection and generosity.

Yet all too often, we assume the worst and slip into cynicism about people's motives and the state of the world. Dr Jamil Zaki, a professor of psychology at Stanford University and director of their neuroscience lab, has studied this closely. When I met him to discuss his work on hope he explained how cynicism is often glamorised as a sign of intelligence or moral superiority.

Zaki's research shows that cynicism comes at a cost. Cynical people tend to perform less well on cognitive tests and are less accurate at judging others. Their assumptions tend to blind them to reality. Media consumption can also further skew our perceptions, making the world seem harsher than it really is.

> ⭐ 'Cynicism is not a neutral position – and although it asks almost nothing of us, it is highly infectious and unbelievably destructive.'
>
> **– Nick Cave**

We often underestimate the goodness of others, especially those we disagree with – and this fuels misunderstanding and division. By contrast, trust can create a virtuous cycle. When we show faith in people it inspires them to live up to that trust. The greatest risk may be not that we trust too much but that we miss the chance to bring out the best in each other.

> **→ Trust loudly**
>
> To counter cynicism, Dr Zaki offers one of my favourite ideas for building trust. It's both simple and radical: trust loudly.
>
> Rather than quietly hoping others will rise to the occasion we can openly express our confidence in them.

For example, I might say to my daughter, 'I believe in you', or to a new team member, 'I'm trusting you with this because I know you can handle it.'

When we give responsibility to others and show our faith in them it increases accountability and strengthens relationships. It also encourages them to live up to the trust we've placed in them. Zaki calls this 'earned trust' and it's a powerful way of drawing out the best in others.

Who will you trust loudly this week?

Start by being trustworthy

If we want a more trusting world, the best place to start is by being trustworthy ourselves. We can't control what others do, but we can choose how we behave.

→ How to be trustworthy

Here are six top tips for how to be more trustworthy in relationships:

1. Follow through. Trust is built on keeping small promises. Show up on time and reply when you say you will.

2. Keep confidentiality. Trust is fragile and hard to rebuild once broken. When someone shares something in confidence, treat it like treasure.

3. Be consistent. Trust grows through steady, predictable behaviour. Say what you mean and do what you say.

4. Tell the truth. Trust requires honesty and integrity, especially when it's hard. Don't just avoid lies, have the courage to be transparent.

> **5. Own your mistakes**. Trust requires accountability. Admit when you've messed up – it doesn't make you weak, it makes you human.
>
> **6. Integrity over self-interest**. Trust reflects our values. Do what's right, not just what benefits you – especially when no one's watching.

Who to trust

Trust always involves a degree of vulnerability. When we trust a friend to turn up and help we take the small risk that they may not follow through. When we trust a romantic partner to remain faithful we accept the possibility of being hurt.

Trusting people we don't know may seem ill-advised, yet it's something millions of us do every day. In general, I believe in starting from a position of goodwill and giving people the benefit of the doubt. But trusting wisely also means paying attention to the signals people show us. A helpful way to do this is to look for patterns of behaviour. We can start with a small step of trust and see how they respond. We can ask others' opinions. We can notice how they behave in different situations. Trust is something we can offer and others can gradually earn through their actions.

> **→ Can I trust them?**
> Here are five top tips for working out who to trust:
> **1. Actions over words**. People show reliability through what they *do*, not just what they say. Look for signs of follow-through – do they show up when they say they will? Do they keep their word?

2. Notice how they treat others. Most people are kind by default, but patterns matter. How do they speak to colleagues, service staff or people they disagree with? Warmth and respect are good indications of character.

3. Look for consistency. Trust grows through steady behaviour over time. One lovely gesture is nice, but consistency reveals more. Do they behave similarly in other contexts, especially when under pressure?

4. Start small. Trust doesn't have to be a big leap. Begin with a small request or low-risk situation. If they handle it with care and respect then that's a good sign you can build on.

5. See how they repair. Everyone slips up. What matters is how people respond. Trustworthy people take responsibility, apologise and try to make amends rather than deny, deflect or blame others.

Rachel Botsman, a leading speaker and author on trust, has a helpful idea which she calls the 'trust pause'. The idea is that when making decisions we remember to take a moment of reflection to ask, 'What trust signals am I seeing? Do I need more information?'

I like this idea of pausing. Maybe we can think of trust as another of our skills for living mindfully – one that we can develop through awareness and practice. Rather than rushing in or just relying on gut feelings, we can slow down and become more conscious about how we give trust and how we earn it too.

> 'The best way to find out if you can trust somebody is to trust them.'
>
> **– Ernest Hemingway**

Trust and boundaries

Being trusting doesn't mean being boundary-less. In fact, having clear boundaries strengthens trust because it creates honesty, safety and mutual respect. When you agree to something, you might say 'but here's what that needs to look like for me' and explain any limits you have. By setting firm boundaries and demonstrating self-respect your trust becomes less fragile and you can offer it more genuinely without the fear of being taken advantage of or becoming overwhelmed.

When people are distrustful it's often understandable. Many trust issues stem from early relationships, especially for people who learned their needs wouldn't be met or were frequently let down. People who have experienced trauma often find it difficult to trust, even with loved ones. Anxiety can also make trust harder. So if you struggle to trust others, you may well have good reasons. Working with a therapist or counsellor to explore the roots of these patterns can be helpful. Even small steps towards rebuilding trust can improve wellbeing and lead to healthier and more secure relationships.

When trust has broken down in a relationship it can feel hard to rebuild. But it's possible and the benefits can be significant, especially when the relationship really matters. The starting point is open and honest communication about what happened. If both people are willing to repair things they can start small and gradually increase the level of trust and vulnerability they share. Once people demonstrate trustworthiness in small ways, the next steps become much easier.

Trusting ourselves

We can't fully trust others unless we also trust ourselves. In fact, self-trust is a foundation for healthy relationships. The mindfulness expert Jon Kabat-Zinn says that trusting ourselves begins with being present and honouring our thoughts and feelings, even when they're difficult. They're not enemies to be conquered, but messengers to be heard. So it's back to those awareness skills again!

When we develop the courage to sit with our experiences – pleasant or painful – without judgement, we discover that we can handle far more than we imagined. We learn to meet each moment with curiosity and openness rather than fear or self-doubt. And as our self-trust grows it becomes easier to trust others and the world around us too. By letting go of control and choosing to be present we uncover a quiet strength: whatever arises, we'll be okay.

> ### → Ways to build and encourage trust
> Here are some practical ways you can help to create more trust and encourage others to be more trusting and trustworthy:
>
> **1. Trust loudly.** Tell people you trust them and let others see you extend trust. This encourages them to act in trustworthy ways and inspires others to trust more too.
>
> **2. Be fully present.** Give people your attention, make eye contact and use open body language. This helps people feel seen and signals approachability.
>
> **3. Assume good intent.** Choose to believe the best about others rather than jumping to judgement. This is how most of us like to be treated.
>
> **4. Get round the table.** Make time for shared meals.

Eating together encourages relaxed conversation and helps lower our defences.

5. Meet people not like you. Spend time in places where you'll mix with people from different backgrounds. Familiarity breaks down stereotypes and builds trust.

6. Use social media differently. Share hopeful stories and resist the urge to pile on. This reminds others the internet can be an encouraging place.

7. Only positive gossip. When someone isn't in the room, highlight their good points and stick up for them. This nudges others to do the same.

8. Let people surprise you. Stay open to the possibility that people may exceed your expectations. Trust grows when we leave room for others to grow.

Even tiny actions can trigger wider ripple effects we may never fully see. But trust me – your actions really do make a difference.

Towards a more trusting world

If we want a happier world, we need high-trust societies. As we saw earlier, trust has fallen in recent decades, especially in the West. But it's not all bad news. Recent data from the British Social Attitudes survey indicates that trust has bounced back to the highest level since 1998, with around half of people now saying that, generally speaking, others can be trusted.

Individually, we may not be able to do much to change national levels of trust, but it's still important to understand what helps, so we encourage these locally and vote for policies that support them.

Here are some wider changes I'd love to see that can help strengthen trust:
- More encouragement and opportunities for volunteering
- More public recognition for people doing good things
- More shared spaces where people can meet beyond their usual circles
- More development of social and emotional skills in schools
- More transparency in government and business
- More humanising and collaboration across divides
- More careful regulation to keep online spaces healthy
- More solutions-focused journalism
- More focus on fairness and strong social safety nets
- More opportunities for local communities to make decisions together.

> 'Rich or poor, living in a trusting society simply makes people happier.'
> – **Paul J. Zak**

A major 2025 review published in *Psychological Bulletin* analysed studies involving more than 2.5 million participants and found a consistent link between trust and happiness. Higher levels of trust are associated with greater happiness and the reverse is true as well, with happier people being more likely to trust others. This pattern holds across cultures, suggesting it may be universal.

Trust lightens our mental load. When we're constantly questioning whether the world around us can be trusted it creates a kind of background noise that wears us down. Trusting more creates space for everyday joy instead of living with constant vigilance. It means less time second-guessing and more energy for being present and making the most of opportunities.

We may not be able to shift the whole culture around us but we can still influence levels of trust. By being trustworthy ourselves, learning how and when to trust, and modelling these behaviours, we help to shape the world around us. And we also pass these habits on to the next generation – the focus of our next chapter.

> **TRUST PEOPLE: CHAPTER SUMMARY**
>
> Ask yourself:
> ❓ **How can I encourage trustworthy behaviour?**
>
> Don't just:
> ✗ Assume everyone is always out to get you.
>
> Try this out:
> ✔ Trust people: you'll find they are surprisingly trustworthy.

Chapter Twenty:

Raise Resilience

How can I help the next generation thrive?

'She did *what*?!'

We'd just had a tech-related parenting disaster and I was mortified.

Although this was before the big rise in public concern about the impact of devices on kids' wellbeing, Kate and I had tried to stay firm and not allow ours to have smartphones until they were at 'big school'.

Having recently finished primary school, our daughter had finally got her first phone and was taking early steps in a new world of online messaging. With hindsight, we should have seen the warning signs. When we got back from our family summer trip she'd opened her phone to find over 1,000 unread messages on her class group chat. Yet what happened next was still a shock.

A local mum contacted us out of the blue saying her son had been the victim of cyberbullying and our daughter was involved. I was stunned. Surely there must be some mistake? It just didn't fit with the kind-hearted girl we knew. But sure enough, someone had created a group chat to talk badly about a boy from her class who they'd disliked. And she'd actively joined in and posted a really unkind photo and message, which inevitably found its way back to the boy. My shock turned to a mix of anger, sadness and embarrassment – we had to put this right.

Inevitably the conversation with our daughter was painful. We were angry, but we also tried to listen. She explained that the boy had been mean to her and she'd been relieved to see others in the group felt similarly. To her credit, she accepted what she'd done was wrong and hurtful. She apologised to him and went along with her punishment of being grounded for a while, with no phone! We told her how upset we felt, but also reassured her that we still loved her and things were going to be okay. We all make mistakes, it's how we respond to them that matters.

This is just one of countless times I've felt insecure, flawed or guilty as a parent. Although I didn't see it clearly then, this moment touched on many of the fundamentals of raising happy, well-adjusted children: unconditional love, clear boundaries and the space to explore, fail and grow.

The world they're growing up in

Growing up has always been tough. Yet I look back on my own childhood with a feeling that life was just much simpler. Today's youngsters are coming of age in a world that's more complex and uncertain than ever, with new challenges on their path to adulthood. Despite being more 'connected', many young people are spending less time with friends in person and taking longer to reach traditional markers of adulthood – like going out unsupervised, dating, learning to drive or getting their first paid job.

Compared to previous generations, teens appear to be engaging in fewer risky behaviours but are more worried and perfectionistic.

In this chapter we'll look at the fundamentals that children need to live happy and meaningful lives. We can't develop these qualities on their behalf but we can help them grow through our love, challenge and modelling.

> **→ We're all in this together**
> The material in this chapter may feel most relevant for parents or carers trying to raise and support young people. But even if you don't have young people in your life right now, I hope you'll read on – or at least check out the part titled 'It takes a village'. Helping the next generation learn how to live well benefits everyone.

People tend to assume that if they can protect their children from difficulties and provide them with material things and the best opportunities to get ahead they'll be happier. Although well-intentioned, this isn't the best approach. Our role is *not* to create short-term happiness by giving children everything they want or preventing them from failing. It's much better to help them build the skills themselves to lead a good life. This includes coping with difficult emotions and being resilient when things go wrong.

As we saw in part one, there are lots of practical skills we can learn to be happier, so this is teachable in the sense that we can model good wellbeing habits for young people, such as self-awareness and kindness. These aren't side topics or luxuries – they're every bit as important as learning to read, write or add up. The earlier we start to build these foundations the better. For example, family meals, shared experiences and honest conversations can help to build healthy relationship skills from the very earliest years.

We can also teach children about concepts that are proven to support emotional resilience, such as the 'growth mindset'.

> ### → Encouraging a growth mindset
> Stanford University psychologist Carol Dweck distinguishes between two different mindsets:
> - **Fixed mindset** – believing your abilities are static
> - **Growth mindset** – believing abilities can be developed with effort
>
> When young people believe in their potential to grow – rather than being stuck with a fixed set of talents or intelligence – this empowers them to try new things, persevere and recover from setbacks. Dweck emphasises that how we speak to children makes a profound difference. It can often be much more helpful to focus on effort rather than achievement.
>
> When you praise achievement (e.g. 'you're so smart'), you encourage a fixed mindset, where kids fear failure or stick to what they already feel good at. But when you praise effort (e.g. 'you worked so hard at this') you build their belief that they can improve and their willingness to keep trying.
>
> Having a growth mindset helps children view mistakes as opportunities for growth, rather than as reflections of their limits or inner worth. We can also teach them about their brain's neuroplasticity, helping to reinforce the idea that their brain can grow and change through continued effort. We're not trying to encourage false positivity – we're acknowledging their struggle and reinforcing the belief that progress is possible with persistence.

As well as supporting their academic development we can also cultivate character strengths that help young people thrive and contribute. Angela Duckworth, the renowned psychologist and author of *Grit*, explained to me how she categorises these as strengths of *heart* (such as honesty and kindness), strengths of *mind* (such as curiosity and openness) and strengths of *will* (such as self-control and perseverance). Importantly, these are not fixed at birth or unchangeable – they can be intentionally developed, much like our intellect or physical strength.

> 'It's not our job to toughen our children up to face a cruel and heartless world. It's our job to raise children who will make the world a little less cruel and heartless.'
>
> **– L.R. Knost**

What children and young people need to thrive

Parenting advice tends to be full of platitudes and contradictions, and each child is unique and every family is different. But I believe there are three core 'nutrients' children need to grow up happy and well-adjusted, beyond the physical basics of food and shelter. I call these unconditional love, challenge and boundaries.

Nutrient 1: Unconditional love

The absolute foundation of any child's development is to feel loved unconditionally. Families come in all shapes and sizes and a child's specific home situation is less important than having at least one primary carer who consistently shows them genuine warmth and affection. Harvard professor Arthur C. Brooks drew my attention to a major study showing that parental warmth and affection explain a surprisingly large share of the differences in children's psychological adjustment.

When kids grow up knowing that someone loves them completely and unwaveringly this gives them a secure platform from which to explore, take risks and grow. In years gone by, parenting experts warned against 'spoiling' children with affection, but we now know that having a deep sense of being loved and accepted helps young people develop the self-worth and emotional stability they need to flourish.

As Angela Duckworth says, 'You cannot love your children too much.'

Nutrient 2: Challenge

However, love alone is not enough. Children also need challenge. Real wellbeing doesn't come from kids having an easy life or being protected from hardship. If we make life too easy or comfortable they never learn how to overcome difficulties. Instead we can help them step into discomfort with the right support behind them.

It's natural to want to keep our children safe from harm, but our culture of overprotection can undermine their resilience, depriving them of the little hardships that build strength. As the social psychologist Jonathan Haidt says, we need to 'prepare the child for the road, not the road for the child.'

We can do this by exposing young people to new experiences and giving them greater freedom and responsibility – the earlier the better. We can ask them to help out at home and encourage them to start taking on jobs and earn money. We can nudge them to pursue effortful, meaningful goals – for example through sport, music, study or volunteering. We can allow them to take appropriate risks, to try things out – and, yes, to fail at things too.

Through navigating challenging situations children can learn to reframe negative thoughts and difficulties. In his research on learned optimism, Professor Martin Seligman showed that when young people view setbacks as opportunities to grow they're better placed to navigate future challenges. This is about more than just resilience to cope and survive, it's developing what author Nassim Taleb calls 'antifragility' – the ability to grow stronger from manageable stress and challenge.

Nutrient 3: Boundaries

Challenge involves freedom to explore and take risks. But children thrive most when they can do this in a way that still feels safe. When we set clear boundaries, with warmth and honesty, this gives kids a sense of safety and structure, even if they push back. Within the safety of these boundaries they then have opportunities to experiment, play, fail, learn and develop autonomy. Wise boundaries are an expression of love, even when they appear limiting.

As kids develop into teens, one inevitable set of boundaries relates to them being out alone and staying safe. We can give them freedom to go out but with clear agreements on curfew time and checking in if plans change. Once they show their ability to be trusted and stay in touch we can gradually expand their autonomy and relax the rules.

Other examples of healthy boundaries could include the freedom to use phones but with limits on screen time, like avoiding use at mealtimes or in bedrooms overnight. Or ensuring homework gets done before gaming or socialising. We can also set important boundaries around how to communicate, for example, being free to disagree so long as this is respectful, rather than shouting or hurling insults. Boundaries can also be two-way, for example, parents agreeing to respect their child's space and privacy while also maintaining the right to intervene if their safety or wellbeing is at risk.

In each case the aim is to offer autonomy in a way that builds self-management skills – with the incentive of more freedom if things go well.

Learning the hard way

When I was growing up I used to disappear for hours, going out for adventures with a friend called Adam. He lived round the corner and was a bit of a bad influence. I remember three incidents – and my mum's response to them – that taught me invaluable lessons.

One time we invented a daft game called 'back-wheel tag', which inevitably lasted only as long as it took for me to ride my BMX into Adam's back wheel, at which point I went flying dramatically over my handlebars, ending up in a heap on the tarmac covered in cuts. When I stumbled home bleeding, Mum calmly patched me up and reminded me to cycle safely. She continued to let me go out on my bike but gave me a clear instruction: not to cross the busy main road without an adult. I promised not to.

Then one day Adam invited me to watch an Indiana Jones movie at Neil's house, which was across that main road. I knew I shouldn't but I couldn't resist. The film was fun, but I felt guilty and when Mum found out she was furious. I'd really let her down. There were consequences and I wasn't allowed out on my bike for a while.

So instead we made catapults and enjoyed firing stones at trees. After a while Adam suggested shooting them across the road to see if we could hit cars or passers-by without being seen. At first I was keen, but the moment we nearly hit something I felt a strong instinct that 'this isn't right'. I found the courage to tell Adam I didn't want to damage things or hurt people and I walked away.

Each of these little moments really says less about me and more about my parents. Mum showed a blend of love, patience and courage to let me fail and learn, while also modelling a sense of right and wrong that helped me develop my own values. I was given clear boundaries and, although these felt frustrating, they communicated to me that I was cared for but also that I was expected to take responsibility.

The dangers of overparenting

Recently there's been a rise in so-called 'helicopter parenting', where we hover over our kids like a helicopter, constantly monitoring and intervening. Although well-meaning, this approach can limit a child's development. When I met education expert and former Stanford dean Julie Lythcott-Haims, she described this over-involvement as a major factor behind the rising anxiety and lack of self-sufficiency she sees in students.

Children need real-world experiences, including unsupervised play, independent problem-solving and risk-taking. This can feel uncomfortable for us as adults. But that instinct to swoop in to rescue them in any anxiety-inducing situation robs them of the chance to grow. We also don't need to protect children from experiencing uncomfortable feelings. Research from UCL suggests that when schoolchildren are taught that stress and sadness are normal parts of life, they tend to have better mental health.

Kids don't step into adulthood on their eighteenth birthday. They grow into it gradually as they develop the confidence and skills to handle life's ups and downs. Rather than trying to control outcomes or prevent all hardship we need to nurture their sense of agency and gradually hand over responsibility, starting early. Encouraging independence starts with simple tasks in childhood and builds from there. We can offer age-appropriate challenges, from putting toys away and feeding pets to getting themselves ready for school and helping with chores around the home. In other words, they need to learn how to do things that aren't easy.

The trick is to let them wrestle with challenges without stepping in too soon while also being supportive. We're not disengaging, we're letting go – and showing love through empowerment as much as protection. By supporting rather than controlling we help them to think for themselves and take responsibility.

When it comes to work and study we naturally want to protect our kids from being overwhelmed or chasing unattainable perfection. We often say, 'Just do the best you can', but this can feel vague or even unhelpful. Instead, we can say, 'This matters, so try as hard as you can', while reminding them they're loved regardless of the outcome. Effort and persistence matter, so we can give them space to experience setbacks and try again.

> **Tips for raising happy children**

Here are some ways to help nurture secure and resilient little humans:

- **Love without conditions**. This is the emotional bedrock for their wellbeing.
- **Provide boundaries**. Children feel safe when there are clear, consistent limits.
- **Let them play and mess up**. This builds creativity, problem-solving and resilience. Resist the urge to rush in and rescue.

- **Shape their inner voice**. How we speak to our children becomes the way they speak to themselves. Focus on warmth and encouragement.
- **Praise effort, not outcomes**. Recognising persistence, rather than labelling them as 'clever' or 'good', helps to build a growth mindset.
- **Model emotional intelligence**. By naming and managing our own feelings we teach them how to do the same for themselves.
- **Look for what's good**. Having a regular time to reflect on good things builds a natural sense of gratitude and appreciation.
- **Ask them to help**. Children like to feel useful. When we give them age-appropriate responsibilities it builds confidence and character.

Although it's not right for everyone, one great way to boost family wellbeing is to get a dog. Learning to look after a pet helps kids learn responsibility and confidence – and it's a great way to get them outside more too. Our golden retriever Charlie has been a huge source of joy for our kids growing up with him. Few things teach children as much about affection and kindness as loving a dog. Pets also offer children a chance to see the cycle of life, from puppy or kitten through to adulthood and eventually saying goodbye to a much-loved companion. I have such fond memories of Wanda, the dog who was part of our family for most of my first two decades.

Teenage years

I'll always remember the classic Harry Enfield comedy sketch where Kevin turns thirteen and immediately switches from being a polite and sweet-natured boy to a sullen and grumpy teenager. 'It's so unfair!' Adolescence is often seen as a time when we just need to weather the inevitable storm, and to some extent that's true.

My own teenagers have all had challenging moments, from extremes of anger and anxiety to euphoric, alcohol-fuelled parties. From first boyfriends and girlfriends to breakups and broken hearts. From days stuck alone in bedrooms to nights out where they didn't come home. But these years are also an amazing time of growth and opportunity, and being a dad to teens has brought some of the most memorable moments of unexpected learning and laughter that I've ever experienced.

As kids get older the role of a parent evolves, from being their 'manager' to becoming more of a 'mentor'. Yet their need for love and connection remains. Even the coolest and most self-reliant teens still want to feel loved, listened to and accepted. They may try to push us away, but they don't want us to fully let go. As Julie Lythcott-Haims says: 'Be their base, not their boss.'

The active-listening skills we covered earlier are vital here. Teenagers want to be heard, not fixed. As they start to develop their own daily habits we can also encourage them to adopt many of the actions we looked at in part one, including mindfulness and gratitude practices or healthy habits around food and sleep.

As parents we don't need to be perfect. In fact it's vital that we show vulnerability, admit our mistakes and model self-care.

→ Tips for growing teenagers

Here are some ways to help them grow and take responsibility as they get older:

- **Keep loving unconditionally** (even when they push you away). Be the stable backdrop to all the messiness, especially when they seem distant.
- **More autonomy** (still with boundaries). Teens thrive on a mix of structure and freedom, so let them test limits and involve them in decisions.
- **Encourage antifragility**. They don't need to be protected from discomfort, so let them experience uncertainty and challenge, with support if needed.
- **Co-create digital rules**. Teens need to navigate the digital world, so rather than imposing rules, help them develop their own healthy screen habits.
- **Respect their identity journey**. They're figuring out who they are, so allow them to express themselves. Be curious rather than judgemental.
- **Talk about feelings and choices**. Teenage brains are laying foundations for adulthood, so have conversations about emotions, relationships and values.
- **Focus on character over results**. Success is more than grades, so praise courage, effort, kindness, grit or empathy.
- **Notice what you're modelling**. They're watching how you handle stress and relationships. Try to model the behaviours you'd like them to adopt.

Tech challenges

Today's young people are the first generation to come of age with smartphones and constant connectivity. They spend huge amounts of time in digital spaces that are deliberately designed to capture their attention and hijack their dopamine systems. Teens now face an overload of content and opportunities for comparison at all hours of the day and night. They're more connected than ever, yet many also feel more isolated, overwhelmed and anxious.

In his groundbreaking book *The Anxious Generation*, Jonathan Haidt identifies two major shifts driving the huge rise in youth mental-health problems. The first is the decline in unsupervised, real-world play, which is essential for developing skills in socialising, problem solving and resilience. Parents have become more overprotective and today's kids are not playing outside as much as previous generations. The second is what he calls a 'phone-based childhood', which undermines mental health in multiple ways – from reduced attention spans and disrupted sleep to unhealthy social comparisons, cyberbullying and loneliness. Put simply, we've become overprotective of children in the physical world while failing to protect them adequately online.

Psychologist Jean Twenge has found strong associations between increased screen time – especially smartphones and social media – and rising anxiety, depression and self-harm in young people. These trends are particularly pronounced for girls, which I've seen first-hand as dad to two teenage girls trying to navigate all this.

The answer isn't to demonise technology. Devices aren't going away and they're also not inherently bad. Technology brings new opportunities, from creativity and connection to learning and self-expression. What young people really need is guidance to stay safe online and to balance their digital life with their real-world activities. Haidt recommends avoiding smartphones until secondary school and delaying social media use until at least age 16. Kate and I just about managed this with our teens, but it was a real battle of wills at times. Setting healthy boundaries around avoiding tech use at night is also crucial, especially given how vital sleep is for their mental wellbeing.

Amy Blankson, co-founder of the Digital Wellness Institute, reminded me that we also need to model the behaviour we want to see. Kids copy what they observe, so our own tech habits matter too.

It takes a village

Today's children are the doctors, entrepreneurs, carers, neighbours and leaders of tomorrow, so their wellbeing affects everyone's future. As the saying goes, it takes a village to raise a child. Those who aren't parents or carers themselves can still play a vital role in helping the next generation to develop the empathy and resilience needed to build a better world.

By caring about young people we're acting with intergenerational responsibility. It's a form of hope in action. Children who are loved, supported and emotionally balanced grow into adults who are more likely to contribute to society. Spending time with young people also helps to keep us young and maintain our sense of wonder and playfulness. Having relationships across the generations has been shown to benefit our cognition and health while also strengthening social cohesion.

We can also encourage the right priorities in schools too. As the educator Sir Anthony Seldon has long argued, if we want a future generation that thrives we must teach life skills for happiness as intentionally as we teach maths or literacy. Thankfully more schools are now recognising this and giving this greater priority.

> **→ Supporting young people (when you're not the parent)**
>
> Here are some ways to be a steady and encouraging presence:
> - **Show up and care**. One caring adult can make a huge difference. You don't need all the answers, just keep showing up.
> - **Listen without fixing**. Young people need someone who really listens to them, without interruption, judgement or advice.
> - **Show interest**. Curiosity builds connection, so show interest in the things they love, from sport and music to new apps or unusual trends.
> - **Accept their identity**. They're figuring out who they are, so celebrate their uniqueness and let them know you see them and accept them.
> - **Be a safe haven**. Having a 'different adult' in their life can be a sanctuary. Aim to provide a safe place for humour and warmth, free from pressure.

Modelling what matters

Young people learn less from what we say and more from what we do. So if we want them to learn skills for happier living we need to model the actions from this book. We can show them what it means to get the basics right, with healthy habits around food, sleep and exercise. We can model daily practices like mindfulness and expressing gratitude. We can prioritise time with family and friends. We can show them how fulfilling it is to help others and be part of something bigger. We can name our feelings, show resilience in tough times and be willing to be vulnerable.

We don't need to be perfect or always right. And we don't need to hide our inner insecurities from them – it's more important that we're honest. We can let them see us as a 'work in progress' with good intentions, but also able to admit when we're wrong. Children are watching and they notice how we speak to strangers, respond to frustration or work our way through disagreements. So each time we own our mistakes, show a love of learning or respond with encouragement rather than judgement, we're teaching them to do the same.

Our attitudes and words also shape how they see and speak to themselves. This quote from author Peggy O'Mara sums it up powerfully:

'The way we talk to our children becomes their inner voice.'

Whether you're a parent, carer, relative, friend, teacher or concerned citizen, you can play a role in nurturing the wellbeing of the next generation.

Perhaps the most powerful thing you can do for young people is to show up as the most wholehearted and authentic version of yourself. You can share the actions you've found helpful and be open about your issues too. It's not about being perfect, it's about being present.

RAISE RESILIENCE: CHAPTER SUMMARY

Ask yourself:
❓ **How do I help children feel secure and resilient?**

Don't just:
✗ Pass on your own emotional baggage to the next generation.

Try this out:
✔ Give children a healthy mix of love, boundaries and freedom.

Chapter Twenty-One:

Get Together

How can I be part of something bigger?

'You haven't got time for this, you're too busy and stressed,' my tired brain insisted.

As usual on a Tuesday, I was due to head out to my local community choir, which I'd been part of for a few years. But I really didn't feel like it. I was shattered after a long day where nothing had gone to plan. I'd arrived home late, feeling tense, and eaten a rather rushed dinner – so the last thing I wanted to do was dash out again.

But then I remembered the mental note I'd made about choir being *especially* helpful on tough days. So I dragged myself out, and almost as soon as I stepped into the room I remembered why it was the right choice. Here were 30 or so friendly faces of people from across our community who I'd gradually been getting to know. I was a few minutes late, so they were already singing a warm-up song and immediately it put a smile on my face. The stress I'd been feeling began to fade as we sang together.

Our group, Singing it Back, was led by Mary, a talented local friend who believes passionately that everyone can enjoy singing. She teaches the parts by singing them and the choir 'sings it back', so you don't need to read music. That week we were rehearsing for her plan to stage a surprise flashmob at the local shopping centre, to entertain passers-by with classics like 'Big Spender' and 'Price Tag'.

Two hours later, I returned home still humming the tunes that were now stuck in my head, feeling like a completely different person. Not only had I sung my heart out, I'd reconnected with friends, neighbours and strangers and we'd experienced something together. The singing wasn't flawless, but it was fun. I felt uplifted and calmer. But above all, I felt a sense of belonging – like I was part of something bigger.

Built to belong

We are wired to connect with each other. Feeling connected to others is one of the strongest predictors of life satisfaction. When we feel part of a community, anxiety decreases, resilience increases and life feels more meaningful. Without a sense of belonging, we suffer – socially, emotionally and physically. Research suggests loneliness may be as harmful to health as smoking 15 cigarettes a day, so belonging isn't a 'nice-to-have' – it's a public health necessity and vital for a happier society.

Throughout this book, we've explored many of the building blocks for happier living. In part one we focused on inner happiness, because self-care forms the foundation for showing up well in our communities. When we meet our own emotional and physical needs we have so much more to offer others.

In part two we turned to relationships and the importance of building our 'social fitness'. We explored how active listening helps people feel heard, how to navigate relationship challenges, how kindness creates ripple effects and how people are more trustworthy than we assume.

Now we're taking this one step further – from our close circles of loved ones and colleagues to the wider community we belong to. They say happiness is an 'inside job', and that's true, but it's also shaped by our connections with the people and society around us. At a time of increasing division we need togetherness more than ever.

> 'Alone, we can do so little; together, we can do so much.'
>
> – **Helen Keller**

What's going wrong?

Although we evolved to live in cooperative groups, modern life encourages self-sufficiency and competition. As we've embraced individualism – and learned to order whatever we want from our phone while sitting on the sofa – we seem to have forgotten how much we need each other. Much of the technology and convenience that has made life easier has also been keeping us apart. We spend more time online and less time together in shared spaces.

Our culture of competitive busyness also means we often have less time or energy left for others. When we feel overworked or overwhelmed we're less likely to talk to our neighbours or join in with local activities. As a result, many of us have become less embedded in community life. Research suggests that, compared to previous generations, fewer people now take part in local groups, clubs, choirs, faith communities or volunteering networks. Despite being more digitally connected than ever, many people feel more isolated and unseen. Rates of loneliness have risen, with devastating consequences for emotional wellbeing and physical health.

When we do engage it's often in more adversarial ways. We get stuck in online echo chambers and have less contact across our ideological differences. Social media tends to undermine respectful dialogue and reinforce an 'us vs them' mentality. By contrast, being together in person reduces misunderstanding and helps us find common ground.

As Brené Brown says: 'People are hard to hate close up. Move in.'

Too often, we underestimate the importance of community and fail to realise just how much it contributes – not only to our personal happiness, but to our collective wellbeing. Independence is valuable, but believing we need to do everything alone fuels loneliness and weakens social ties. Life is happier when we embrace our interdependence.

The power of community

One of the simplest ways to expand your circle of connection is through shared experiences. For example, joining a club, doing sport together, singing in a choir, being part of a faith community or helping at a local food bank.

When we're part of a group with a shared purpose, even a small one, we can experience what the French sociologist Émile Durkheim termed 'collective effervescence' – the uplifting energy that arises when we get in sync with others. It's that goosebump moment together at a live concert, the solidarity of a protest march, the warmth of a candlelit service, the shared laughter around a meal or the friendly banter in a pub quiz team.

These moments remind us that we're not alone, and their benefits go far beyond just personal happiness. Connected communities are more trusting, cohesive and resilient. They're better at responding to crises, supporting vulnerable members and maintaining a sense of shared identity and solidarity.

> 'We are made for goodness. We are made for love. We are made for friendliness. We are made for togetherness.'
>
> **– Desmond Tutu**

When we give time to get involved in our community we create ripple effects that benefit others and boost our own wellbeing too. We don't need to agree on everything. Community often begins simply by turning up, side by side, for something that matters.

At Action for Happiness we developed a course run by volunteers in their local communities. It introduces many of the practical ideas in this book, but crucially it also brings people together to explore them as a group. The course was evaluated in a full randomised controlled trial published in a peer-reviewed journal. Participants showed significant increases in wellbeing alongside lower symptoms of depression and anxiety. But that wasn't all. The study also found increases in prosocial behaviour, including compassion and social trust. When people come together to support one other they don't just feel better, they often become kinder, more connected and more trusting members of society. That benefits everyone.

Faith, rituals and beyond

Faith groups have traditionally been powerful forces for bringing people together. All the great religions encourage shared rituals, sacred spaces and collective worship, which create a deep sense of belonging. Rituals bring people together to celebrate important milestones and they can provide great comfort in difficult times.

Faith and cultural traditions also offer some of the most enduring lessons about community. Hindu scriptures encourage caring for guests as we would for the Divine. Christian teachings ask us to love our neighbour as we would ourselves. The Muslim principle of *zakat* embodies the importance of helping others through charity. The Jewish emphasis on *hesed* lays out an obligation to care for each other. And the African philosophy of *ubuntu* – which means 'I am, because we are' – emphasises our interdependence as human beings.

I grew up in a Christian home and was involved with our local church for many years. Although I'm no longer an active believer I still recognise the huge value in these practices of gathering, singing, caring and showing up for something bigger. It's not just the religious service itself, it's the friendly conversations afterwards, mixing across the generations and feeling accepted. During my lifetime there's been a steep decline in the proportion of people who attend religious gatherings. I can understand the desire to move beyond dogma, as I have myself, but I also worry that we risk losing some of the important traditions, ethical principles and shared moments that used to bind us together. Individualism can't fill the hole left when we abandon communal spaces and rituals.

The good news is that togetherness isn't only found in religious settings. There are many other opportunities for connection where we can get together locally and find meaning alongside others. We can join a walking group, book club or repair café. We can volunteer at a community garden or campaign for improvements locally. We can get involved in a neighbourhood association or organise street gatherings.

What matters is less the activity itself and more the sense of shared purpose and mutual benefit. By committing to something bigger than ourselves we build trust and a sense of belonging. We form new friendships and support each other through life's ups and downs. We make things, stand up for things and celebrate things together.

I love watching football on TV, but when I'm in the Holte End cheering on Aston Villa with thousands of other fans, that sense of togetherness is something else. I'll always remember the first time my son ended up hugging random people next to him as we all got caught up celebrating a brilliant goal against Newcastle – a truly magical moment.

So look for ways to join in. By moving our focus from 'me' to 'we', we become part of the story rather than just watching on passively from the sidelines. Whether it's singing hymns or football chants, praying together for those in need or helping out at a homeless shelter, when we do things together, everyone benefits. It builds solidarity and bridges divides.

The happiness of volunteering

One of the most consistently rewarding things we can do – both for ourselves and others – is to volunteer our time or energy to support a cause we care about. As we saw in chapter eighteen, doing good feels good, but this goes deeper too. Volunteering gets us actively involved and helps us to meet likeminded people, pursue meaningful goals and contribute to something meaningful together. This is community in action.

Evidence shows that volunteering, especially in social and community settings, has powerful benefits for psychological, emotional and even physical health. A meta-analysis of 40 studies involving tens of thousands of participants found volunteering to be associated with higher wellbeing, lower levels of depression and even a reduced risk of mortality.

Regular volunteers also tend to report greater life satisfaction as well as being less likely to feel lonely. Research published in the World Happiness Report found people who had volunteered recently were happier than those who hadn't, even after controlling for other factors. As well as bringing a greater sense of agency and purpose, volunteering often involves teamwork and collaboration, which boosts our sense of belonging.

Volunteering doesn't mean sacrificing all your free time to a cause. You can find ways to connect and give back that fit into your schedule. For me, that looks like a weekly Friday food run to support our local food bank. A quick collection at some nearby supermarkets and a drop-off at the centre takes just an hour out of my week, yet it makes a meaningful difference for others. And as a bonus, my daughter has often joined me to help out – along with her great playlists for the car journey!

Even though this small weekly contribution is rewarding, it isn't always easy or joyful. Sometimes I find it tough to muster the time and energy for another to-do at the end of a long week. Occasionally I have to recognise my own limits and prioritise other urgent needs. But one of the powerful things about building community connections is that I can call on a neighbour or friend to help out when I need it.

Where to start

If you're feeling a bit disconnected from your local community at the moment, don't worry. You don't need to jump headlong into every aspect of local life. You can begin with one or two small steps.

You could start by simply saying hello to someone new or asking a neighbour how they're doing. You might choose to put devices away, look up more and really give people your attention when you're with them. You could do a quick search for a local group that aligns with your interests – it could be anything, from art or local history to walking or yoga. You don't need to commit up front, just go along to one session, meet a few people and see how it feels. You could also check your local volunteer centre, or look online, to see if there's a charity or cause that's looking for a bit of extra help.

> **→ Reflection on your community**
>
> Take a few minutes to stop and reflect on your local community. Think about the different ways your community affects your happiness and wellbeing, and how it affects other people you care about. You might want to include local services like healthcare, education or transport. How do these affect or enhance your life?
>
> Now ask yourself two questions:
> - Which aspects of your community have a positive impact on quality of life?
> - Where would you like to see change, or could help make things better?

Using your skills to help others is a brilliant way to meet like-minded people and be part of something meaningful. It doesn't need to be time-consuming and can often be fun. For example, I love the growing numbers of 'Men's Sheds' – community spaces where people come together to work on practical projects and repair things. Alongside woodworking and mending there's plenty of banter and companionship too.

If you're already involved in your community, that's great. Hopefully you've seen the positive impact this can have for you and others. This might be a good time to look for ways to get more deeply involved, for example through more regular volunteering. Or you could help to set something new in motion, such as a local meetup, a get-together with neighbours or even a street party.

In chapter twelve we looked at the importance of maintaining our 'social fitness' in much the same way as physical fitness. The obvious place to start with this is staying in touch with family and friends. But it also helps to expand our circles and make a conscious effort to check in regularly with neighbours and others we know, beyond just our nearest and dearest.

> **➔ Practical ways to build community wellbeing**
> - **Small friendly acts**. Start with simple acts of kindness, like smiling at a stranger, holding a door open or asking someone how they're doing.
> - **Get to know neighbours**. Pause for a chat on the street or over the fence. Invite someone over for tea or join a neighbourhood event.
> - **Join a local group**. Try a nearby book club, choir, sports team, parenting group or meetup linked to a hobby or interest.
> - **Choose the in-person option**. If something can be done either online or face to face, prioritise being together in the real world.
> - **Ask as well as offer**. Be willing to ask for help as well as offering it. Build mutual support by lending and borrowing items from neighbours.

- **Volunteer your time and skills.** Support a local initiative such as a food bank, youth group, mutual aid network or clean-up project.
- **Meet more different people.** Look for chances to connect with people from different backgrounds and take an interest in their perspectives.
- **Make connection a habit.** Broaden your 'social fitness' by regularly checking in with local friends and neighbours.

Communities of love not fear

When we witness injustice in society, getting together with others to campaign can be a powerful and uniting force for social change. However, it's better to unite in ways that encourage understanding and solutions rather than stoking identity-based divisions. Although it's understandable when people gather around a shared grievance, coming together in anger ultimately has a corrosive effect. It turns groups against each other and reinforces tribal divides. Righteous anger may feel powerful and necessary, but it can cloud our judgement, crowd out compassion and take a toll on our wellbeing. When our community life fractures, this breeds distrust and pessimism. It makes it harder for us to rise together in response to common challenges.

We may not be able to change what's going on in our country or around the world, but we do have a choice about how to respond locally. Rather than joining in with tribal antagonism we can choose a different path, where we turn towards instead of away from each other. Where we choose hope over despair and love over fear.

As the former US Surgeon General Vivek Murthy said eloquently: 'To build community requires love.' He doesn't mean love in a sentimental sense, but rather as a guiding force with the strength to build, help and heal. We can rebuild our 'common life' by choosing to spend more time with people who are different to us – to get to know them and see things from their perspective. This is love as courage, generosity and hope.

I was once on a long flight feeling tense and generally frustrated with other passengers. So I put headphones on and my playlist randomly cued up a song by the band Athlete called 'I Love'. The chorus is strangely beautiful and keeps repeating the words 'I love everybody here'. As I sang along silently, my tension eased and I suddenly felt an overwhelming sense of warmth towards all these other fellow human beings. There we all were, sitting in a giant metal tube hurtling through the sky at over 500 miles an hour, each of us with our own unique worries, quirks and hopes.

That moment transformed my attitude from one of hostility and disconnection to one of acceptance and goodwill. I was so much happier for the rest of the flight and I even had a few friendly chats with people nearby. I now try to remember that song whenever I'm travelling or in a busy public space. It helps me recognise the humanity in people around me. I stay calmer and often end up sharing a smile or a friendly conversation.

Focusing on love over fear doesn't mean ignoring what's wrong. But it reminds us we have a choice over the sort of community we want to be part of and contribute to. Rather than joining an online pile-on you could join a local befriending scheme. Rather than complaining about an unfriendly neighbour you could help set up a supportive WhatsApp group for your street. What choices will you make?

> 'You cannot get through a single day without having an impact on the world around you. What you do makes a difference, and you have to decide what kind of difference you want to make.'
>
> **– Jane Goodall**

Personal wellbeing matters, but we also need community at a deep level. We can eat well, exercise, sleep eight hours a night and adopt the best healthy habits, but without community it's hard to feel whole. Life is simply more meaningful when shared.

From me to we

Our own small contributions to local life really matter. But if we want a happier society we can't just rely on each of us to do more as individuals. We also need to rebuild and enhance community life, including the wider systems, policies and institutions that support it. We want a world where thriving communities are accessible to all and where connecting locally is a natural part of everyday life.

Our public spaces really matter for this. Community halls, leisure centres, libraries, green spaces and local high streets are the places where connection happens, often in unplanned ways. Research shows that access to shared spaces can increase social interaction and inclusion, which are vital ingredients for building trust and reducing isolation. Yet as life has become more fast-paced, digital and self-centred, many of these real-world spaces and places are at risk of being underfunded or lost. Creating environments that encourage people to gather isn't just good urban planning, it's an investment in social cohesion and happiness.

So we need to build and restore our 'social infrastructure' – like libraries and local community spaces that allow people to meet and interact. We need policies that empower neighbourhoods and projects where local residents can easily get involved – with funding, support and recognition. We need workplaces that prioritise social connection and employers that actively encourage volunteering.

In the next chapter we'll look at some of the wider structural and policy changes that can help to create a happier society for everyone. We can't do all this ourselves, but it's vital to know what kind of society we want and to recognise where we can take action to encourage this. Together we can help to create a culture where people really want to contribute, not just consume. Where we thrive together, not just by ourselves.

> **GET TOGETHER: CHAPTER SUMMARY**
>
> Ask yourself:
> **? How can I help people get together in my community?**
>
> Don't just:
> ✗ Ignore your neighbours and avoid meeting new people.
>
> Try this out:
> ✔ Be an active member of your local community.

Chapter Twenty-Two:

Be the Change

Can I help create a happier society?

Wow, this is a big moment, I thought to myself, feeling real hope and excitement.

It was a year after I'd joined up with Richard Layard to launch Action for Happiness and here we were together at the United Nations in New York. I couldn't quite believe it. We'd come for the first ever UN Conference on Happiness, and all 193 countries had just adopted a new resolution to officially recognise happiness as a fundamental human goal and a global measure of progress. Having spent years as a leading proponent of wellbeing economics, Richard had co-authored the first ever World Happiness Report, which was being launched at the conference with great fanfare.

I felt honoured to be there in support. Richard has been a hero of mine ever since I read his first book on happiness in 2005. After working together for many years, he'd become a mentor and close friend too. The range of things he's achieved is remarkable. He was the driving force behind the UK's Improving Access to

Psychological Therapies programme and a key player in getting policymakers around the world to take wellbeing much more seriously. He's published groundbreaking reports and books, spoken at countless events and had extensive media coverage. In short, he's helped to shift wellbeing and mental health from fringe concerns to mainstream priorities.

But what I love most about Richard is the *way* he does all this. He's deeply passionate, intellectually rigorous and incredibly hard-working – yet he also embodies the values we need for a happier society. He's warm-hearted, modest, friendly, generous and optimistic. I once went to visit him when he was stuck at home with a broken foot from his weekly tennis game. I was expecting him to be frustrated, but he greeted me with his usual warm smile and told me it was a great opportunity to work on his new book and watch the Olympics. As I write this, he's in his 90s, yet still working energetically every day to make a difference. He could easily have retired decades ago, but for Richard a happy life is a purposeful one.

We can't all be like Richard in terms of his professional capabilities – and nor do we need to be. We can still follow his example, by trying to use our own unique talents to make a difference. Richard consistently models two characteristics needed above all to make life happier: agency and altruism. Likewise, we can recognise that our actions matter (agency) and use our gifts to help others (altruism).

This chapter is about how each of us – wherever or whoever we are – can take small but meaningful steps towards a better world. It's about standing up for what matters, even if your voice shakes. It's about turning ideals into action. And most of all, it's about recognising that change doesn't start out there with someone else. It starts with us.

> ⓢ 'Fight for causes that you believe in. Your planet, your country, your community. They all need us as activists, you know. And it's okay to be angry at injustice, but perhaps start with an act of kindness.'
>
> – **Bono**

The state of our world

Over the last century, our world has taken many encouraging steps forwards. New technologies, medical breakthroughs, falling child mortality, longer lifespans and meaningful progress on a range of social issues. Yet almost everywhere we look there is still a dreadful amount of suffering. And there are serious concerns about our future – around conflict, climate and economic systems that are unfair and unstable.

In this book we've explored many ways to make life happier. We've looked at how our own happiness is shaped by our daily actions. We've also explored how interconnected we are and how good relationships contribute to our collective happiness. But it's hard to be authentically happy when there's so much injustice in the world. Outrage and anger are understandable responses. It's also hard to stay hopeful in the face of existential threats, like future risks from AI-powered destruction or environmental breakdown.

So how can we as individuals possibly make a difference? I certainly don't have answers to the big problems. I feel hopeless watching innocent lives lost in needless conflicts. I feel angry at huge disparities in wealth and quality of life between groups. I feel outrage at the denial of man-made environmental disasters and watching our leaders fail to do what's needed. And I feel especially sad watching polarised debates that stoke hatred and fuel 'us vs them' storylines.

But here's something important to keep in mind:

Things are often not as bad as they seem in the news – they have the potential to get better and usually do over longer periods of time.

This isn't wishful thinking, it's realistic optimism. We live in a media ecosystem that incentivises a focus on bad news and outrage. Things are far from perfect, but they're often not as awful as the headlines suggest. Max Roser, the economist, philosopher and founder of *Our World in Data*, sums it up well:

'The world is awful. The world is much better. The world can be much better. All three of these statements are true at the same time.'

The news focuses on the first of these, highlighting what's going wrong and rarely mentioning the positive developments. But as Roser notes, as well as being realistic about how things are we also need to notice what's improving and focus on positive ways to help make some of the awful things better too.

Shutting ourselves away from reality isn't the answer. As concerned citizens, it's important that we stay aware of what's going on, both locally and globally. But it's not healthy or useful to spend our lives scrolling through the world's traumas and feeling outraged. It rarely improves the situation and it certainly doesn't help us or the people around us. Hostile words amplified online don't change people's minds or move debates forwards constructively.

I try to remind myself that armchair doomscrolling and outrage are not moral acts in themselves. When we get too caught up in all the trauma and injustice this undermines our ability to act. It can stop us taking positive steps in our own lives and communities.

> 'Wading around in all the distress of the world paralyses people, and stops them acting in their community. When I'm online I am definitely a less good artist, a less good friend, a less good father, and a less good sibling and son. I am a not-happy, over-stressed person, and I think you should try to be a happy, under-stressed person for the people you love.'
>
> – Tim Minchin

Our instinct is often to attack those we disagree with or call for their views to be cancelled. Having enemies is convenient because it lets us pretend that all the badness in the world is in them. As a result we may decide it's okay to treat others harshly when we feel our behaviour is morally justified. Or that it's fine to abuse the 'bad people' and their followers, provided we're a warrior for truth and justice.

But is it really? Maybe the more moral thing to do is focus on being the best we can be – as caring partners, parents, friends, colleagues, neighbours and citizens.

I like the word 'citizens'. It implies not just that we belong somewhere but that we also have rights and responsibilities to each other. I've been inspired by the work of Jon Alexander and the New Citizen Project, which encourages us to see ourselves as active citizens rather than passive consumers.

> 'Start where you are. Use what you have. Do what you can.'
>
> – Arthur Ashe

When it comes to making life happier for everyone, it turns out there's a lot we can do together. But before looking at our own potential contributions to this, let's start by looking at some of the wider changes we need to see.

Towards a happier world

As we think about the state of the world it's tempting to dismiss happiness as a side issue. But this isn't a luxury topic for the privileged few. The deeper reason we care about big issues like health, the economy, justice, education, work or equality is because of how much they contribute to – or undermine – overall human happiness.

You don't need to just take my word for it. Researchers have been measuring happiness levels around the world for decades and this work provides vital insights into where things are going wrong, but also how things could be better.

As you'd expect, levels of happiness vary hugely across nations. The least happy countries tend to be those where basic human needs – like food, shelter and safety – are unmet or under threat. At the time of writing, the least happy countries include Afghanistan, Sierra Leone, Lebanon, Zimbabwe, Yemen and the Democratic Republic of the Congo, all facing extreme poverty, conflict or both.

The happiest countries are typically in Northern Europe: Finland, Denmark, Iceland, Sweden and Norway regularly top the rankings. The Netherlands, Austria and Switzerland also do well, as do Australia, New Zealand and Canada. In recent years, Latin American nations – like Costa Rica and Mexico – have risen in the rankings, along with Eastern European countries such as Lithuania, Slovenia and Czechia.

Much of the variation in happiness can be explained by six key factors researchers track: GDP per capita, social support (having someone to count on), healthy life expectancy, freedom to make life choices, generosity and perceptions of corruption.

Although the happiest countries tend to have good standards of living, there are wealthy countries where happiness is lower than you'd expect from their income levels – for example Singapore and the United States. Again this shows there's more to happiness than money. Levels of freedom and corruption really matter too. More authoritarian regimes, including Russia and China, score significantly lower in the happiness rankings. People want to be free to live their lives.

If we want a happier world we need a vision for how things could be better. So what is it about places like Finland and Denmark that helps people thrive? Trust is almost certainly a key ingredient. Far higher proportions of Finns and Danes report that 'most people can be trusted' compared with people in the US or UK.

Fortunately, a growing body of research now shows which public policies can help to make societies happier. These range from the basics of peace, safety and democracy to approaches that improve wellbeing in specific areas, like workplaces, healthcare, communities and public services.

Before we explore these in more detail, let's pause for a moment.

> ### ➔ What might a happier society look like?
> Take a moment to visualise a better and happier version of your country. Try to bring to mind some specific changes you'd like to see. For example:
> - What would education be like?
> - How might family life be different?
> - What would healthcare focus on?
> - How could our working lives be better?
> - How would we treat each other in our communities?
> - What would the government be prioritising?

I'm now going to run through some of the key areas, sharing the priorities as I see them, drawing on research evidence and the experts I've worked with.

Democracy and government

For those of us lucky enough to live in a democracy, even a flawed one, we tend to take it for granted far more than we should. The foundations of a happy society include free and fair elections, respect for human rights, freedom of expression and rule of law. All of the happiest countries are democracies, while a large proportion of the least happy are authoritarian.

Recent anti-democratic trends are deeply worrying. If we undermine the institutions that support our freedoms, we risk the very way of life that most reliably supports human flourishing. It's vital that we uphold democratic norms and don't allow these precious foundations to be dismantled by populists who drift into autocracy.

So what is the role of good government? On this, I'm firmly with Thomas Jefferson, who said its purpose was 'the care of human life and happiness'. We need governments that prioritise people's wellbeing above all else. This includes a strong economy and good public services, but also so much more.

The starting point is to measure wellbeing and take it as seriously as GDP or inflation. Fortunately, a growing number of countries are doing this, and bodies like the OECD now recommend it. When deciding how to spend public money, policymakers should evaluate which options will most cost-effectively enhance wellbeing, using measures like the WELLBY (wellbeing-adjusted life-year). Through this lens, investment in mental-health services often provides far better value than, say, spending on a new train line.

> 'Create all the happiness you are able to create; remove all the misery you are able to remove.'
>
> – Jeremy Bentham

The economy

There's a lot of confusion about money and happiness. The conventional view is that economic growth is the main route to improving quality of life. Others argue that prioritising growth at all costs leads to more inequality, social division, environmental damage and financial crises. Some even call for us to move 'beyond growth'.

My view is that growth will remain appealing – humans have always wanted to strive, improve and make things better. The key question is: *What* are we growing and *why*? The economy should be the means to an end, not the end in itself. Its role is to serve people, not the other way around. Our leaders should focus on growing overall wellbeing, not just GDP.

None of this downplays the importance of a strong economy. Decent household incomes and well-funded public services are vital. But rather than chasing growth for its own sake we should focus on economic stability and shared prosperity. Boom and bust cycles hurt everyone and research shows that wellbeing falls more sharply in downturns than it rises in good times. Although some inequality is inevitable, high levels are corrosive. Rising disparities in wealth erode trust, fuel resentment, create political upheaval and weaken social cohesion. Wellbeing is higher when prosperity is broadly shared rather than concentrated in the hands of a few.

Healthcare

As a Brit, I love our National Health Service. I remain convinced that universal healthcare is essential for a happy society. No one should have to weigh up their finances before receiving life-saving treatment. Yet in the UK, as in many countries, it often feels like we have a Physical Illness Service rather than a system supporting overall wellbeing. Two major shifts are vital here. Both are underway, but much more progress is needed.

The first is recognising that health is about our minds as well as our bodies. Mental illness causes enormous suffering, yet often fewer than a third of those affected receive appropriate help. People should have access to proven therapies, medication and support. Mental ill health, including depression and anxiety, should be treated with the same seriousness as physical conditions.

As well as being underfunded, mental health has been separated off from mainstream healthcare. Yet for many physical disorders, psychological factors play a significant role, including chronic back pain (I can vouch for that one!), insomnia, headaches, digestive issues and chronic fatigue. Stress has been linked to Type 2 diabetes, cardiovascular disease, immune dysfunction, cognitive decline and even some cancers.

The second shift is moving from treatment to prevention. Earlier in the book we looked at the basics: sleep, healthy eating and exercise. These lifestyle factors, along with other habits such as tobacco and alcohol use, have a surprisingly large effect on long-term health. While life expectancy has risen, our 'healthspan' – how long we stay in good health – has not kept pace. Focusing on prevention helps people stay healthier and happier for longer while also reducing the pressure on healthcare systems.

Education
Since I was at school, the education system has shifted heavily towards assessments, inspections and league tables. Although the aims were noble, this narrow focus on attainment means that

academic outcomes often overshadow broader learning. Three things need to change.

First, schools must support children's emotional and social development and mental wellbeing. These matter just as much as academic skills and also contribute to better performance at school. Second, we need to help young people develop actual life skills, not just exam-passing abilities. The curriculum should cover practical topics including personal finance, communication skills, emotional resilience, healthy phone habits and navigating social media. Thirdly, schools should cultivate character, helping young people develop prosocial values beyond just individual achievement. Academic excellence matters, as does a strong work ethic, but life demands more than cognitive intelligence.

Sir Anthony Seldon, co-founder of Action for Happiness and a pioneer of wellbeing education, says we must help children develop their 'multiple intelligences'. Drawing on the work of Howard Gardner, he encourages schools to go beyond verbal and logical skills, to nurture musical, linguistic, interpersonal, spatial and physical intelligence too. The modern world doesn't just need university graduates, but those with vocational skills honed through practical opportunities like apprenticeships. We need young people who can take responsibility, get on with others and solve problems, with the emotional intelligence to thrive in the real world.

Employment and workplaces

Work is not only a vital source of income but also fundamental to our wellbeing. It gives us opportunities to build relationships, develop skills and use our creativity. It provides structure, routine and crucially also a sense of identity and meaning. Being out of work, whether through unemployment, ill health or incapacity, is almost always bad for happiness. We lose our purpose, not just our pay. So as a society we must minimise unemployment and help people return to work as quickly as possible. The rise in NEETs (young people Not in Education, Employment or Training) is particularly concerning and needs urgent attention.

Good work brings stability, decent income, social connection and opportunities for personal growth, yet many companies still have unhappy or even toxic cultures. Line managers have a vital role here. As the saying goes: 'People join companies but leave managers.' Nobody wants to work for someone who is rude, unfair, micromanaging or lacks empathy.

Good managers give freedom within clear guidelines, encourage positive relationships and help people understand how their work makes a difference. This isn't a fluffy, box-ticking exercise. As my friend and workplace wellbeing expert Nic Marks says: 'Happiness is a serious business.' Research shows that happier employees are more loyal, productive, collaborative and give better customer service. Happier companies tend to be more profitable and even generate higher long-term shareholder returns. As businesspeople like to say, it's a clear win–win!

Welfare

A thriving economy must also support those who aren't able to support themselves. Strong, fair and inclusive welfare systems are vital. Scandinavian countries rank highly for happiness in part because they offer comprehensive welfare support across unemployment, housing, sickness, disability, healthcare and family benefits.

A strong social safety net doesn't just catch people when they fall – it helps them live with dignity and contribute more to society. But support should also empower people, encouraging and enabling them to move into meaningful work where possible. Welfare should be a launchpad, not a trapdoor. Crucially, systems must be accessible, inclusive and human-centred. People need support that's easy to navigate, free from shame or excessive bureaucracy, and grounded in compassion.

Leisure and culture

Culture and creativity aren't luxuries – they're lifelines. Music, art, sport, storytelling and shared rituals bring joy, meaning and connection. Every community should have access to these things, not just the privileged few.

Public funding for libraries, arts centres and music should be seen as investments in collective wellbeing. Likewise, green spaces, parks, sports clubs and community venues offer vital ways for people to move, meet and feel part of something bigger. A thriving culture of leisure nourishes us emotionally and spiritually.

Families and relationships

The earliest years of a child's life are crucial, when brain development is fastest and neural pathways are shaped by nurturing relationships. Research shows that emotional wellbeing in childhood is a stronger predictor of adult life satisfaction than exam results or income. So family support must be a foundation, not an afterthought. We need to help new parents and vulnerable families through parenting programmes, peer support and home-visiting schemes. Countries that invest in early intervention, parental leave and affordable childcare tend to have higher wellbeing and less inequality.

Experiencing conflict, neglect or instability during childhood can have long-lasting effects, but supportive relationships can buffer and repair these risks. Warmth, consistency and emotional safety matter far more than family structure. Relationship struggles are normal, but many couples only seek help when problems are entrenched. We need earlier, more accessible support that reduces the risk of family breakdown.

Above all, we need strong social networks that support parents and help to create a 'village', where children have multiple caring adults in their lives and families feel connected and able to support each other, especially in tough times.

Community

Humans are social animals. We all need people we can count on, yet increasing numbers of people say they have no one to call in a crisis. Tackling loneliness must be a public health priority. This means creating environments that encourage connection: walkable streets, shared spaces, local initiatives and community centres that bring people together. A culture of volunteering can foster solidarity, purpose and friendship.

When people feel a sense of belonging and pride in where they live – supported by good housing, safe neighbourhoods and clean air – wellbeing follows.

Migration and population change

People migrate in order to seek out better lives for themselves and their families. The World Happiness Report shows that when people move to happier countries their wellbeing tends to rise. In many countries, including here in the UK, generations of migrants have successfully integrated and made vital contributions to national wellbeing – from business and public service to providing essential roles in health or social care.

Yet migration has become a polarising issue and is often exploited politically. Hostility can arise when people are struggling and looking for someone to blame. It's also understandable that rapid change can feel unsettling, and people may worry about fairness or social cohesion, particularly if they see migrants arriving through irregular routes. The key is successful integration – helping newcomers feel welcome while ensuring everyone understands and upholds shared values such as respect for the rule of law, non-discrimination, and freedom of speech or belief. National pride is no bad thing, so long as it's inclusive rather than divisive.

Migration is likely to keep increasing in the years ahead, especially with ageing populations, declining birth rates and more forced movement. Countries that create effective routes for legal migration, help new arrivals integrate successfully and maintain community stability will be the ones that thrive. For all its flaws, I'm grateful to live in multicultural Britain and I hope we continue to be a country that, on the whole, remains proud to be welcoming and tolerant.

The environment and future generations

As well as shifting our focus from the economy towards wellbeing, we must also care about future generations and the natural world. This means prioritising sustainability, not just because the climate crisis demands it but because community and environmental wellbeing go hand in hand.

Many of the actions that bring authentic happiness, like walking, mending, planting, sharing or volunteering, also support a healthier planet. Living sustainably is great for our wellbeing. Also, when people feel happier and more connected, they're more likely to care for the natural world. Research shows that people with higher wellbeing are more inclined to behave in pro-environmental ways.

So we need more wellbeing experts encouraging care for the natural world and more environmental activists promoting the importance of wellbeing. Spending time in nature, walking or cycling instead of driving, growing food, swapping books, singing, meditating – these are things that enrich our lives while also reducing our carbon footprint. Our happiness and the future of our planet are inextricably linked.

> **→ Happier World Wishlist**
>
> My personal list for positive changes I'd like to see in the world goes on, covering everything from using technology for good to rethinking the criminal justice system to affordable public transport and more community spaces. What's on your Happier World Wishlist?

But what can I do?

Although we want to see these big system changes, we can also 'be the change' in the way we approach our lives in our homes, workplaces and communities. As we've seen, one of the greatest ways to be happier ourselves – and to contribute to a better world – is to look beyond ourselves and find joy in helping others. Even small acts of friendship and kindness make a meaningful difference.

Although we may start small, we can gradually expand our circles of influence so our impact begins to ripple out further. A key part of this is recognising the agency we already have and developing what psychologists call an internal 'locus of control'. When we believe everything is determined by external forces it's easy to feel helpless. But when we see that our effort and inner attitude can shift things we become more resilient and more willing to act. We're not denying the real difficulties, we're simply focusing on what we can do. We can take time to get to know our neighbours or volunteer for a local cause we care about. We can join a community group or campaign for changes that improve wellbeing in our neighbourhood.

In fact, in each of our roles – from families to workplaces to public life – we have the potential to use our skills, passion and influence to help make life happier. Once we recognise how much this all matters we can be more aware of what's needed and more ready to get involved.

> **→ What you can do**
> Here are some practical ways you can make a difference in your roles:
> - **As a leader or manager**: embed wellbeing in the workplace culture, recognise effort, support autonomy and lead with empathy.
> - **As a teacher or educator**: teach social and emotional skills, encourage growth mindset and mindfulness, look beyond academic achievement.
> - **As a health worker**: treat patients holistically (body and mind), encourage prevention, prioritise mental health and show compassion.
> - **As a co-worker or teammate**: offer appreciation, support others, avoid blame, help build a culture of teamwork and trust.
> - **As a parent or carer**: show unconditional love with clear boundaries, model emotional regulation, active listening, gratitude and kindness.
> - **As a friend**: check in regularly – especially in difficult times – be honest and available, celebrate success and offer support without judgement.

- **As a neighbour**: greet and look out for people around you, be a friendly presence, host or support local gatherings and groups.
- **As a consumer**: reduce unnecessary consumption, choose experiences over things, support ethical companies, use tech mindfully.
- **As a scientist or researcher**: explore evidence-based insights on human flourishing, raise awareness, help shape policy and culture.
- **As an artist or creator**: inspire hope through creativity, highlight shared humanity, challenge harmful narratives and share beauty.
- **As a citizen**: volunteer your time, vote for policies that prioritise wellbeing, advocate for justice and inclusion, share the ideas in this book.

As we wrap up this second part of the book I'll leave you with the inspiring words of Jane Goodall, the incredible zoologist and primatologist:

'The greatest danger to our future is apathy. We can't all save the world in a dramatic way, but we can each make our small difference, and together those small differences add up. Every single person makes an impact on the planet every single day.'

The question is: What kind of impact do you want to make?

BE THE CHANGE: CHAPTER SUMMARY

Ask yourself:
❓ **Where can I encourage a greater focus on wellbeing?**

Don't just:
✗ Stay overwhelmed with anger about all that's wrong in the world.

Try this out:
✔ Promote what you love rather than bashing what you hate.

PART 3:
HAPPIER FOR GOOD

Bringing all of these ideas together

Chapter Twenty-Three:

Make it Last

How can we keep making life happier?

'I really don't think I can do this. And besides, will anyone care?'

I was sitting at my desk feeling lost, having a crisis of confidence. Writing a book, it turns out, is even harder than it sounds. I felt like an imposter.

Yes, these ideas helped change my life, but who am I to assume anyone else wants to hear them from me? Surely the world doesn't need another happiness book!

Yes, this feels urgent to me, but maybe others see it as blindingly obvious or trivial. Our world is burning and here I am writing about the power of tiny actions and trusting people. Have I lost the plot?

In that moment of self-doubt I decided to take my own advice. I turned away from my desk, paused, took a mindful breath and just noticed what was going on. I let myself feel the insecurity and acknowledge it.

As I sat there I found that alongside my doubt was a deeper, stronger conviction. I'm not a guru with all the answers, but I've had the privilege of working with hundreds of experts and helping lots of people find ways to be happier. And I genuinely want everyone to discover how life-changing this can be.

Moments later, out of the blue, a reminder popped up on my phone with feedback from a talk I'd given a few months earlier. I'd forgotten all about it, but people from the Action for Happiness community had sent me messages of gratitude and encouragement.

'Truly inspiring,' said one. 'This was so helpful,' said another. 'I think I was meant to hear what you had to say tonight,' wrote a third. Seeing their words brought tears to my eyes and a warm feeling inside.

Their appreciation didn't just lift my mood, it brought me back to the moment of my original Good Life Crisis all those years before. I suddenly realised just how much had changed since then. That moment of waking up had sparked a shift in my life that was still unfolding two decades later.

I'd made a decision to Make Life Happier, not just for myself but through the way I live and the things I focus on. Although the significance wasn't clear at the time, that choice has shaped almost everything I've poured my energy into since. My personal habits, my relationships, my work – the whole direction of my life.

I may not have changed *the* world, but my whole world has changed. And I've been able to help others along the way. Even if this book inspires just one more person to make this their focus, it will have been worth it.

Maybe that person is you?

A life's work, not just a lifehack

This book didn't promise a quick fix or perfect formula for a happy life. Happiness isn't a tick-box goal or a finish line to rush towards. By exploring ways to make life 'happier', rather than 'happy', we've focused on our direction of travel rather than the destination.

At its core this is about a way of *being*, supported by everyday skills and choices we can continue to develop throughout our lives. We make life happier not by eliminating unhappiness but by responding to life's inevitable challenges with more awareness, kindness and purpose. Along this journey, we've explored ways to become more mindful and intentional, to embrace both the joy and the messiness, to show up with compassion for ourselves and others, and to see our lives as part of something bigger.

In part one, Happier Inside, we began with the idea of 'waking up' and asking what truly matters. We looked at how to get off autopilot and become more aware of our thoughts, feelings and habits. We recognised that we don't need to wait for perfect conditions to change how we feel. Our actions shift our mood and our attention shapes our reality.

Along the way, we explored the importance of:
- Choosing to look for what's good, even in difficult times
- Staying grounded in realistic optimism rather than forced positivity
- Getting the basics right with sleep, nutrition, exercise and devices
- Taming the inner critic by talking to ourselves more like a friend
- Focusing on what we can change and choosing how we respond

- Experimenting with different actions to find out what works best.

These skills are foundational, but self-care is not enough — true happiness expands outwards and connects us to others and to the wider world.

So in part two, Happier Together, we explored the social dimensions of happiness, beginning with the vital importance of relationships and why we need to work on our 'social fitness' just as much as our physical fitness.

We covered relational skills including:
- How to listen so people really feel heard
- Understanding needs and navigating relationship difficulties
- Showing vulnerability and being willing to trust
- The extraordinary power of everyday kindness
- Repairing old wounds, learning to forgive and move forwards
- Being part of a community and contributing to a happier society.

These themes helped us reveal a deeper truth: lasting happiness comes from *connecting more deeply* to ourselves, to each other and to something bigger than us. This is the heart of happier living. And it's also the heart of this final chapter. We may be reaching the end of the book, but this is just the beginning of what's possible.

How to be happier for good

I've thought long and hard about this phrase, 'happier for good' — in fact it was my original title for this book. There's an intentional double meaning here — both aspects matter deeply and each supports the other.

'Happier for good' is firstly about building a sense of inner happiness that can last. Those small habits you've been experimenting with – like mindfulness, gratitude, listening, connecting, helping, letting go – can fundamentally change the way you experience your daily life. These aren't quick fixes to help you feel better temporarily, they're lifelong skills to help you live more wisely and meaningfully, for good.

'Happier for good' is also about being a force for good in the world. It means taking what you've learned and using it to enrich not just your own life but the lives of others. It's choosing to leave places better than you found them. It's creating ripples through small acts of generosity and kind intentions and recognising these ripples spread outwards and contribute to wider change. When you flourish, others benefit. And when you help others flourish this enhances your own wellbeing.

Changing the world from the inside out

This brings us back to the central idea of this book: self-care and caring for others go hand in hand. They're not competing priorities, they reinforce each other. When we take care of ourselves we have more capacity to give. We're calmer, less reactive, more able to show up for others. And when we help others to feel happier we discover a deeper fulfilment that no self-centred striving can ever provide.

In our frantic and competitive world, one person's gain is usually seen as another's loss. In economics this is called a 'zero-sum game'. Thankfully, when it comes to happier living, we can be part of a 'positive sum', where everyone benefits. It's a virtuous circle, the ultimate win–win. Put simply: the more we give, the more we grow; and the more we grow, the more capacity we have to give.

Imagine a world where this way of living became the norm. A world where people are more in tune with their thoughts and feelings. Where conversations are rooted in empathy. Where children feel loved and resilient. Where schools and workplaces prioritise wellbeing. Where mental health is valued as much as physical health. Where communities are vibrant and neighbours trust each other. Where love and kindness are seen as strengths, not soft options. Where we work together for the greater good.

This wouldn't just make us feel better and more connected to each other, it would transform many of the social challenges we face today. When societies have higher wellbeing and stronger relationships this helps to reduce things we don't want: like crime, polarisation, family breakdown, addiction and unemployment. And it leads to more of what we do want, like productivity, good health, social cohesion, volunteering, compassion and democratic participation. Happier people tend to be more prosocial, open-minded, environmentally conscious and engaged as citizens.

This world is possible. In fact it's already present in many lives and communities. You don't need to wait for change – you can start small and help build it from the inside out.

Aim big, start small

When we think about making a difference in the world it's easy to feel overwhelmed. The challenges around us – like conflict, loneliness, corruption, inequality or climate change – seem impossibly vast. But small changes add up to profound shifts over time. They ripple outwards, like concentric circles from a single drop of water.

You can think of your impact in these four simple circles:

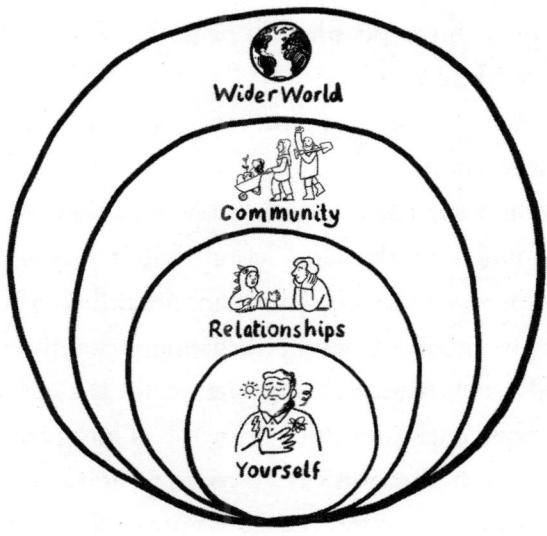

1. Yourself (Happier Inside)
Changing the world starts within. When you wake up from autopilot, notice your thoughts, manage your emotions and build healthy habits, you lay the foundation for living more wisely. When you treat yourself with kindness you're better able to be there for others. Self-care isn't selfish, unless that's all you do! You can't pour from an empty cup, but there's no point having a full cup if it just sits there. So think of self-care not just as something for you but also as a way to help you contribute to a happier world through service and care for others.

2. Your relationships (Happier Together)
Your second circle is the people closest to you: family, partners, friends and colleagues. This is where you practise listening, empathy and kindness. Where you navigate challenges, repair misunderstandings and build trust. By showing up with authenticity

and compassion you model behaviours that others can see and adopt. Each thoughtful and friendly interaction creates ripples that spread – not just to the people you're with, but onwards to others they connect with too.

3. Your community

Beyond your closest ties is the local world you belong to: your neighbours, your workplace, your wider social circles and community. Here you can help to encourage belonging, inclusion and collective wellbeing. It might be through friendly conversations, sharing meals, volunteering, supporting local causes, or helping to create a more caring culture at work. These don't need to be grand gestures and you don't need to be a high-profile influencer. By showing up and showing you care you're already a role model.

4. Your wider world

The outermost circle is the global community you're part of – our shared humanity. You may not have direct political power but you do have influence: as a voter, citizen, consumer or campaigner. You can align your choices with your values and support wellbeing-focused policies. You can channel anger into positive action. You can bridge divides, encourage tolerance and amplify marginalised voices. You can show decency where others shout. You can live sustainably and support efforts to protect the environment. You can seek and share things that are true amid misinformation. Each small step contributes to a more just and compassionate society.

> *'Just as ripples spread out when a single pebble is dropped into water, the actions of individuals can have far-reaching effects.'*
>
> **– The Dalai Lama**

Ethics in action

You've probably heard the phrase, often attributed to Gandhi: 'Be the change you wish to see in the world.' Some dismiss this as simplistic, but it's actually a radical and powerful idea. As you expand your outlook into those wider circles, your daily choices can help to build a better tomorrow for all of us.

As we zoom out to the bigger picture it becomes clear that self-improvement needs a moral compass. Without an ethical foundation, personal development can become misguided or even harmful. Mindfulness, for example, is a vital life skill. But mindful awareness without moral grounding could produce more skilful manipulators or fraudsters.

The core idea of this book is really an ethical one: we should aim to live in ways that increase happiness and reduce suffering. This means paying close attention not only to our inner world but also to the impact of our choices on others. A helpful way to do this is to keep in mind three ethical principles. These are secular, yet they echo timeless wisdom across many traditions:

1. **Avoid harming others**: I will move through the world with awareness and do my best not to cause hurt through my words or actions.
2. **Increase wellbeing**: I will act in ways that uplift others, through kindness, encouragement and helping to make things better.
3. **Recognise interdependence**: I will remember that we're all part of a shared human community and helping others strengthens my own wellbeing too.

Our world urgently needs more agency and altruism – a sense of moral duty to make things better. We don't need to wait, blame others, or just hope things will change. We can begin where we are. In his inspiring book *Moral Ambition*, Rutger Bregman urges us to contribute meaningfully to humanity rather than chasing wealth or status. This is about action, not just good intentions. He writes: 'It's not what you think is right that counts, but what you're prepared to do about it.'

Making things better starts in everyday moments. When you pause before reacting, you create space to respond more calmly. When you listen without interrupting or have a brave conversation, you help someone feel supported. When you choose to forgive, show compassion and trust people, you create a healthier culture. And when you show up and speak out, you can make a real difference.

These choices matter more than you may realise. The evidence backs this up, too: social norms shift when enough individuals start to behave differently. As we've seen, gratitude can spread and kindness is contagious. Listening and encouragement can open doors that facts and arguments never will.

So ask yourself: Who do I want to be? What do I want to be known for? What do I bring into a room, a home, a conversation, a workplace?

My hope is that you'll choose to Make Life Happier and help these ideas spread. You can't do everything but you can always do something. Be the pebble and see how far your ripples can spread.

> ### → Your Good Life Crisis
>
> At the start of this book, I shared my Good Life Crisis – the unexpected turning point that changed everything. I stopped trying to be who I thought I *should* be and started asking who I really *wanted* to be. The journey since hasn't

always been easy but it's been life-enhancing in ways I could never have imagined.

You don't need a crisis to make that shift. This is your invitation right now to step off autopilot, let go of other people's expectations and focus on what matters. So pause for a moment and take a few deep, relaxing breaths.

Then ask yourself:
- What really matters most in my life?
- What do I want to spend more time focusing on?
- How can I help make things better?

These are big questions, but the answers often come more easily than we expect. In our busy lives we don't often pause to think about the big picture, yet the truth is usually already there inside us when we stop and listen.

You can't change everything overnight. I certainly didn't. But as we've seen throughout this book, small actions add up to big changes. So once you know the direction you want to head in, focus on taking the first small steps forwards. Or put differently: before you put more effort into rushing up the ladder of your career or life, make sure it's leaning against the right building.

Balancing purpose and pleasure

As we've seen throughout this book, we miss out on deeper happiness if we only pursue a pleasurable or easy life. But we also miss out if we strive constantly without taking the time to actually enjoy living. Professor Paul Dolan is an expert in behavioural science and has done extensive research on happiness. In his book

Happiness by Design, he describes happiness as having two core ingredients: *pleasure* and *purpose*.

Some activities are pleasurable, but not particularly purposeful – like watching a favourite show, enjoying a drink or sharing a joke. Others feel purposeful but aren't necessarily pleasurable – like being up all night with a sleepless child, finishing a difficult project or standing up against injustice. When you're deciding how to spend your time it's worth asking: 'Does this bring pleasure, purpose – or both?' And if the answer is *neither*, why are you giving time to it?

As we get busy pursuing meaningful projects it's important to just pause every now and then to appreciate what's good. I love the concept of 'glimmers', coined by social worker Deb Dana. Glimmers are the tiny moments that spark joy when we notice them – the smell of fresh coffee, a stranger's smile, sunlight through leaves or being greeted by your pet at the door.

Why not take a moment right now to notice a glimmer, however small, and allow yourself to just feel happy in this moment.

Final reflections

So here we are. Thank you for joining me on this journey and making it to the end of the book. Across these 23 chapters you've explored your inner world, looked more closely at your relationships and considered how you contribute to wider society.

Now it's time to ask yourself:
- What has changed in me?
- What will I carry forwards in my life?
- What small next step will I take right now?

This book isn't an instruction manual, it's a set of guideposts for the journey of a lifetime and an invitation to take your next step forwards – and then to keep going.

As I reflect on my own journey in writing this book, one thing has become completely clear. The deeper thread running through everything is love. Not sentimental love, and not just romantic love. I mean love for ourselves (Happier Inside), love for each other (Happier Together) and love for this fragile, beautiful world we all share. Life is precious and short. Let's make the most of it.

You've made it this far, and the world urgently needs more people like you. People who care enough to live with intention and love. People who recognise that small actions contribute meaningfully to big aims. People who keep waking up every day and choosing to make life happier for themselves and everyone around them.

In the famous words of Margaret Mead: 'Never doubt that a small group of thoughtful, committed citizens can change the world. It's the only thing that ever has.'

Let's step out into the world and make life happier – for ourselves, for others, for good.

MAKE IT LAST: CHAPTER SUMMARY

Ask yourself:
❓ **Which happiness actions will I turn into lifelong habits?**

Don't just:
✗ Read about happiness without putting any of it into practice.

Try this out:
✔ Remember: life is precious, so wake up and live wholeheartedly right now.

23 questions to ask yourself

1. What advice would my 'future self' give me about how to live today?
2. What's going on for me beneath the surface?
3. Which actions actually leave me feeling happier?
4. What am I thankful for (or taking for granted)?
5. How can I respond constructively to this situation?
6. What would I say to a self-critical loved one? (Now say it to yourself.)
7. Will this still matter a year from now?
8. What positive change do I want to try out today?
9. How can I make my most important habits non-negotiable?
10. What behaviours help me to feel calm and safe?
11. What are the greatest sources of meaning in my life?
12. Which relationships do I need to give more priority to?
13. Can I reflect back what people are saying so they feel heard?
14. What is my underlying need and how can I express this clearly?
15. What mask am I wearing and who can I reveal my feelings to?
16. What wounds am I still carrying from past relationships?
17. What anger am I holding on to that I can choose to let go of?
18. What's the most compassionate way I can respond to this?
19. How can I encourage trustworthy behaviour?
20. How do I help children feel secure and resilient?
21. How can I help people get together in my community?
22. Where can I encourage a greater focus on wellbeing?
23. Which happiness actions will I turn into lifelong habits?

23 things to avoid. Don't just . . .

1. Keep ploughing on without thinking about what really matters.
2. Live on 'autopilot' and stay disconnected from your mind and body.
3. Try to feel differently without doing anything differently.
4. Focus only on what's wrong or what might go wrong.
5. Believe positive thinking will bring you everything you want.
6. Use a harsh inner voice to motivate or punish yourself.
7. Push away uncomfortable feelings or pretend things are fine.
8. Assume your existing habits are the best way forwards.
9. Fail to turn your helpful actions into lasting habits.
10. Allow anxiety to leave you feeling unable to do the things you want.
11. Spend your whole time trying to meet others' expectations.
12. Assume your relationships will stay strong without working on them.
13. Give unwanted advice or make your own points when someone's talking.
14. Assume you know what someone needs or they know what you need.
15. Keep things bottled up inside, worrying that people will judge you.
16. Continue replaying the same old relationship conflicts and traumas.
17. Keep carrying the burden and anger of seeing yourself as a victim.
18. Focus only on what's best for you rather than helping others.
19. Assume everyone is always out to get you.
20. Pass on your own emotional baggage to the next generation.
21. Ignore your neighbours and avoid meeting new people.
22. Stay overwhelmed with anger about all that's wrong in the world.
23. Read about happiness without putting any of it into practice.

23 practical steps to try out

1. Focus on the things that matter most. Let go of other stuff.
2. Choose to live mindfully and learn to 'tune in' to your mind and body.
3. Do something positive, however small. Then take the next step.
4. Appreciate precious moments rather than taking them for granted.
5. Be a realistic optimist. See life as it is but focus on what could go right.
6. Show yourself the same kindness and care you'd give to a good friend.
7. Let go of things outside of your control, and focus on what you can change.
8. Experiment with new behaviours and find what works best for you.
9. Make sure the actions you find helpful become part of your daily life.
10. Learn ways to lower anxiety in your body, mind and environment.
11. Find and pursue meaningful goals that give you a sense of purpose.
12. Focus on your 'social fitness' and invest time in your relationships.
13. Help people feel heard and understood by really listening to them.
14. Aim to understand people's needs and be clear about your own needs.
15. Have more conversations that matter and share your inner feelings.
16. Acknowledge your 'inner child' to accept and let go of old wounds.
17. Forgive and let go, not to condone it but to set yourself free.
18. Discover the joy of helping and notice how kindness ripples out.
19. Trust people: you'll find they are surprisingly trustworthy.
20. Give children a healthy mix of love, boundaries and freedom.
21. Be an active member of your local community.
22. Promote what you love rather than bashing what you hate.
23. Remember: life is precious, so wake up and live wholeheartedly right now.

REFERENCES

INTRODUCTION

Action for Happiness, registered charity 1175160, actionforhappiness.org.

Cohen, S., Doyle, W.J., Turner, R.B., Alper, C.M., & Skoner, D.P. (2003), 'Emotional Style and Susceptibility to the Common Cold', *Psychosomatic Medicine*, 65(4), 652–657.

Guven, C. (2012), 'Reversing the Question: Does Happiness Affect Consumption and Savings Behavior?' *Journal of Economic Psychology*, 33(4), 701–717.

Lyubomirsky, S., King, L., & Diener, E. (2005), 'The Benefits of Frequent Positive Affect: Does Happiness Lead to Success?' *Psychological Bulletin*, 131(6), 803–855.

Steptoe, A., Wardle, J., & Marmot, M. (2005), 'Positive Affect and Health-Related Neuroendocrine, Cardiovascular, and Inflammatory Processes', *Proceedings of the National Academy of Sciences of the United States of America*, 102(18), 6508–6512.

PART 1: HAPPIER INSIDE

1. Wake Up: What am I doing and what matters most?

Benedetti, F. (2014), *Placebo Effects: Understanding the Mechanisms in Health and Disease*, Oxford University Press.

Borrell-Carrió, F., Suchman, A.L., & Epstein, R.M. (2004), 'The Biopsychosocial Model 25 Years Later: Principles, Practice, and Scientific Inquiry', *Annals of Family Medicine*, 2(6), 576–582.

de Heer, E.W., Gerrits, M.M., Beekman, A.T., Dekker, J., van Marwijk, H.W., de Waal, M.W., Spinhoven, P., Penninx, B.W., & van der Feltz-Cornelis, C.M. (2014), 'The Association of Depression and Anxiety with Pain: A Study From NESDA', *PloS one*, 9(10), e106907.

Ricard, M. (2015), *Happiness: A Guide to Developing Life's Most Important Skill*, Atlantic Books.

Shakespeare, W. (2006), *Hamlet* (A. Thompson & N. Taylor, Eds.). Bloomsbury. (Original work published 1603).

Siegel, R.D., Urdang, M. & Johnson, D.R. (2001), *Back Sense: A Revolutionary Approach to Ending the Cycle of Back Pain*, Broadway Books.

Tedeschi, R.G., & Calhoun, L.G. (2004), 'Posttraumatic Growth: Conceptual Foundations and Empirical Evidence', *Psychological Inquiry*, 15(1), 1–18.

2. Look Inside: What's going on in my mind and body?

Goldberg, S.B., Riordan, K.M., Sun, S., & Davidson, R.J. (2022), 'The Present and Future of Mindfulness-Based Interventions: A Summary of 10-Year Systematic Reviews', *Perspectives on Psychological Science*, 17(1), 108–130.

Hölzel, B.K., Carmody, J., Vangel, M., Congleton, C., Yerramsetti, S.M., Gard, T., & Lazar, S.W. (2011), 'Mindfulness Practice Leads to Increases in Regional Brain Gray Matter Density', *Psychiatry Research*, 191(1), 36–43.

Kabat-Zinn, J, (2013), *Full Catastrophe Living: Using the Wisdom of Your Body and Mind to Face Stress, Pain, and Illness* (revised ed.), Bantam Books.

Lewis, C.S. (2012), *The Great Divorce*, Collins. (Original work published 1945).

Remskar, M., Western, M.J., & Ainsworth, B. (2024), 'Mindfulness Improves Psychological Health and Supports Health Behaviour Cognitions: Evidence from a Pragmatic RCT of a Digital Mindfulness-Based Intervention', *British Journal of Health Psychology*, 29(4), 1031–1048.

Russo, M.A., Santarelli, D.M., & O'Rourke, D. (2017), 'The Physiological Effects of Slow Breathing in the Healthy Human', *Breathe*, 13(4), 298–309.

Sezer, I., Pizzagalli, D.A., & Sacchet, M.D. (2022), 'Resting-State fMRI Functional Connectivity and Mindfulness in Clinical and Non-Clinical Contexts: A Review and Synthesis', *Neuroscience and Biobehavioral Reviews*, 135, 104583.

3. Decide to Act: How can my actions change how I feel?

Dalai Lama & Cutler, H. C. (1998). *The Art of Happiness: A Handbook for Living*. Riverhead Books.

Diener, E., Lucas, R.E., & Scollon, C.N. (2006), 'Beyond the Hedonic Treadmill: Revising the Adaptation Theory of Wellbeing', *The American Psychologist*, 61(4), 305–314.

Dweck, C.S. (2006), *Mindset: The New Psychology of Success*, Random House.

Folk, D. & Dunn, E. (2023), 'A Systematic Review of the Strength of Evidence for the Most Commonly Recommended Happiness Strategies in Mainstream Media', *Nature Human Behaviour*, 7. 1–11. 10.1038/s41562-023-01651-4.

King, V. (2016), *10 Keys to Happier Living: A Practical Handbook for Happiness*, Headline Publishing.

Kvam, S., Kleppe, C.L., Nordhus, I.H., & Hovland, A. (2016), 'Exercise as a Treatment for Depression: A Meta-Analysis', *Journal of Affective Disorders*, 202, 67–86.

King, M. L., Jr. (as cited in Reynolds, B. A., Ed., 1988). *And Still We Rise: Interviews with 50 Black Role Models*. USA Today Books.

Mazzucchelli, T.G., Kane, R.T., & Rees, C.S. (2010), 'Behavioral Activation Interventions for Wellbeing: A Meta-Analysis', *The Journal of Positive Psychology*, 5(2), 105–121.

Schultz, W. (2015), 'Neuronal Reward And Decision Signals: From Theories To Data', *Physiological Reviews*, 95(3), 853–951.

Sin, N.L., & Lyubomirsky, S. (2009), 'Enhancing Wellbeing and Alleviating Depressive Symptoms with Positive Psychology Interventions: A Practice-Friendly Meta-Analysis', *Journal of Clinical Psychology*, 65(5), 467–487.

4. See the Good: What am I taking for granted?

Baumeister, R.F., Bratslavsky, E., Finkenauer, C., & Vohs, K.D. (2001), 'Bad is Stronger Than Good', *Review of General Psychology*, 5(4), 323–370.

Boggiss, A.L., Consedine, N.S., Brenton-Peters, J.M., Hofman, P.L., & Serlachius, A.S. (2020), 'A Systematic Review of Gratitude Interventions: Effects on Physical Health and Health Behaviors', *Journal of Psychosomatic Research*, 135, 110165.

Brault, R. (1986), 'Quotable Quotes', *Reader's Digest*, September 1986 Issue.

Emmons, R.A., & McCullough, M.E. (2003), 'Counting Blessings Versus Burdens: An Experimental Investigation of Gratitude and Subjective Wellbeing in Daily Life', *Journal of Personality and Social Psychology*, 84(2), 377–389.

Harris, S. (2014), *Waking up: Searching for Spirituality Without Religion*, Simon & Schuster. See also Harris's guided practices in the Waking Up app.

Seligman, M.E.P., Steen, T.A., Park, N., & Peterson, C. (2005), 'Positive Psychology Progress: Empirical Validation of Interventions', *American Psychologist*, 60(5), 410–421.

5. Keep it Real: Is staying positive always helpful?

Byrne, R. (2006), *The Secret*, Atria Books. [Note: listed here as discussed critically, rather than recommended.]

Macy, J.R., & Johnstone, C. (2022), *Active Hope: How to Face the Mess We're in With Unexpected Resilience and Creative Power* (revised ed.), New World Library.

Navarro, T. (2019), *Kintsugi: The Japanese Art of Embracing the Imperfect and Loving Your Flaws*, St Martin's Publishing Group.

Radmacher, M.A. (2009), *Courage Doesn't Always Roar*, Conari Press.

Samuel, J. (2017), *Grief Works: Stories Of Life, Death And Surviving*, Penguin Random House UK.

Sirois, M.A. (2016), *A Short Course in Happiness After Loss (And Other Dark, Difficult Times)*, Green Fire Press.

6. Tame That Critic: Why am I so hard on myself?

Gilbert, P. (2009), *The Compassionate Mind*, Constable & Robinson.

Kross, E. (2021), *Chatter: The Voice in Our Head, Why it Matters, and How to Harness it*, Crown.

Neff, K.D. (2011), *Self-Compassion: The Proven Power Of Being Kind To Yourself*, William Morrow.

Neff, K.D., & Germer, C.K. (2018), *The Mindful Self-Compassion Workbook*, Guilford Press.

Nhat Hanh, T. (2007). *The Art of Power*. HarperOne.

Tod, D., Hardy, J., & Oliver, E.J. (2011), 'Effects of Self-Talk: A Systematic Review', *Journal of Sport and Exercise Psychology*, 33(5), 666–687.

7. Reframe Difficulty: Is there a different way of looking at this?

Achor, S. (2013), *Before Happiness: The 5 Hidden Keys to Achieving Success, Spreading Happiness, and Sustaining Positive Change*, Crown Business.

Aurelius, M. (2011). *Meditations* (R. Hard, Trans.). Oxford University Press. (Original work written c. AD 170).

Beck, J.S. (2021), *Cognitive Behavior Therapy: Basics and Beyond* (3rd ed.), Guilford Press.

Ben-Shahar, T. (2007), *Happier: Learn the Secrets to Daily Joy and Lasting Fulfillment*, McGraw-Hill.

Chapman, B.P., Fiscella, K., Kawachi, I., & Duberstein, P.R. (2013), 'Emotion Suppression and Mortality Risk Over a 12-Year Follow-Up', *Health Psychology*, 32(6), 621–628.

David, S. (2016), *Emotional Agility: Get Unstuck, Embrace Change, and Thrive in Work and Life*, Avery (Penguin Random House).

Frankl, V. E. (2008). *Man's Search for Meaning*. Rider. (Original work published 1946).

Greenberger, D., & Padesky, C.A. (2016), *Mind Over Mood: Change How You Feel By Changing the Way You Think* (2nd ed.), Guilford Press.

Marcus Aurelius (2006), *Meditations* (G. Hays, Trans.), Modern Library. (Original work written c. 161–180 CE.)

Schwarz, N., & Clore, G.L. (1983), 'Mood, Misattribution, and Judgments of Wellbeing: Informative and Directive Functions of Affective States', *Journal of Personality and Social Psychology*, 45(3), 513–523.

Smith, J. (2022), *Why Has Nobody Told Me This Before?*, Penguin Michael Joseph.

Tutu, D. via Schroder, J. (2024), 'Do a Little Bit of Good', *Becoming the Journey*.

Tutu, D., & Tutu, N. (1989). *The Words of Desmond Tutu*. Newmarket Press.

8. Do Experiments: How do I find what works best for me?

Dunn, E.W., Aknin, L.B., & Norton, M.I. (2008), 'Spending Money on Others Promotes Happiness', *Science* (New York, N.Y.), 319(5870), 1687–1688.

Dunn, E.W., Gilbert, D.T., & Wilson, T.D. (2011), 'If Money Doesn't Make You Happy, Then You Probably Aren't Spending it Right', *Journal of Consumer Psychology*, 21(2), 115–125.

Epley, N., & Schroeder, J. (2014), 'Mistakenly Seeking Solitude', *Journal of Experimental Psychology*: General, 143(5), 1980–1999.

Power, T.J. (2024), *The DOSE Effect: Small Habits to Boost Your Brain Chemistry and Help You Live Happier*, London, England: Penguin Life.

Sheldon, K.M., & Lyubomirsky, S. (2021), 'Revisiting The Sustainable Happiness Model and Pie Chart: Can Happiness Be Successfully Pursued?', *The Journal of Positive Psychology*, 16(2), 145–154.

Sun, M.-L., Li, J.-Y., Wang, W.-W., Li, J.-G., & Yang, J.-M. (2024), 'Intermittent Fasting and Health Outcomes: An Umbrella Review of Systematic Reviews and Meta-Analyses of Randomized Controlled Trials', *eClinicalMedicine*, 67, 101955.

Twain, M. in Paine, A.B. ed. (1935), *Mark Twain's Notebook*, Harper & Brothers.

Whillans, A.V., Dunn, E.W., Smeets, P., Bekkers, R., & Norton, M.I. (2017), 'Buying Time Promotes Happiness', *Proceedings of the National Academy of Sciences of the United States of America*, 114(32), 8523–8527.

9. Build Habits: How can I keep the good things going?

Clear, J. (2018), *Atomic Habits: An Easy & Proven Way to Build Good Habits & Break Bad Ones*, Avery.

Dai, H., Milkman, K.L., & Riis, J. (2014), 'The Fresh Start Effect: Temporal Landmarks Motivate Aspirational Behavior', *Management Science*, 60(10), 2563–2582.

Duhigg, C. (2012), *The Power of Habit: Why We Do What We Do in Life and Business*, Random House.

Durant, W. (2022). *The Story of Philosophy*. Dover Publications. (Original work published 1926).

Fogg, B.J. (2020), *Tiny Habits: The Small Changes That Change Everything*, Boston, MA: Houghton Mifflin Harcourt.

Graybiel, A.M. (2008), 'Habits, Rituals, and The Evaluative Brain', *Annual Review of Neuroscience*, 31, 359–387.

Kelly, K. (2023). *Excellent Advice for Living*. Viking.

Milkman, K.L. (2021), *How to Change: The Science of Getting From Where You Are To Where You Want To Be*, London, England: W.H. Allen.

10. Cultivate Calm: How can I be less anxious?

Balban, M.Y., Neri, E., Kogon, M.M., Weed, L., Nouriani, B., Jo, B., Holl, G., Zeitzer, J.M., Spiegel, D., & Huberman, A.D. (2023), 'Brief Structured Respiration Practices Enhance Mood and Reduce Physiological Arousal', *Cell Reports Medicine*, 4(1), 100895.

Brewer, J. (2021), *Unwinding Anxiety: New Science Shows How to Break the Cycles of Worry and Fear to Heal Your Mind*, Avery.

Chatterjee, R. (2019), *Feel Better in 5: Your Daily Plan to Feel Great for Life*, Penguin Life.

Chen, S. et al. (2024), 'Dynamic Changes And Future Trend Predictions of the Global Burden of Anxiety Disorders: Analysis of 204 Countries and Regions From 1990 to 2021 and the Impact of the COVID-19 Pandemic', *EClinicalMedicine*, 79, 103014.

Gloster, A.T., Walder, N., Levin, M.E., Twohig, M.P., & Karekla, M. (2020), 'The Empirical Status of Acceptance and Commitment Therapy: A Review of Meta-Analyses', *Journal of Contextual Behavioral Science*, 18, 181–192.

LeDoux, J.E., & Pine, D.S. (2016), 'Using Neuroscience to Help Understand Fear and Anxiety: A Two-System Framework', *American Journal of Psychiatry*, 173(11), 1083–1093.

Niebuhr, R. (c. 1943). Quoted in Sifton, E. (2003). *The Serenity Prayer: Faith and Politics in Times of Peace and War*. W. W. Norton & Company.

Pennebaker, J.W., & Chung, C.K. (2011), 'Expressive Writing: Connections to Physical And Mental Health', in H.S. Friedman (Ed.), *The Oxford Handbook of Health Psychology* (pp. 417–437), Oxford University Press.

Porges, S.W. (2011), *The Polyvagal Theory: Neurophysiological Foundations of Emotions, Attachment, Communication, and Self-Regulation*, W.W. Norton & Company.

11. Find Meaning: Where am I really heading?

Aristotle. (2020). *The Nicomachean Ethics* (A. Beresford, Ed.). Penguin. (Original work written ca. 350 BCE).

Burkeman, O. (2021). *Four Thousand Weeks*. Penguin.

Burton, M.L., & Wedemeyer, R.A. (1991), *In Transition: From the Harvard Business School Club of New York's Career Management Seminar*, HarperCollins.

Crofts, N. (2008), *What is my Purpose? Know It, Live It*, Online e-book.

Einstein, A. (1932, as cited in Calaprice, A., 2010, p. 231). *The Ultimate Quotable Einstein*. Princeton University Press.

Frankl, V.E. (2004), *Man's Search for Meaning: The Classic Tribute to Hope From the Holocaust* (Original work published 1946), Rider.

Layard, R. (2011), *Happiness: Lessons From a New Science* (2nd ed.), Penguin Press.

Locke, E.A., & Latham, G.P. (2002), 'Building a Practically Useful Theory of Goal Setting and Task Performance', *American Psychologist*, 57(9), 705–717.

Martela, F., & Steger, M.F. (2016), 'The Three Meanings of Meaning in Life: Distinguishing Coherence, Purpose, and Significance', *The Journal of Positive Psychology*, 11(5), 531–545.

NASA (2023), 'Our Solar System', *Solar System Exploration: NASA Science*, science.nasa.gov/solar-system.

Thurman, H. via Bailie, G. (1995), *Violence Unveiled: Humanity at the Crossroads*, The Crossroad Publishing Company.

Ware, B. (2012), *The Top Five Regrets of the Dying: A Life Transformed By the Dearly Departing*, Hay House Inc.

PART 2: HAPPIER TOGETHER

12. Prioritise People: Am I focusing enough on my relationships?

Brooks, A.C. (2021), 'The Type of Love That Makes People Happiest', *The Atlantic*.

Collins, H., & Whillans, A. (2022), 'The Rewards of Social Diversity: High-Intensity Socializers are Happier Than Low-Intensity Socializers,' *Proceedings of the National Academy of Sciences* (PNAS), 119(43), e2202523119.

Epicurus, as cited in Diogenes Laertius. (1925). *Lives of Eminent Philosophers* (R. D. Hicks, Trans.). Harvard University Press. (Original work written c. 3rd century CE).

Gable, S.L., Reis, H.T., Impett, E.A., & Asher, E.R. (2004), 'What Do You Do When Things Go Right? The Intrapersonal and Interpersonal Benefits of Sharing Positive Events', *Journal of Personality and Social Psychology*, 87(2), 228–245.

Gottman, J.M., & DeClaire, J. (2001), 'The Relationship Cure: A 5-Step Guide to Strengthening Your Marriage, Family, And Friendships', *Harmony*.

Grover, S., & Helliwell, J.F. (2019), 'How's Life at Home? New Evidence on Marriage and the Set Point for Happiness', *Journal of Happiness Studies*, 20(2), 373–390.

Holt-Lunstad, J., Smith, T.B., & Layton, J.B. (2010), 'Social Relationships and Mortality Risk: A Meta-Analytic Review', *PLoS Medicine*, 7(7), e1000316.

Epley, N., & Schroeder, J. (2014), 'Mistakenly Seeking Solitude', *Journal of Experimental Psychology: General*, 143(5), 1980–1999.

Sandstrom, G.M., & Dunn, E.W. (2014), 'Is Efficiency Overrated? Minimal Social Interactions Lead to Belonging and Positive Affect', *Social Psychological and Personality Science*, 5(4), 437–442.

Uvnäs-Moberg K. (1998), 'Oxytocin May Mediate the Benefits of Positive Social Interaction And Emotions', *Psychoneuroendocrinology*, 23(8), 819–835.

Waldinger, R., & Schulz, M. (2023), *The Good Life: Lessons from the World's Longest Scientific Study of Happiness*, Simon & Schuster.

13. Listen Actively: Do I really hear what people are saying?

Brown, B. (2012), *Daring Greatly: How the Courage to be Vulnerable Transforms the Way we Live, Love, Parent, and Lead*, Gotham Books.

Dolan, P. (2025), *Beliefism: How to Stop Hating the People we Disagree With*, Little, Brown Book Group.

Edmondson, A.C. (2018), *The Fearless Organization: Creating Psychological Safety in the Workplace for Learning, Innovation, and Growth*, Wiley.

Hanh, T.H. (1996), *Living Buddha, Living Christ*, Ebury Publishing.

Kasriel, E. (2025), *Deep Listening: Transform Your Relationships With Family, Friends and Foes*, Thorsons.

Kelly, K. (2023), *Excellent Advice For Living*, Viking.

Mehl, M.R., Vazire, S., Holleran, S.E., & Clark, C.S. (2010), 'Eavesdropping on Happiness: Wellbeing is Related to Having Less Small Talk And More Substantive Conversations', *Psychological Science*, 21(4), 539–541.

Plett, H. (2020), *The Art of Holding Space: A Practice of Love, Liberation, and Leadership*, Page Two.

Rogers, C.R., & Farson, R.E. (1957), 'Active Listening', Industrial Relations Center of the University of Chicago.

Whyte, D. (2019), *Consolations*, Canongate Books.

Yeomans, M., Brooks, A.W., Minson, J., & Gino, F. (2017), 'It Doesn't Hurt to Ask: Question-Asking Increases Liking', *Journal of Personality and Social Psychology*, 113(3), 430–452.

14. Understand Needs: Can I help to resolve our difficulties?

Chatterjee, R. (2019), *Feel Better in 5: Your Daily Plan to Feel Great For Life*, Penguin Life.

Chatterjee, R. (2025, April 18). FRIDAY FIVE: Let's talk about stress, meaningful chats, and morning mindsets [Newsletter].

Dass, R., 'Ram Dass Quotes', Blog: *Ram Dass*.

Gable, S.L., Reis, H.T., Impett, E.A., & Asher, E.R. (2004), 'What Do You Do When Things Go Right? The Intrapersonal and Interpersonal Benefits of Sharing Positive Events', *Journal of Personality and Social Psychology*, 87(2), 228–245.

Grant, A. (c. 2021). In toxic relationships, people give blame but don't take responsibility. [Social Media Post].

Leu, L. (2015), *Nonviolent Communication Companion Workbook: A Practical Guide for Individual, Group, or Classroom Study* (2nd ed.), PuddleDancer Press.

Perel, E. and Miller, M. A. (2018), How to Fix the Fights You're Sick of Having, Blog: *Esther Perel*.

Robin, C., & Bradford, D.L. (2017), *Connect: Building Exceptional Relationships With Family, Friends, and Colleagues*, Portfolio.

Rosenberg, J. (2018), *90 Seconds to a Life You Love: How to Master Your Difficult Feelings to Cultivate Lasting Confidence, Resilience and Authenticity*, Little, Brown Spark.

Rosenberg, M.B. (2015), *Nonviolent Communication: A Language of Life* (3rd ed.), PuddleDancer Press.

15. Remove the Mask: Can vulnerability be my source of strength?

Brown, B. (2006), 'Shame Resilience Theory: A Grounded Theory Study on Women and Shame', *Psychology of Women Quarterly*, 30(1), 43–55.

Brown, B. (2010), *The Gifts of Imperfection*, Hazelden.

Brown, B. (2012), *Daring Greatly: How the Courage to Be Vulnerable Transforms the Way We Live, Love, Parent, And Lead*, Gotham Books.

Collins, N.L., & Miller, L.C. (1994), 'Self-disclosure and Liking: A Meta-Analytic Review', *Journal of Personality and Social Psychology*, 66(3), 457–475.

Gottlieb, L. (2019), *Maybe You Should Talk to Someone*, Houghton Mifflin Harcourt.

16. Heal Those Wounds: How do my past relationships shape me?

Ainsworth, M.D.S., Blehar, M.C., Waters, E., & Wall, S. (1978), *Patterns of Attachment*, Lawrence Erlbaum.

Bowlby, J. (1969/1982), *Attachment and Loss (Vol. 1: Attachment)*, Basic Books.

de Botton, A. (2024), *Essays in Love*, Pan Macmillan.

Gottlieb, L. (2019), *Maybe You Should Talk to Someone*, Houghton Mifflin Harcourt.

Gottman, J.M., & Silver, N. (2015), *The Seven Principles for Making Marriage Work*, Harmony.

Hendrix, H., & Hunt, H.L. (2019), *Getting the Love You Want: A Guide for Couples* (revised ed.), Random House.

Maté, G., & Maté, D. (2022), *The Myth of Normal: Trauma, Illness & Healing in a Toxic Culture*, Avery/Penguin Random House.

Richards, J. (2022, June 17). Raising resilient boys with John Richards. [podcast episode]. In *The Business Elevation Show with Chris Cooper*. VoiceAmerica Business.

Samuel, J. (2017), *Grief Works: Stories of Life, Death and Surviving*, Penguin Random House UK.

Schwartz, R.C. (2021), *No Bad Parts: Healing Trauma and Restoring Wholeness with the Internal Family Systems Model*, Hay House.

van der Kolk, B.A. (2014), *The Body Keeps the Score*, Viking.

17. Let it Go: How can I forgive and move on?

Building Bridges for Peace: https://buildingbridgesforpeace.org

Goleman, D. (2006), *Emotional Intelligence: Why it Can Matter More Than IQ*, Bantam.

Haidt, J. (2021), *The Righteous Mind* (updated ed.), Penguin.

Lerner, H.G. (2017), *Why Won't You Apologize?: Healing Big Betrayals and Everyday Hurts*, Simon & Schuster.

Luskin, F. (2002), *Forgive for Good: A Proven Prescription for Health and Happiness*, HarperCollins.

Nussbaum, M.C. (2016), *Anger and Forgiveness: Resentment, Generosity, Justice*, Oxford University Press.

Toussaint, L., Worthington, E.L., & Williams, D.R. (2015), 'Forgiveness and Health: Scientific Evidence and Theories Relating Forgiveness to Better Health', *Social and Personality Psychology Compass*, 9(6), 316–330.

Tutu, D. (1999), *No Future Without Forgiveness*, Doubleday.

18. Spread Kindness: How can I be helpful and inspire others too?

Aknin, L.B., Dunn, E.W., Whillans, A.V., Grant, A.M., & Norton, M.I. (2013), 'Prosocial Spending and Wellbeing: Cross-Cultural Evidence for a Psychological Universal', *Journal of Personality and Social Psychology*, 104(4), 635–652.

Curry, O.S., Rowland, L., Van Lissa, C.J., Zlotowitz, S., McAlaney, J., & Whitehouse, H. (2018), 'Happy to Help? A Systematic Review and Meta-Analysis of the Effects of Performing Acts of Kindness on the Wellbeing of the Actor', *Journal of Experimental Social Psychology*, 76, 320–329.

Dalai Lama, & Chan, V. (2012). *The Wisdom of Compassion*. Riverhead Books.

Darley, J.M., & Batson, C.D. (1973), '"From Jerusalem to Jericho": A Study of Situational and Dispositional Variables in Helping Behavior', *Journal of Personality and Social Psychology*, 27(1), 100–108.

Darwin, C. (2004), *The Descent of Man* (Original work published 1871), Penguin Classics.

Fowler, J.H., & Christakis, N.A. (2010), 'Cooperative Behavior Cascades in Human Social Networks', *Proceedings of the National Academy of Sciences*, 107(12), 5334–5338.

Grant, A.M. (2013), *Give and Take: Why Helping Others Drives Our Success*, Penguin.

Hamilton, D.R. (2017), *The Five Side Effects of Kindness: This Book Will Make You Feel Better, Be Happier and Live Longer*, Hay House UK.

Harding, K. (2019), 'The Power of Kindness – with Dr Kelli Harding', Action for Happiness event.

Harding, K. (2019), *The Rabbit Effect: Live Longer, Happier, and Healthier with the Groundbreaking Science of Kindness*, Atria Books.

Harrison, S. in conversation with Naomi Haile (2024), 'What Truly Makes Us Happy, Surprising Research on Happiness, "Old Happy" and How it Ruins Our Lives', Podcast: *Power of Why with Naomi Haile*.

Helliwell, J.F., Layard, R., Sachs, J., De Neve, J.-E., & Wang, S. (eds.), (2025), *World Happiness Report 2025: Caring and Sharing for Wellbeing*, University of Oxford: Wellbeing Research Centre.

Jinpa, T. (2015), *A Fearless Heart: How the Courage to Be Compassionate can Transform our Lives*, Hudson Street Press.

Keltner, D., & Marsh, J. (2015), 'The Evolutionary Roots of Compassion', *Current Opinion in Psychology*, 6, 193–198.

Lutz, A., Brefczynski-Lewis, J., Johnstone, T., & Davidson, R.J. (2008), 'Regulation of the Neural Circuitry of Emotion by Compassion Meditation: Effects of Meditative Expertise', *PLoS ONE*, 3(3), e1897.

Marmot, M., & Wilkinson, R.G. (eds.), (2005), *Social Determinants of Health* (2nd ed.), Oxford University Press.

Moll, J., Krueger, F., Zahn, R., Pardini, M., de Oliveira-Souza, R., & Grafman, J. (2006), 'Human Fronto–Mesolimbic Networks Guide Decisions About Charitable Donation', *Proceedings of the National Academy of Sciences*, 103(42), 15623–15628.

Whillans, A.V., Dunn, E.W., Sandstrom, G.M., Dickerson, S.S., & Madden, K.M. (2016), 'Is Spending Money on Others Good for Your Heart? Health Behavior, Cardiovascular Risk, and Prosocial Spending,' *Health Psychology*, 35(6), 574–583.

Zak, P.J. (2012), *The Moral Molecule: The Source of Love and Prosperity*, Dutton.

19. Trust People: Do I see and encourage the good in others?

Bi, S., Maes, M., Stevens, G.W.J.M., de Heer, C., Li, J.B., Sun, Y., & Finkenauer, C. (2025), 'Trust and Subjective Wellbeing Across The Lifespan: A Multilevel Meta-Analysis of Cross-Sectional and Longitudinal Associations', *Psychological Bulletin*, 151(6), 737–766.

Botsman, R. (2017), *Who Can You Trust? How Technology Brought Us Together and Why it Might Drive Us Apart*, Portfolio/Penguin.

Brown, B. (2018), *Dare to Lead*, Ebury Publishing.

Cave, N. (2022), Issue #190, The Red Hand Files.

Cohn, A., Maréchal, M.A., Tannenbaum, D., & Zünd, C.L. (2019), 'Civic Honesty Around the Globe', *Science*, 365(6448), 70–73.

Faulkner, G., Fagan, M., McKenna, J. Brussoni, M., Bélanger, K., Gunnell, K., Tremblay, M. S. & Larouche, R. (2025). 'Stranger Danger or Good Samaritan? A Cross-Sectional Study Examining Correlates of Tolerance of Risk in Outdoor Play Among Canadian Parents', *BMC Public Health* 25(1), 627.

Finkelhor, D., Hammer, H., & Sedlak, A.J. (2002), 'Nonfamily Abducted Children: National Estimates and Characteristics. U.S. Department of Justice', Office of Juvenile Justice and Delinquency Prevention.

Helliwell, J.F., Layard, R., Sachs, J.D., De Neve, J.-E., Aknin, L.B., & Wang, S. (eds.), (2025), 'World Happiness Report 2025', University of Oxford: Wellbeing Research Centre.

Hemingway, E. (1981). *Ernest Hemingway: Selected letters, 1917–1961*. Scribner.

Holle, R.L. (2016), 'The Number of Documented Lightning Fatalities in the United States', *International Journal of Disaster Risk Reduction*, 16, 127–132.

Policy Institute at King's College London. (2023), 'The State of Social Trust: How the UK Compares Internationally'.

Yates, J. (2021), *Fractured: Why Our Societies Are Coming Apart and How we Put Them Back Together Again*, HarperNorth.

Zak, P.J., Kurzban, R., & Matzner, W.T. (2005), 'Oxytocin is Associated with Human Trustworthiness', *Nature*, 435(7042), 673–676.

Zak, P. J. (2012), *The Moral Molecule*, Bantam.

Zaki, J. (2020), *The War for Kindness: Building Empathy in a Fractured World*, Crown.

20. Raise Resilience: How can I help the next generation thrive?

Brown, E.L., Lee, E.K., & Yoon, H. (2020), 'Intergenerational Programs and Mental Health: A Systematic Review', *Journal of Intergenerational Relationships*, 18(2), 93–113.

Deighton, J., & Hayes, D. (2025), 'Education For Wellbeing: School-Based Mental Health Interventions Trial Findings', University College London/Anna Freud Centre.

Duckworth, A. (2016), *Grit: The Power of Passion and Perseverance*, Scribner.

Dweck, C.S. (2007), 'The Growth Mindset: A Psychological Perspective on Intelligence, Achievement, and Motivation', *Child Development Perspectives*, 1(3), 170–171.

Haidt, J. (2024), *The Anxious Generation: How the Great Rewiring of Childhood is Causing an Epidemic of Mental Illness*, Penguin Press.

Khaleque, A., 'Perceived Parental Warmth, and Children's Psychological Adjustment, and Personality Dispositions: A Meta-Analysis', *J Child Fam Stud* 22, 297–306 (2013).

Knost, L. R. (2013), *Two Thousand Kisses a Day*, Little Hearts Books.

Lythcott-Haims, J. (2015), *How to Raise an Adult: Break Free of the Overparenting Trap and Prepare Your Kid For Success*, Henry Holt.

Taleb, N.N. (2012), *Antifragile: Things that Gain From Disorder*, Random House.

Twenge, J.M. (2017), *iGen: Why Today's Super-Connected Kids are Growing Up Less Rebellious, More Tolerant, Less Happy—And Completely Unprepared For Adulthood*, Atria Books.

Twenge, J.M. (2024), *Generations: The Real Differences Between Gen Z, Millennials, Gen X, Boomers, and Silents—and What They Mean for America's Future*, Atria Books.

21. Get Together: How can I be part of something bigger?

Chan, E.H.W., & Lee, G.K. (2024), 'Understanding the Relationship Between Urban Public Space and Social Cohesion: A Systematic Review', *International Journal of Community Wellbeing*, 7, 155–212.

Goodall, J., & Berman, P. (1999). *Reason for Hope: A Spiritual Journey*. Warner Books.

Holt-Lunstad, J., Smith, T.B., & Layton, J.B. (2010), 'Social Relationships and Mortality Risk: A Meta-Analytic Review', *PLoS Medicine*, 7(7), e1000316.

Jenkinson, C.E., Dickens, A.P., Jones, K., Thompson-Coon, J., Taylor, R.S., Rogers, M., & Bambra, C. (2013), 'Is Volunteering a Public Health Intervention? A Systematic Review and Meta-Analysis of the Health and Survival of Volunteers', *BMC Public Health*, 13, 773.

Krekel, C., Neve, J-E., Fancourt, D., & Layard, R. (2021), 'A Local Community Course That Raises Wellbeing and Pro-Sociality: Evidence From a Randomised Controlled Trial', *Journal of Economic Behavior & Organization*, Volume 188, 2021, 322–336.

Lash, J. P. (1980). *Helen and Teacher*. Delacorte Press.

Putnam, R.D. (2000), *Bowling Alone: The Collapse and Revival of American Community*, Simon & Schuster.

Tabassum, F., Mohan, J., & Smith, P. (2016), 'Association of Volunteering With Mental Wellbeing: A Life-Course Analysis of a National Population-Based Longitudinal Study in the UK', *BMJ Open*, 6(8), e011327.

Tutu, D., & Tutu, M. (2010). *Made for Goodness*. Rider.

World Health Organization (2025), 'From Loneliness to Social Connection: Charting a Path to Healthier Societies', Report of the WHO Commission on Social Connection.

22. Be the Change: Can I help to create a happier society?

Adams, T. (2024), 'Interview: Tim Minchin: 'Maybe scrolling the traumas of the world is not in itself a moral act', *Guardian*.

Ashe, A. (attributed) via BrainyQuote, 'Arthur Ashe Quotes'.

Alexander, J., & Conrad, A. (2022), *Citizens: Why the Key to Fixing Everything is all of Us*, Canbury Press.

Bentham, J. (1983). *Deontology* (A. Goldworth, Ed.). Clarendon Press. (Original work written c. 1814–1831).

Bono (2020), 'A Message from Bono: RTE Home School Club', *RTE Kids*. YouTube Video.

De Neve, J.-E., Ward, G., De Keulenaer, F., Van Landeghem, B., Kavetsos, G., & Norton, M. I. (2018), 'The Asymmetric Experience of Positive and Negative Economic Growth: Global Evidence Using Subjective Wellbeing Data', *Review of Economics and Statistics*, 100(2), 362–375.

Durlak, J.A., Weissberg, R.P., Dymnicki, A.B., Taylor, R.D., & Schellinger, K.B. (2011), 'The Impact of Enhancing Students' Social and Emotional Learning: A Meta-Analysis of School-Based Universal Interventions', Child Development, 82(1), 405–432.

Edmans, A. (2011), 'Does the Stock Market Fully Value Intangibles? Employee Satisfaction And Equity Prices', *Journal of Financial Economics*, 101(3), 621–640.

Frijters, P., Krekel, C., Sanchis, R. et al., 'The WELLBY: A New Measure of Social Value And Progress', *Humanities and Social Sciences Communications* 11, 736 (2024).

Gardner, H. (1993), *Frames of Mind: The Theory of Multiple Intelligences* (10th anniversary ed.), Basic Books.

Helliwell, J.F., Layard, R., & Sachs, J. (eds.), (2018), 'World Happiness Report 2018, Chapter 1: Happiness and Migration: An Overview', Sustainable Development Solutions Network.

Helliwell, J.F., Layard, R., Sachs, J.D., De Neve, J.-E., Aknin, L.B., & Wang, S. (eds.), (2025), 'World Happiness Report 2025', University of Oxford: Wellbeing Research Centre.

Layard, R., Clark, A.E., Cornaglia, F., Powdthavee, N., & Vernoit, J. (2014), 'What Predicts a Successful Life? A Life-Course Model of Wellbeing,' *The Economic Journal*, 124(580), F720–F738.

Marks, N. (2025), *Happiness is a Serious Business: Why Happy Teams are More Successful and how to Build Them*, Rethink Press.

Organisation for Economic Co-operation and Development (2025), *Guidelines on Measuring Subjective Wellbeing* (2025 update), OECD Publishing.

Oswald, A.J., Proto, E., & Sgroi, D. (2015), 'Happiness and Productivity', *Journal of Labor Economics*, 33(4), 789–822.

Roser, M. (2023), 'The World is Awful. The World is Much Better. The World Can Be Much Better', Our World in Data.

Roser, M., & Ortiz-Ospina, E. (2018), 'Global Development: Indicators, Trends, and Challenges', Our World in Data.

United Nations General Assembly. (2011), 'Happiness: Towards a Holistic Approach To Development', (A/RES/65/309), United Nations.

World Health Organization, (2022), 'World Mental Health Report: Transforming Mental Health For All', WHO.

Zawadzki, S.J., Steg, L., & Bouman, T. (2020), 'Meta-Analytic Evidence for a Robust and Positive Association Between Individuals' Pro-Environmental Behaviors and Their Subjective Wellbeing', *Environmental Research Letters*, 15(12), 123007.

PART 3: HAPPIER FOR GOOD

23. Make it Last: How can we keep making life happier?

Bregman, R. (2025), *Moral Ambition: Stop Wasting Your Talent and Start Making a Difference*, Bloomsbury Publishing.

Dalai Lama. (2013, May 10). Just as ripples spread out when a single pebble is dropped into water, the actions of individuals can have far-reaching effects. Post on X.

Dana, D., & Porges, S.W. (2018), 'The Polyvagal Theory in Therapy: Engaging the Rhythm Of Regulation', W.W. Norton & Company.

Dolan, P. (2014), *Happiness by Design: Finding Pleasure and Purpose in Everyday Life*, Allen Lane.

Acknowledgements

This book has been shaped by far more people than I can possibly name here, and I am deeply grateful to all who have contributed in ways large and small.

My heartfelt thanks to Carole Tonkinson and her brilliant team at Bonnier and LEAP for their belief in this project and their guidance throughout. I'm also enormously grateful to my agent, Jane Graham Maw, whose wisdom and steady encouragement have made such a difference from the very beginning.

A very special thank you to Chelsey Pippin, who helped me turn ideas into words and patiently worked with me to draw thoughts out of my head and onto the page. Thanks also to Phoebe Halstead at ARC Studio for the wonderful chapter illustrations.

Action for Happiness sits at the heart of this book. I'm profoundly grateful to my co-founders – Richard Layard, Anthony Seldon and Geoff Mulgan – for their original vision and for believing in me. Our incredible Patron, the Dalai Lama, has been a constant source of inspiration and it has been wonderful to have his support.

I'm thankful to everyone who has been part of our extraordinary Trustee Board over the years – Vanessa King, Nic Marks, Radha Modgil, Mike Nolet, Julie Bentley, Kate Thompson, David Stead, Louisa Sampson and Judy Gibbons.

To my wonderful colleagues in the Action for Happiness team – Alex Nunn, Sarah Vero, Tanya Battatt, Gaby Deschamps, Joshua French, Jo Holloway-Green, Jess de Ayala, Clair Cohen, Tracy Ampah, Laura Walker, Val Payne and Peter Harper – thank you for your commitment, creativity and friendship.

To all the incredible researchers, teachers and thinkers whose work I've drawn upon – thank you for helping us understand what it means to live well. I'm also grateful to those who reviewed early drafts of this book and offered invaluable feedback and encouragement, especially Jane Griffiths, Peter Harper, Tracy Ampah and Judy Gibbons.

And above all, thank you to the thousands of volunteers and members around the world who have helped build Action for Happiness into a thriving global community. Your compassion, courage and commitment give life to these ideas every day.

On a more personal note, heartfelt thanks to my amazing Mum for all the love and encouragement – and for always showing me how to be grateful, optimistic and kind.

To my wonderful wife Kate, thanks for everything – including your patience and support during the long stretches when this book demanded more time and headspace than I ever intended. I couldn't have done this without you.

And to Emily, Daisy and Harry, thanks for tolerating all my funny habits and for bringing so much joy into my life. You remind me every day what really matters.

About the Author

Dr Mark Williamson is co-founder and Director of Action for Happiness, taking it from a concept on paper in 2010 to a thriving, global mass movement with over 800,000 members across 100+ countries. Mark has collaborated with many of the world's leading happiness experts and teachers, including the Dalai Lama, and he has hosted live events with over 500,000 people taking part.

Prior to Action for Happiness, Mark had a wide range of experience across commercial and non-profit organisations, from start-ups to large multinationals. He was Director of Innovation at the Carbon Trust and founder of online initiative What You Can Do. He spent nine years as a management consultant at Accenture and also worked for Hewlett Packard Labs and Orange. He has an MBA from IMD business school in Switzerland, where he received the President's Award. He has a PhD and first-class honours degree in Engineering from the University of Bristol. He is a Sainsbury Management Fellow, Chartered Engineer and Fellow of the RSA. In 2010 Mark gave up the corporate world and changed direction to focus on happiness and wellbeing. In 2022 he was awarded an additional Honorary Doctorate in recognition of his work with Action for Happiness.

Mark lives in Kingston with his wife Kate and they have three children: Emily, Daisy and Harry. He loves cycling and football and is a long-suffering Aston Villa fan. He's also passionate about music and plays guitar in a band called The Report.